1989

Poetry in the Age
of Democracy

Poetry in the Age of Democracy

The Literary Criticism of Matthew Arnold

Mary W. Schneider

University Press of Kansas

Published by the University Press of Kansas (Lawrence, Kansas
66045), which was organized by the Kansas Board of Regents and
is operated and funded by Emporia State University, Fort Hays
State University, Kansas State University, Pittsburg State
University, the University of Kansas, and Wichita State University

Library of Congress Cataloging-in-Publication Data

Schneider, Mary W., 1925–
  Poetry in the age of democracy : the literary criticism of Matthew
Arnold / Mary W. Schneider.
    p. cm.
  Bibliography: p.
  Includes index.
  ISBN 0-7006-0380-8 (alk. paper)
  1. Arnold, Matthew, 1822–1888—Knowledge—Literature. 2. English
poetry—19th century—History and criticism—Theory, etc.
3. Classical poetry—History and criticism—Theory, etc. 4. Poetry.
I. Title.
PR4024.S295   1989
821′.8—dc19   88-29096
                                                         CIP

Printed in the United States of America
10 9 8 7 6 5 4 3 2 1

To
James Madison Willis
and
Mary E. Park Willis

Contents

Preface   ix

1   Literary Critics and Democratic Ideas   1

2   The Balliol Group   17

3   "Poetry as Such": Arnold's Early Criticism   32

4   Subjects from the Past   59

5   "That Natural Heart of Humanity": Homer
     and the Ballad Poets   86

6   The Great Work of Criticism   103

7   The Activity of Poetry   135

8   The Classic and Classical Poetry   173

Notes   193

Bibliography   213

Index   221

Preface

In this study of the literary criticism of Matthew Arnold, I look at the answers that Arnold gave to the question of the kind of poetry—and more broadly, literature—necessary in a democratic age. The clearest results, in my view, could be achieved by a study of his literary criticism, rather than his social criticism or theological essays. For this reason I have not included *Culture and Anarchy*, the books on religion, or the poetry. Although I do not mean thereby to deny that the thought of Matthew Arnold may tend towards a unified whole, I do not believe that a principle can be easily moved from literary criticism to philosophy or theology or that literary terms can be translated, without some change, into philosophical or theological terms: for example, what is "excellence" in literary criticism is not the same as "perfection" in moral or religious thought. Certainly, such exchanges do take place in Arnold's writing, yet much of his effort, I have concluded, went to separating literary criticism and poetry from history, philosophy, and theology. Nor have I set out to make all of Arnold's thought a unified whole. I might add that if a magisterial study of Arnold's thought is to succeed, it must, to some extent, depend on investigations of special problems. In the same way, Arnold's critical thought needs to be studied in the context of European and American thought, both of his own time, including such figures as Thomas Carlyle and Ralph Waldo Emerson, and of the early period of the Romantics and the eighteenth century, including such writers as Samuel

Taylor Coleridge, Heinrich Heine, Samuel Johnson, Johann Wolfgang von Goethe. Much good work, indeed, has been done on such studies; and more might be done on the French prose writers, particularly Voltaire, and the French historians, such as Jules Michelet. I thought it useful, however, to begin nearer home, as it were, and to compare Arnold's literary criticism with that of his friends, in order to illuminate the kinds of questions that were asked and the answers that were given. Because these friends were, in fact, classical scholars, which Arnold himself was not, as well as literary critics, the problem, so limited, reveals not only some shared assumptions but also significant differences in a long-continued debate about the place that poetry should hold in the new age.

My research for this book was begun in 1980/81 on a sabbatical leave from the Department of English at Kansas State University; I am grateful for this leave and for funds and travel grants provided by the Graduate School. The librarians at Farrell Library have been cordial and efficient in obtaining the materials that I required. The Beinecke Library at Yale and the Houghton Library at Harvard generously allowed me to use the Arnold and Clough materials in their collections. I owe special thanks to Richard D. McGhee for his support of this study and for his encouraging reports on an early chapter. I am grateful to Christopher Clausen for reading the manuscript and for many helpful suggestions. An anonymous reader for the University Press of Kansas offered useful criticism. John Farrell gave some excellent advice about the general argument.

Since I began my work on Arnold, I have learned much from the Arnoldians; my particular debts to those who have written on Arnold criticism is acknowledged in the text. R. H. Super's edition of the prose works, beginning with the first volume on the classical criticism of Arnold, has been invaluable. Among those critics whose work I have followed with interest, I mention, in addition to the books of Professors McGhee, Farrell, and Clausen, those of David J. DeLaura, Warren Anderson, and William Madden, Sidney Coulling, and Ruth apRoberts. To G. Robert Stange I owe thanks for his patient reading of my early essays on Arnold's poetry and for his own fine book on Matthew Arnold.

A somewhat different version of part of chapter 6 appeared in the Arnold centenary volume of *Victorian Poetry* under the title "The Real Burns and 'The Study of Poetry.' " Some of the material in chapter 6 appeared in the *Arnoldian* under the title "Arnold's Imaginative Reason and Sellar's *Roman Poets*"; I am grateful to the editors of *Victorian Poetry* and of the *Arnoldian* for permission to use this material.

My husband, Harold W. Schneider, has been infinitely patient and understanding at the same time that he has held up the highest standards of criticism.

Chapter One

Literary Critics
and Democratic Ideas

Greatest among the Victorian critics, Matthew Arnold is also the most diverse; like the Greek hero Odysseus, type of the ancient Athenians, Arnold had a curious mind, and his criticism is a series of explorations and travels into new territory. Aware of the many possibilities of human life, and opening up to others the knowledge of them, Arnold undertook in his lectures and essays a wide variety of subjects. No single study of Arnold's criticism can do entire justice to all of his work, and those who have studied all or part of the criticism have traced but one of his courses. What I have done is to follow Arnold's exploration of the place of criticism and poetry in a democratic age.

Arnold's criticism can be followed from his earliest letters and the prefaces to his poems to his criticism of Homer and to the early and later essays on criticism and poetry that make up the main body of his critical work. In his earliest letters, Arnold was mainly aware of the difficulties of being a poet in the Victorian world; he was trying to find his own voice. In these letters to his friend Arthur Hugh Clough, Arnold began to define his conviction that whatever else poetry may be or do, it is first of all an art. Making a place for the art of poetry became his central concern in the 1850s, when, in his important essays, he thought about the function of poetry in a democratic age, turning to the examples of the Athenian democracy and the Roman republic and to Aristotle as the defender of tragic poetry in the polis. Drawing first on the

1

theories of the historians, Arnold came close to making poetry, as the interpreter of life to a democratic age, all but a kind of history, a position that he later modified and eventually abandoned. In the essays on Homer, Arnold turned to the questions raised in Homeric criticism—namely, whether the Greek epic poet was in fact like the English ballad poets and whether the true poetry for a democratic age was a kind of ballad poetry celebrating the life of the ordinary people. Arnold here defended Homer as a master of the grand style; in effect, Arnold denied that the great democracy of Athens was educated by a ballad poetry and that the coming democracy of England could be nurtured on such poetry.

In Arnold's formal criticism, in his two collections titled *Essays in Criticism*, Arnold affirmed his own belief in the work of criticism and poetry, an activity realizing the possibilities of all the people in a great democratic age. Turning again to the great literary critic of Athens—Aristotle—Arnold began to delineate a theory of the way in which all of the people may share in both criticism and creation. In the second collection, Arnold defined the limits of poetry, a poetry that is neither morality nor philosophy but that offers a criticism of life; he examined the democratic poets from Burns to Byron and set forth once more the idea that the only poetry for a democratic age is the best possible poetry or any age—the classic.

Throughout his poetic life and in all of his criticism, Arnold had argued that poetry was art and was to be judged as art and that only this poetry would suffice for a great democratic age. Whereas others were arguing for a poetry of or by the people—or at least for the people—a kind of folk or ballad poetry, a literature suited to the limited knowledge and taste of the people, Arnold argued from the beginning that poetry is a free activity, not bound by any program or any idea or by any form, beyond the requirement of what he called poetic truth and poetic beauty. Only in this way can great poetry be written, and only great poetry can suffice for a democratic society.

Although some notable critics have looked at Arnold's ideas about democracy, few have connected Arnold's literary criticism to the question of a literature for a democratic society. Benjamin E. Lippincott, in his analysis of Arnold's criticism of Victorian democracy, argued that Arnold welcomed the coming of democracy and that he set about showing how English society might be changed to bring about a sound order. Lippincott rightly emphasized Arnold's contribution to reform in education, from the elementary schools to the universities, aiming to wrest from the aristocracy the control over the public schools and the universities by establishing state schools and universities.[1] What Lippincott did not fully see, however, is that Arnold's literary criticism is connected to his social thought; Arnold wrote his essay "Democracy" at about the time that he began to write literary criticism, and he considered including it in his first series of critical articles, *Essays in Criticism*.[2]

Lionel Trilling did grasp both the importance of Arnold's social and political thought and the direction that it took in his social criticism. Trilling saw that Arnold welcomed the age of democracy and upheld the "ideas of 1789"; and Trilling thought that Arnold, in his 1857 lecture "On the Modern Element in Literature," outlined a program for a literature for the people. Arnold's demand for adequacy, Trilling said, is new, and Trilling brilliantly connected this new literature to the needs of democracy. Literature that offers an "intellectual deliverance," that orders the world, is needed in order to command the attention of individuals in a democratic state, individuals who possess reason: "Democracy is based on the intellect; it can progress only by the intellect, by the circulation of sound ideas so clear and distinct as to win general agreement."[3] Trilling used *England and the Italian Question* (1859) to show that Arnold insisted that reason, not force, was "the instrument of the democratic masses" (p. 149). And literature, which offers an "adequate interpretation" of the times, is the guide for the "idea-moved" masses, in that it clarifies ideas as well as calms and composes the mind (p. 150). Literature, too, Trilling interpreted Arnold as saying, must hold up an ideal for the people. Trilling thought that the lectures on Homer were also directed toward the literature of a democracy, attempting to free the people from eccentricity of ideas and taste (pp. 157–58). Here Trilling drew a lively picture of Arnold attacking an "American" vulgarity and eccentricity in the person of the unfortunate Francis W. Newman, the translator of Homer; but Trilling did not see that Arnold was attacking not only the criticism of Newman but a larger movement, a movement towards a popular poetry that was happily encouraged by Arnold's friends in the Oxford group. Trilling was at his best when he wrote about Arnold and the ideas of the French Revolution, as in the essay on Heine, rightly seeing that Arnold valued Heine as a soldier in the war to free humanity, who knew the importance of ideas in the new democracy (p. 190). Trilling also saw political themes in Arnold's later criticism, noting that "Literature and Science" again affirms the ideas of the French Revolution and seeing that Byron was of all the Romantic poets still praised for his faithfulness to the ideas of 1789 (p. 340).

Trilling's weakness as a critic is that he failed to see that Arnold's literary criticism was not isolated from his social thought. Thus, Trilling saw the 1853 Preface as being concerned primarily with Romantic subjectivity and Classical objectivity but did not see how the essay laid the groundwork for later theories about tragedy and democracy. Trilling saw that Arnold's call for the grand style was not aristocratic (p. 139), but he thought that Arnold, then as later, was working out a "religious theory of art" (p. 139). Trilling thus dismissed *Merope* as a frigid classical imitation (p. 143); by not connecting the drama to the 1857 lecture, he separated the poem from the criticism that was meant to provide an aesthetic for a drama for the people. Trilling's analysis of the essays in criticism again separated the essays into those dealing with social issues and those dealing with literature; and he held to his thesis that Arnold saw poetry as essentially religious. Trilling's desire to make of Arnold's essays a unified whole made him set up equivalences that are not really justified by the text: poetry is a "criticism of life," the highest expression of the "imaginative reason"; "criticism of life" means making "ethical and spiritual judgments," essentially philosophical ones (pp. 175–79). Trilling thus ignored the distinctions that Arnold carefully worked out as he developed his ideas. Trilling confused "criticism" with poetic "criticism of life"; he linked both to "imaginative reason" and thus reduced Arnold's distinctive terms to general philosophic terms in ethical and theological systems.

In the same way, in commenting on the second series of essays, Trilling accepted the view that Arnold intended poetry to take the place of religion and that poetry must become religious (pp. 340–41). Arnold's "truth and seriousness" was made transcendental; "seriousness" was taken as "solemnity"; yet Arnold's idiosyncratic taste was thought to determine his practical criticism of poetry, in his preference for the sad or melancholy (p. 341). Further, Trilling saw in "The Study of Poetry" a Romantic hero—William Wordsworth—and Arnold's longing for Wordsworth's sense of the supernatural (p. 343). Trilling's analysis of Arnold's practical failures in his social criticism pursued a similar path, seeing Arnold as either retreating into metaphysics from the actual world or as falling into contradictions when his principles came into conflict with his personal sympathies. Thus, Trilling interprets Arnold's "disinterestedness" as not taking up a cause. Trilling thought Arnold was inconsistent in saying that Lucius Cary Falkland had been crippled by his own "disinterested" appraisal of the Royalist cause (p. 186). Actually, Falkland's case proves Arnold's point—namely, that criticism must keep apart from practical action; Falkland, by committing himself to the cause of the Royalists, was no longer acting as an observer or critic. For a man of action, his hesitation, his indecision, and his ability to see both sides of a question were handicaps. Falkland's irresolution made him, in Arnold's view, a tragic figure, in implied contrast to the Caesars and Cromwells of the world.

On the matter of John William Colenso, bishop of Natal, Trilling again saw a contradiction in Arnold's holding that a democracy depends on the "idea-moved masses" yet saying that ordinary people cannot follow an intellectual demonstration of the kind that Colenso offered. Therefore, according to Trilling, Arnold thought that Colenso's work was harmful in destroying the support of " 'old moral ideas, [which] leaven and humanise the multitude' " (p. 194; *PW*, 3:44). In this instance, however, Trilling had less respect for the capacity of the people than Arnold had. Few, Trilling said, can lead an intellectual life; whereas Arnold meant only that people cannot deal with the ideas of a discipline until they have been trained in that discipline, like Jane Austen's Catherine Morland, who did not know anything until she had been taught it. Trilling left out of account here what Arnold always thought essential—education—although in an earlier discussion, Trilling had given a detailed analysis of the failure of British education during the early nineteenth century. Here, Trilling did not take into account Arnold's conviction that until there is a good system of public schools, the "idea-moved masses" could not reason well enough even to decide questions of their own welfare but, always attracted to new ideas, would be easily led into quirky or fanatical systems. Few may lead the intellectual life of philosophers; but many might, with education, follow practical social and political arguments.

Much critical analysis of Arnold has tended to follow Trilling, by identifying criticism and culture, by seeing Arnold as making of poetry a sad, melancholy religion or offering consoling illusions, or by trying to compensate for a failed romanticism by turning to a false classicism.[4] Few have followed Lippincott and Trilling in trying to understand Arnold's program for democracy. A notable exception is R. H. Super, who has made available in his edition of Arnold's prose the texts that make any new study of Arnold possible. In *The Time-Spirit of Matthew Arnold*, Super described Arnold as "the liberal of the future": "Arnold's liberalism, then, rested on the double conviction that it was the only condition compatible with human dignity."[5] In a later essay on Arnold's critical practice, Super took account of the life of nineteenth-century Europe, of "the ideas of 1789," and of the need for "a new spiritual basis" for life.[6] He saw the critic, in Arnold's theory, as arriving at a synthesis of knowledge, supplying from many fields the materials for poetry (p. 163); in this way the critic finds a new spiritual basis: "The central core of Arnold's criticism is, then, his sense of a writer's value in supplying the spiritual and intellectual needs of the nineteenth century" (p. 175). Although one may assume that the ideals of 1789 are connected to the intellectual needs to be met by criticism and by poetry, Super did not draw out these ideas and, like Trilling, tended to leave Arnold's literary criticism detached from his social thought.

The question of Arnold's relation to the Victorian age was seen by Sidney Coulling as central in Arnold's criticism. Coulling argued that Arnold, although at odds with his time, came to feel a need to sympathize with the age and that this sympathy was expressed in the 1857 lecture "On the Modern Element in Literature," the essay that Trilling found to be important in Arnold's social thought.[7] Coulling did not, however, see Arnold as concerned about finding a literature for the age of democracy. Even in Coulling's analysis of the essays on Homer, he thought that Arnold had primarily been concerned with the question of whether Homer was, as Francis Newman argued, "quaint, garrulous, prosaic, and low." Coulling did not take up the fact that Newman thought that Homer was "a popular poet, and thus he should be translated into the ballad metre," that is, a popular poet should be translated into a popular form (pp. 77-79). Because Coulling appears to have viewed classical poetry as esoteric, remote from the people, he did not grasp the full significance of Arnold's answer to Newman. Coulling, in examining "The Function of Criticism at the Present Time" as a product of the Colenso controversy, did, however, emphasize the connection of that essay to the "higher criticism," though he took perhaps too narrow a base. Coulling discussed *Culture and Anarchy* as Arnold's answer to the charge that his idea of culture took no account of the "common man" (p. 205). Arnold, Coulling pointed out, answered the criticism of Robert Williams Buchanan, who took from the Spasmodic poets the view that "actual life" was "the true material for poetic art," a view that was absurd if the only true material was the actual life of East London. Coulling thus left Arnold somewhat remote from actual life but was right when he said that Arnold, in *Culture and Anarchy*, had hoped to change the society of England and was unwilling to accept the dreadful life of the poor as a permanent fact of English life.

The tendency to see Arnold as standing above the struggles of the people continues to appear in recent criticism. Dorothy Deering, in "The Antithetical Poetics of Arnold and Clough," perceived an Arnold who turned aside from the modern world and attempted to "rise to the passionless heights beyond self to a pure realm of aesthetic beauty,"[8] whereas Clough "turned with hope to the people of the new industrial world" (p. 29). Deering continued the contrast of the "subjective" poetry of Arnold and the "objective" poetry of Clough, a theme put forth by critics from the nineteenth century to the present.[9] The emphasis on "imaginative reason" as a key to Arnold's criticism also tends to put Arnold above the actual world. William Madden, who took "imaginative reason" as central in Arnold's poetics, attempted to unify Arnold's critical thought by making him part of a tradition of criticism that assumes that all experience could be organized by the "aesthetic consciousness."[10] With heroic effort, Madden united Arnold's various positions into a single statement, and asserted that man's "highest joy" is "the disinterested contemplation of the beauty of life and things" and that this "aesthetic contemplation" is Arnold's "religion of the imaginative reason" (p. 187). A high price is paid for this vision of unity, most of all in giving up the development of Arnold's thought, his taking up and modifying of certain positions. Many scholars have recently found in imaginative reason a key to Arnold's thought and poetry; but too much emphasis on that idea tends to lead away from Arnold's central concerns.

In keeping the focus on literary criticism, I have hoped to avoid the kinds of questions raised by considerations of culture and civilization. Raymond Williams has shown how closely connected are the terms *culture* and *democracy* and has shown also how the terms have changed in meaning since the eighteenth century.[11] Williams's discussion of *Culture and Anarchy* is valuable in giving a broad background for the period, but he did not discuss Arnold's idea of democracy, and he thought that Arnold's program of culture meant "education, poetry, and criticism" (p. 121). The tendency to equate *culture* with education can arise from Arnold's use of *culture* (which Williams recognized) as a growth of the individual towards perfection. It seems unlikely, however, that Arnold thought that the means to culture included chiefly poetry and criticism; even Arnold's idea of criticism can include the best that is thought and said in all disciplines. Little about critical theory can be found in *Culture and Anarchy*; Arnold, who was well aware of his journalistic critics, did not represent himself as a poet or argue the superior virtue of poetry; instead, he spoke, ironically, of his occasional use of poetry and philosophy. Nevertheless, there is in *Culture and Anarchy* a statement that looks ahead to "The Study of Poetry": "Plenty of people will try to give the masses, as they call them, an intellectual food prepared and adapted in the way they think proper for the actual condition of the masses. The ordinary popular literature is an example of this way of working on the masses" (*PW*, 5:112). Although Arnold did not specify the literature, in general he used the world *literature* in a broad sense. Little in the way of literary criticism is to be found in *Culture and Anarchy*, and I do not believe that Arnold's terms *culture, criticism,* and *criticism of life* are interchangeable. Certainly Arnold's *culture* does not mean belles-lettres or even literature in the sense of what is written, whether science or poetry; rather, it keeps the radical sense of growth and development. Arnold, in *Culture and Anarchy*, described some general ideas about human nature and society, but a theory of literary criticism cannot be deduced from those essays.

A good deal of recent work has been based on the assumption that literature is bound to the society that produced it, or to its culture, and cannot be transmitted to another society in a different time, place, or language without loss, or even from one group or class to another. An extreme position is that literature arises from a group or class in a certain time and place and the sole audience for that literature is that class. Indeed, even T. S. Eliot, although he argued for a unified culture or "way of life," took the view that a "minority" culture, that of the hereditary upper-class family, educated at a university, and belonging to the established religion, cannot be widely disseminated without suffering deterioration.[12] The converse view is that the working class will create its own culture, which will differ from that of the other classes, and that out of this culture will come a literature with a special aesthetic consciousness.[13]

The problems in the transmission of a literature from one age to another, specifically from ancient Greece and Rome to Victorian England, were raised by Arnold's friends and critics and continue. For example, Frank Kermode, in *The Classic*, began with Arnold's comments on Vergil as the inadequate interpreter of his age in "On the Modern Element in Literature" but did not take account of Arnold's discussion of the problem in his lectures on Homer or his definition of *classic* in "The Study of Poetry."[14] Arnold, in the essays on how to translate Homer into English, was aware that "mists" separated the Victorians from ancient Greece; certain things, he acknowledged, could not now be known about how the Athenians had read Homer. Arnold's practical solution was to refer such questions to a scholar who had an appreciation of poetry, such as Benjamin Jowett. Even in the 1857 lecture, Arnold distinguished between "manners," which are local and temporal, and thought or feelings, which may be held to be universal.[15]

A similar problem arose in America in respect both to

Greek literature and to British literature. Walt Whitman, the declared poet of democratic America and of the people, to whom America and democracy were "convertible terms," acknowledged the greatness of the Greek poets and of Shakespeare but insisted these were "monarchical" poets, not "consistent with the United States."[16] Yet speaking of the Hellenic poets, Whitman mused on the Athenian audience, in a brief parenthesis: "I sometimes fancy the old Hellenic audience must have been as generally keen and knowing as any of their poets" (*Goodbye, My Fancy*, p. 1261). Whitman also thought about the popular audience: "Sometimes the bulk of the common people (who are far more 'cute than the critics suppose) relish a well-hidden allusion or hint carelessly dropt, faintly indicated, and left to be disinterr'd or not" (p. 1261); Whitman found this style in Aristophanes, Pindar, Shakespeare, Tennyson, and the old ballads. On the one hand, Whitman spoke grandiloquently about a great literature to rise from the coming democracy; on the other hand, he speculated about the way poets had always made an appeal to the "common reader." Whitman, in reported conversations, attacked Arnold as a "dude" who was indifferent to the common man, remarks that are part of a response to Arnold's criticism of American civilization.[17]

But Whitman's ideas about a popular poetry were not altogether opposed to those of Arnold. What Arnold had to say about the United States remains more interesting than what Americans had to say about Arnold. Arnold observed in the United States a democracy forming in a country that he thought to be mainly middle-class, with the strengths and weaknesses of that class. In his early letters, Arnold was dismayed at the "hard unintelligence" of American democracy as it then appeared to him, a democracy that had been formed under the leadership of Andrew Jackson; Arnold takes what Bernard Bailyn has called the view from the center of civilization towards the "marchland." Even in his later essays on the United States, Arnold tended to focus on the "marchland," the new city of Denver and the families in the cabins on the

frontier. Nonetheless, what is important is Arnold's conviction that the significant fact about the United States is its
political and social democracy. The response of American
critics, especially the professed Arnoldians such as Sherman
Paul and William Brownell, showed that Arnold was not
thought to be hostile to the United States or to democracy.

This brief review of work on Arnold shows that some of
the best Arnoldians have recognized Arnold's acceptance of
political democracy. The emphasis of these writers, however,
has fallen on Arnold's social thought rather than on his literary criticism. What I intend to show is that Arnold became
increasingly concerned with the question of a literature for a
democratic age. In developing this thesis, I have followed a
more or less chronological order in the discussion of Arnold's
work and have, at the same time, been concerned with the
essays and criticism of Arnold's friends, most particularly the
Balliol group. One reason for taking the circle into account
is that Arnold's major essays were written in part as answers
to essays or reviews written by Arthur Hugh Clough and John
Campbell Shairp. Moreover, Arnold and his friends were debat-
ing the question that is my principal concern—namely, the
question of literature in a democratic age.

Further, I have concentrated on the importance of Aristotle in Arnold's literary criticism—the *Poetics* in the earlier
criticism; the *Ethics* in the later essays. The importance of
Aristotle cannot be overestimated but has often been missed
by those who have seen Arnold's thought as generally Stoic.
As I shall show, Arnold was trained early in Aristotle, and
when he turned for models to the great poets of the Athenian
democracy, he turned also for guidance to the great literary
critic of Athens, not so much because he thought that only
the literature of the Greek democracy would be consistent
with a new democracy, but because the success of the tragic
writers in winning a popular audience had set an example for
modern writers. Equally important was the fact that Arnold
had to solve the kinds of problems that Aristotle had faced
when he had made a case for Homer and the tragic poets in

a time when both were under attack, not from the populace, but from a far more dangerous opponent, Plato. Aristotle had demonstrated, in answer to Plato, that the poets had a place in the city or in the republic; the theory of catharsis—that is, the purgation of pity and fear—has long been seen as an answer to Plato's charge that tragedy weakened the spirit of the people. Gerald F. Else, whose commentary on the *Poetics* is magisterial, has, in a recent book, gone further in showing how the *Poetics* answered Plato's attack on Homer and Greek tragedy. Aristotle's theory of imitation, Else argued, is "a part of Aristotle's polemic against Plato's intellectual elitism."[18] Arnold's use of Aristotle in the 1853 Preface was not, then, a gesture of frigid classicism but was a recognition of Aristotle's arguments in defense of a poetry in a democratic society. The "laws of poetic truth and poetic beauty," which Arnold speaks about in "The Study of Poetry," have to do with poetic structures, plot and action, and character, which are based on universals. Arnold is like Aristotle in seeing the poet as a maker rather than as a philosopher and in seeing poetry as giving pleasure, which is consistent with the aim of human life as happiness.

Like Aristotle, Arnold held that happiness was to be found in an activity, an *energeia*, at the level of excellence. What Arnold set out to do, finally, was to show how the activity of criticism or of poetry is available to all in a democratic society. Arnold's idea of the function of poetry went beyond the affectivist notions of his early letters—namely, that poetry must animate and console—and beyond the didactic—that poetry must ennoble. Pursuing the idea of the best—not ballad poetry, but Homeric epic—Arnold arrived at the perception that creative activity at the level of excellence is the life of happiness, the good life, not only for the poet or the critic but also for the readers, who in some way share in the sense of creative activity.

Poetry is, however, only one of many possible activities. In his criticism, Arnold's main theoretical task was to separate poetry from other activities. Poetry, he concluded after much thought and even mistaken theory, is not, after all, history; nor, for all of Arnold's intense study of modern European thought, is it philosophy; nor, for all of his inquiry into theological matters, is it religion; nor, for all of his fascination with Lucretius, is it science. Poetry does not replace these activities, even religion, although there is much confusion on this point among later critics. Poetry does not even compete with these activities; each has a function in the ideal society or state. The sorting out of the functions of poetry and criticism was a gradual development in Arnold's criticism, which was not completed until "Literature and Science." Arnold defined the function of poetry in part in order to defend the place of the poet and the critic in the state, although he never quite separated poetry from politics, as Aristotle did not. Even Arnold's literary judgments often had a political bias, notably his determined loyalty to Byron and to Shelley, the great revolutionary poets. Arnold's idea was of a nation in which the poet takes a rightful place among the artisans and the thinkers, with each seeking performance in an activity at the level of excellence and each sharing in an ideal human development, both individual and social.

Although Arnold did not offer a classic definition of democracy, in a review of a history of Greece he quoted with approval the description of the Athenian democracy as allowing " 'the free and independent participation of all in the affairs of the commonwealth' " (PW, 5:275). In the essay "Democracy," which was first published as an introduction to The Popular Education of France (1861), Arnold's examples of democracies were France and the United States. In that book he urged a system of national education in England in order to avoid the dangers of these democracies and to make a "timely preparation" for the passing of power to the people (PW, 2:19). At the present time, Arnold thought, the aristocrats, who were not receptive to new ideas, "leave the people still the multitude, the crowd; they have small belief in the power of the ideas which are its life" (PW, 2:11). Nor was the middle class likely to improve the people, but if the middle class were to win power within the next fifty years, as Arnold thought that it might, it would fail to assimilate the masses, "whose sympathies are at the present moment actually wider and more liberal than theirs" (*PW,* 2:26). What Arnold hoped for, however, was that a "common culture" could be achieved through the fusing of the upper and middle classes (*PW,* 2:89) and through a national system of education (*PW,* 2:22–23, 26). In "The Twice-Revised Code" (1862) Arnold fought against the proposals that he thought would severely limit the education of the poorer classes (*PW,* 2:243). He wrote in a letter that he hoped to have "done something to ward off the heaviest blow dealt at civilization and social improvement in my time" (*Letters,* 1:85). Although Arnold failed to prevent the changes he fought against, it is evident that he was more interested in the extension of education to all the people than in the extension of the franchise.

In "Democracy," Arnold saw the Athenian democracy as one that brought the lower and middle classes into a common life and a common culture. Later, in his reviews of the five volumes of Ernst Curtius's *History of Greece,* Arnold traced the failure of Athenian democracy. The ideal of democracy was one in which "the people by free development and by the practical school of public life might become a set of individuals able each to think and act wisely for himself" (*PW,* 5:277). Pericles, in order to govern the multitudes, became a dictator; and the practical failure of democracy was matched by a theoretical failure: "To give to a whole people entire freedom and the practical school of public life is well." But the great days of Athens, Arnold thought, lived on accumulated resources of "character" forged in the past and used "by the new, vigorous force of democracy, by a whole gifted people with the fresh sense of being alive and astir" (*PW,* 5:281). In the next essay, Arnold, following Curtius's account, pointed out that Socrates and Plato had attempted to recall to Athens the sense of the old virtues, to show that "freedom and movement" are not enough without an ideal to move towards (*PW,* 5:287). Nevertheless, as Arnold acknowledged,

Plato was no friend to the people. In the last of the reviews, Arnold took note of the orator Demosthenes, who "was in vital sympathy . . . with the Athenian democracy," valuing its great past, its leaders, and its historian Thucydides (*PW*, 5:293). Arnold noted the contrast between Plato and Demosthenes and quoted Curtius on Plato, " 'his teachings and aims could only become the possession of a circle of elect' " (*PW*, 5:293). Arnold recognized that the greatness of Demosthenes lay in his not accepting the fall of the city or the democracy— "The grandeur of Demosthenes, and his civic superiority to a man, even, so fascinating as Plato, consists in his having refused to allow himself to entertain such a belief"—and in his working to avoid the fall of Athens, thus saving at least "the ideal of national greatness and of true political effort among mankind" (*PW*, 5:292). The emergence of the orator Demosthenes balanced the despairing note in Arnold's account of the decline and fall of the Athenian democracy; it struck a note of optimism as Arnold observed the beginning of another democracy.

Chapter Two

The Balliol Group

The task that Matthew Arnold set himself in his criticism was to find a place for poetry in a democratic age. Arnold did not, however, see the people as a folk—as a source of natural wisdom. Throughout his career he argued against the poets and the critics who claimed for the common people, as both subject and source, the exclusive territory of poetry. In his criticism he fought steadily on this ground, most often against his own early friends—the Balliol group, or the Oxford set—especially his own good friends the poet Arthur Hugh Clough, the classicists John Campbell Shairp and William Young Sellar, and their ally James Anthony Froude. Arnold, in the Preface to the 1853 *Poems*, his first important piece of criticism, showed why the poet of the people, Alexander Smith, whom Clough had extravagantly praised in a review of Arnold's earlier poems, was not a great poet. In his inaugural lecture as Oxford Professor of Poetry in 1857, Arnold held up as models the great poets of the democratic ages of the past. In the lectures on Homer, answering Shairp, Arnold showed the error of reading Homer as a ballad poet; and he argued against Shairp on the importance of criticism in "The Function of Criticism at the Present Time." And in "The Study of Poetry," Arnold showed why Robert Burns, whom Shairp admired as a poet of the countryfolk, had not achieved the rank of the classic. In regard to the question of a literature for a democratic age, the debate with members of the Balliol group was of primary significance, especially because they shared a common education and had for all their lives been concerned with the education of others.

Matthew Arnold's friends at Balliol left a record of the social life of the group in early letters and in memoirs written late in the century. Thomas Arnold, in *Passages in a Wandering Life* (1900), gave a glimpse of the "little interior company" of Clough, Theodore Walrond, and the two Arnold bothers and recalled that they met at Clough's rooms on Sunday mornings.[1] Thomas Arnold also remembered another society called the Decade, which, between 1843 and 1845, included Matthew Arnold, Shairp, Jowett, and Arthur Penrhyn Stanley (p. 59). The Balliol group was seen somewhat differently by its various members, according to their interests, among them classical scholars such as Sellar or poets and critics such as Francis T. Palgrave. As Oxford scholars, the friends debated the question of the poet as interpreter of the age and as historian of the times—that is, the poet's relation to the people and to the past. Most of them welcomed Clough's *Bothie* but deplored Arnold's *Empedocles on Etna.* They continued the debate throughout their lives, in essays, reviews, and books—a debate that had continuing significance in the development of Arnold's critical thought.

The center of the group was Clough, who was older than the others, who led the way both as teacher and as poet, and who was the first to die and the first to be recreated by his friends in memorial essays. In the recollections of his friends, Clough emerged as a profound thinker who struggled with insoluble problems but was finally baffled, even though he was always noble and sincere in his struggle.[2] The view of Clough as a failed genius, which in part was the result of his early reputation among the Balliol group as a profound thinker on the religious questions that had troubled the young men at Oxford, appears in Palgrave's introduction to Clough's poems and to some extent in Arnold's elegy "Thyrsis." Henry Sidgwick, in his review of the 1869 edition of Clough's poems, concluded that friends were not the best judges of a poet's actual achievements: "There is a natural disposition among personal friends to dwell upon unrealized possibilities, and exalt what a man would, could, or should have done at the expense of what he actually did."[3] Yet Sidgwick, like Clough's friends, saw him as "always trying to solve insoluble problems" (p. 62).

Another side of Clough emerges in Shairp's recollections of the days at Balliol: here Clough is seen as a kind of Victorian Wordsworth, climbing the hills of Wales, the Lake Country, and Scotland, now and then making pen-and-ink sketches, occasionally in silence contemplating nature in its visionary aspects—in storm or sunset on mountain lakes—and natural man in his rural habitat.[4] Clough seemed to Shairp to have a special sympathy for rural life: "Often afterwards he used to speak of his Scotch adventures with great heartiness. There was much in the ways of life he saw there that suited the simplicity of his nature" (p. 212). Clough also found natural gentlefolk, lords and ladies, among the peasants (pp. 205–6). To some extent, Shairp and others made Clough the kind of poet they wanted, on the one hand struggling to resolve questions of faith in a skeptical age and, on the other, drawn to the simple life of the common people, the folk of England and Scotland.

The friendship of Arnold and Clough is recorded chiefly from Arnold's side, mainly in his early letters. On the evidence of these letters, Arnold was not drawn to the Clough of the Balliol group, the profound thinker and doubter in poetry, but rather to the classicist, the poet who was willing to experiment with Homeric style and meter—the Clough whom Arnold commemorated in his last lecture on Homer. He thought that Clough took entirely the wrong track in his attempts to solve the universe, and Arnold cared little for Clough's novelistic treatment of life in the *Bothie* and in *Amours de Voyage*. Although the two agreed on the poet's duty to reach the people, they disagreed on the kind of poetry that was necessary. In the formal criticism, the frank but friendly exchanges of letters became forceful attacks on each other's poetry and critical positions, Clough's first from the other side of the Atlantic in a review of Arnold's poems. Yet from the early days of their friendship, Arnold and Clough shared a certain common background: not only are there images common to both poets but also some critical ideas.

Not one of the group, but important in the Oxford life, was Benjamin Jowett. Jowett's pupils included those who belonged to the set of Clough, Arnold, Sellar, Palgrave, and Walrond; in 1841 Jowett was a member of the Decade, which then included Stanley.[5] Jowett had been present at Dr. Arnold's inaugural lecture at Oxford (*LL*, 1:86), and although he did not agree with Arnold's ideas on church and state (*LL*, 1:150-51, 154), he admired Arnold's work at Rugby and to some extent thought that he himself was carrying on a similar work at Balliol (*LL*, 2:43). In 1878, reading again Stanley's *Life of Arnold*—"which always catches hold of me when I take it up again"—Jowett remarked that the *Life* had "idealized" the profession of teaching: "There were weak points in Arnold and his friends intellectually, but in that one respect of inspiriting others with ideals, there has been no one like him in modern times" (*LL*, 2:161). With his good friend Stanley, Jowett traveled in Europe. When in 1848 they made a trip to Paris, Stanley was carrying an introduction to Jules Michelet from Matthew Arnold (*LL*, 1:134). There is not much evidence of a close friendship between Arnold and Jowett; as Jowett himself said, "it was not until long afterwards that he learned to take Matthew Arnold seriously" (*LL*, 1:88–89).

In his essays on translating Homer, Arnold proposed Jowett as the arbiter of taste in judging a translation; but Jowett rarely commented on Arnold's work. In a letter on *Literature and Dogma*, Jowett criticized Arnold's use of etymology and commented, "Arnold is too flippant to be a prophet" (*LL*, 2:80–81—1875). On Arnold's death, however, Jowett wrote about the "serious side" of Arnold's character of "hard work, independence, and the most loving and careful fulfilment of all the duties of life" (*LL*, 2:227–338). Arnold's visits to Jowett at Balliol may have been rather dutiful, although Arnold once expressed regret that Jowett did not return his visits. In 1871, Arnold wrote from Harrow to decline Jowett's invitation to meet Tennyson, giving the reason that the Walronds were coming: "The sort of visit you have promised to make and never do make."[6] In 1873, Arnold is mentioned as one of Jowett's visitors at Balliol. And in 1875, Arnold, with other Balliol men, appeared at a banquet on the opening of the new Hall, when he and Alexander Grant, the editor of Aristotle's *Ethics*, responded to the toast "Literature and Science," proposed by Thomas Hill Green. Stanley quoted Clough's poem "One port, methought, alike they sought" (*LL*, 2:103–5). Jowett, among his old friends and pupils, "was supremely happy." Years later, on the death of Sellar in 1890, Jowett recalled the "remarkable band" that had included Grant and Arnold, commenting, "I am pleased to think that they stood together and had a strong affection for one another through life, and that Balliol College was accidentally the center of this connexion" (*LL*, 1:141).

Arnold was probably not much influenced by Jowett's work on Greek thought and literature, most of which was published too late to have had a direct influence on Arnold's criticism. On the other hand, the instruction of Jowett at Balliol may have led Arnold to certain classical writers. In 1847, Jowett began the study of Plato's *Republic*, thus initiating a change from Oxford's exclusive concentration on Aristotle (*LL*, 1:132). As early as 1845, however, Arnold was reading the *Republic*, probably for the Oriel fellowship.[7] On the other hand, in 1845, Jowett was lecturing on the pre-Socratic philosophers (Faber, p. 160), and Arnold's first long poem was on one of the pre-Socratics, Empedocles. Jowett's favorite subjects for lectures included Sophocles, Aristophanes, Thucydides, and Plato (*LL*, 1:200, 241, 250); and Arnold later set up these Greek writers as standards of excellence. Late in his life, Arnold was reading Aristotle's *Politics*; in 1887 he entered in his *Note-Books*, "Aristotle's Politics i–iii (with Jowett)" (pp. 619–21). Although Jowett may have been a guide both early and late in Arnold's reading, even more important to Arnold than the work of Jowett himself may have been the scholarship of Jowett's pupils, especially that on Lucretius and Aristotle. Jowett encouraged the work of Alexander Grant on the *Ethics* (*LL*,

1:283-84) and suggested that he undertake a translation of all of Aristotle (*LL*, 2:44). Grant dedicated the new edition to Jowett (*LL*, 2:270). Jowett also followed the work of Sellar on Lucretius (*LL*, 1:129). Jowett was important to the classical scholars of the Oxford set, and it was this "remarkable band" that he himself remembered.

Sellar was perhaps the least well known of the group. "Who is Sellar?" John Ruskin once asked, as he came across a reference to Sellar in Palgrave's work on landscape.[8] Like Shairp, Sellar had come from Scotland to Balliol, where he became one of Jowett's pupils and his lifelong friend. In 1850, Sellar returned to Scotland. After the publication of *The Roman Poets of the Republic* (1863), he was appointed to the chair of Latin at Edinburgh. There he became a friend of Grant's. Among the younger scholars were Richard Claverhouse Jebb and S. H. Butcher. Sellar's early work on Lucretius and Vergil provides a context for Arnold's criticism of Rome and the Roman poets. In working out an aesthetic for the philosophic poetry of Lucretius, Sellar arrived at an idea of the imaginative reason. Sellar's last work, on Horace and Ovid, is infused with lines from Arnold's poetry and criticism, as Sellar illuminated the literature of the Romans by comparing them to the Victorians. Sellar saw in Ovid something like Arnold's treatment of mythology and, in Arnold's criticism, the qualities of Horace. Sellar himself, as Andrew Lang has reported, turned increasingly to the poetry and criticism of Arnold: "Among his contemporaries, he [Sellar] most appreciated Mr. Matthew Arnold. One of the last books that Sellar read was the Second Series of Essays in Criticism . . . : 'There is nobody like him,' he said, as he laid them down."[9] Sellar remains the least known of the set and, in some ways, the most like Arnold. Although at Balliol, Sellar followed Shairp and others in his admiration for Clough's *Bothie* and remained loyal to the memory of Clough, his own solid criticism of the Roman poets led him to respect Arnold's work.

Shairp, whose early friendship with Clough we have noted, made himself Clough's heir and carried further some of Clough's ideas in his own later criticism. Shairp and his friends had liked *The Bothie* partly because it recalled to them the summer life of the Oxford students and the intellectual life under Clough's guidance. In 1845, Shairp and Clough were in Scotland on a visit to Theodore Walrond's family at Calder Park; in 1847, Clough had a reading party in Scotland, near Loch Ness, where Shairp, Walrond, and Thomas Arnold visited Clough. According to Shairp, Clough had used some incidents from this visit in *The Bothie*.[10] In 1846, Shairp became an assistant master at Rugby, where Matthew Arnold was toiling for a time in his father's school. Shairp returned to Scotland in 1856, first going to Glasgow and then, in 1857, to St. Andrews, where he became professor of Latin in 1861 and, in 1868, principal of the United College. In 1877, Shairp, with Matthew Arnold's help, was elected professor of poetry at Oxford and was reappointed in 1882.

Shairp published two collections of poetry, *Kilmahoe: A Highland Pastoral* (1864), which was reviewed by Sellar, and a posthumous book, which was edited by Palgrave, *Glen Dessaray and Other Poems* (1888). Shairp's poetry illustrated his ideas about the subjects and themes of popular poetry drawn from the lives of the Scottish people and set in the landscape of the Highlands. Beginning in 1864 with an essay on Wordsworth, Shairp developed these ideas in a number of essays on poetry: *Studies in Poetry and Philosophy* (1868); *Poetic Interpretation of Nature* (1877); *Aspects of Poetry* (1881), a collection of his Oxford lectures; and *Sketches in History and Poetry* (1887). Shairp cut a broad swath in his criticism, writing both on Latin poetry and on English as well as Scottish poetry, always with a strong sympathy for popular forms and for rural themes. Between Shairp and Arnold there was an undeclared but unresolved quarrel. Shairp reviewed Arnold's early poems, attacking its classical forms and themes; Arnold's major pieces of criticism contain answers to Shairp, beginning with "The Function of Criticism at the Present Time"; and Shairp not only attacked Arnold's criticism but also answered Arnold's *Culture and Anarchy* with his own *Culture and Reli-*

gion. Shairp's monograph on Burns gave Arnold fuel for "The Study of Poetry," and Shairp replied in one of his last essays, "English Poets and Oxford Critics" (1882). In many ways, Shairp illuminates the criticism of Arnold, not only by his somewhat heavy-footed paraphrases of Arnold's ideas but also by helping Arnold to define and to defend his own critical principles. In this exchange, more than any other, one sees the essential conservatism of the advocates of poetry of and for the people, in contrast to Arnold's genuine belief that in a democratic poetry the best poetry was none too good for the people.

One of the Oxford set, though not of the Balliol group, James Anthony Froude, in his career at Oriel and later as editor and historian, served as observer of the members of the group. His early letters add to the legend of Clough as a profound religious thinker.[11] Froude was then in the midst of his own religious crisis and the consequences of the publication of his *Nemesis of Faith:* he resigned, he was denounced, and his book was burnt on February 27, 1849.[12] Froude also added to the caricature of Arnold as shallow in thought and experience: the calm and resignation of Arnold's poems, Froude declared, was too easily won; "he has never known what a storm is." Froude also thought that Arnold's poetic art was facile; writing to Clough, Froude said, "On the whole he shapes better than *you* I think—but you have marble to cut out—and he has only clay" (*Correspondence*, 1:251). Froude's reviews of the early poems by Arnold and by Clough generally support the views of the letters. As editor of *Fraser's Magazine*, Froude published some of Arnold's essays based on his early Oxford lectures. As a historian of the Elizabethan Age, Froude may have helped Arnold decide that Shakespeare's age was one of the great epochs. On the other hand, Froude's theories about literature and history were the opposite of Arnold's and Froude became one of the circle of Carlyle. Like Shairp, Froude helps to show the difference between the Balliol group and its greatest poet and critic.

Francis T. Palgrave was closer to Jowett than to anyone

else in the group except Sellar.[13] Palgrave's chief interest, however, lay in poetry; in 1849, Froude reported that Palgrave was ready to put Arnold and Clough above the popular poet Philip James Bailey, the author of *Festus (Correspondence,* 1:251). Palgrave became a friend and admirer of Tennyson. G. D. Boyle, dean of Salisbury, recalled conversations sometime in 1865 or 1866 in London: the talk began with the Oxford set but ended in reading Tennyson:

> The merits of Matthew Arnold's poetry, and his first volume of *Essays in Criticism,* the place of Clough in poetry, and the revival of interest in Wordsworth's poetry and Coleridge's philosophy, in two fresh and suggestive essays by his old Balliol friend, J. C. Shairp, were the theme of many talks, prolonged sometimes to late hours, and always ending in rapturous readings from *Maud* and *In Memoriam,* and enlivened by personal recollections of the last visit to the Isle of Wight, and the last conversations held with the great poet. *(FTP,* p. 38)

When Tennyson's "Lucretius" appeared in 1866, Arnold was dismayed to find that the poet laureate had preempted Arnold's own subject, on which he had been at work, he said, for twenty years; and he suspected that Palgrave, with whom he had discussed his plans, had carried word to Tennyson.[14] Palgrave's letters and journals indicate that he often visited his friends and kept track of the work of the Balliol group. For instance, he wrote to Grant in 1863 about Sellar's Edinburgh appointment *(FTP,* p. 83); to Grant in 1875 on the publication of Grant's essays on Aristotle's *Ethics (FTP,* p. 140–41); and to Sellar on his Vergil in 1877 *(FTP,* p. 147). Palgrave wrote a memoir for the 1862 *Poems* by Clough, which was published first in *Fraser's Magazine* in March *(FTP,* p. 71). On October 25, 1884, Arnold wrote to Palgrave on the latter's retirement, suggesting a literary professorship. Arnold quoted from what he called an old Sicilian song: " 'The future is not ours and the past is lost' " *(FTP,* p. 173). In 1885, Palgrave was elected

132, 247

professor of poetry at Oxford, succeeding Shairp; in 1877, Palgrave had stepped aside in favor of Shairp, as he had in 1867 for his uncle Francis Doyle (*FTP*, pp. 99, 188). In 1888, Palgrave wrote from Rome on Arnold's death and later gave the commemoration speech, in Latin, on Arnold (*FTP*, pp. 209–10).

Palgrave's own poetry has been little remarked. His poems on English history appeared in 1880 and 1881, titled *Visions of England*. Henry James, according to his letter, read them to Fanny Kemble (*FTP*, pp. 158, 163). Palgrave's Oxford lectures were collected in 1897 as *Landscape in Poetry*, which again were read by Henry James (*FTP*, pp. 254–58). Probably the most influential of Palgrave's work, however, was the *Golden Treasury*, first published in 1861 (*FTP*, p. 65). Christopher Clausen has given considerable attention to this collection, seeing it as an important cause of the shift in taste towards lyric poetry and showing how it has influenced lyric poets and the novelists of the twentieth century.[15] Clausen has recognized the importance of Palgrave in establishing a popular poetry. On this evidence, Palgrave belongs with Shairp and Clough's friends in helping to achieve the ascendance of the lyric over the epic or narrative poem. Yet Palgrave himself aimed at the longer narrative poem on a historical subject, the kind of poetry with which Scott had achieved popularity in his day. These minor poets illustrate the ways in which the poets chose certain subjects and forms in order to reach a national audience: Shairp through his Highland poems, Palgrave through his poems about English history, and Clough in later poems, modeled after Chaucer, titled *Mari Magno*, on the lives of the emigrants from England. These were the subjects that these poets urged in their criticism and, in some ways, were the subjects of the popular broadside ballads: current topics, historical and patriotic subjects, and lives of the ordinary folk. The poetry illustrates these poets' criticism, especially their differences with Arnold.

However different the courses that each of the group took in later years, all had been trained in Aristotle; all knew the *Poetics* and the *Ethics*. The prominence of Aristotle in Arnold's critical thought appears, in this context, to be thoroughly natural, but it is important to see how Arnold and Clough, especially, read and responded to Aristotle.

The importance of Aristotle as a guide to right choices in life is evident in Arnold's early life and education. Thomas Arnold, who referred familiarly to the Greek philosopher as "Old Tottle," had studied the ancient historians by the light of the political theory of Aristotle and had a "long cherished intention of bringing the 'Politics' of this favourite Aristotle to bear on the problems of modern times and countries."[16] Equally important was the study of Aristotle at Oxford.[17] Matthew Arnold spoke, with his accustomed irony, of "the bad old times, when we were stuffed with Greek and Aristotle" (*PW*, 5:126–27).[18]

More important than the *Politics* here was the *Ethics*. Clough in *The Bothie* (1848) gave a lively description of the undergraduates who, on a reading party in Scotland, had been stuffed with Aristotle until they are ready to escape, "Weary of Ethic and Logic, of Rhetoric yet more weary"; but they had promised to return, "Three weeks hence, with the rain, to Prudence, Temperance, Justice, / Virtues Moral and Mental."[19] They cannot, however, anywhere escape Aristotle as a moral guide, and Adam the tutor instructs them to take their precepts from the *Ethics*. The young hero, Philip Hewson, accepts his tutor's advice, somewhat impatiently: "Let us all get on as we can, and do what we're meant for. / Or, as is said in your favourite weary old Ethics, our ergon" (pt. IX, ll. 85–86, p. 51 of 1848 ed.). He repeats his resolve, with variations in Clough's epic manner: "Let us get on as we can, and hunt for and do the ergon" (pt. IX, l. 97, p. 51 of 1848 ed.). By *ergon*, it should be said, Philip does not mean duty; he means finding the work that he can best do, in which he is to find his "good," a good proper to his own nature. This good is what Adam speaks about: "Yes, we must seek what is good, it always and it only;/ Not indeed absolute good, good for us, as is said in the Ethics./ That which is good for ourselves, our proper selves, our best selves."[20] Although Philip is skeptical about making Aristotle a sufficient guide for everyday life and although he sees that finding the good—or knowing one's best self—is no easy task, Clough suggests in *The Bothie* that the young Oxford scholars took seriously the quest laid upon them by their study of Aristotle, most particularly in their search for an activity in which they could find their own good life. Ironically, perhaps, Clough, when he looked for employment in the United States, again found himself teaching the *Ethics*.

Arnold's letters to Clough show the young poet following Aristotle in working out his poetics as an ethical problem, an activity that engaged his best self and constituted the life that was good for himself and humankind. Writing to Clough from Thun in 1849, Arnold clearly is thinking in the terms of the *Ethics*; he speaks about finding his own way, according to his own nature, and of making choices aiming at his own good as well as the social good. He ends by paraphrasing Aristotle, as he urges Clough, "Let us neither be fanatics or yet chalf [sic] blown by the wind," but rather let us make our moral choices wisely and independently. Keeping more literally to Arnold's Greek (as far as one can understand what he meant to say), let us make moral choices like the man of practical wisdom *(phronimos)*. Arnold in part quotes Aristotle's definition of virtue,[21] and appears to be thinking about moral choice.

The full context of the letter shows how much Arnold's thought about practical wisdom is based on the *Ethics*; it indicates also how much his poetics are part of his moral effort. His own plan to live by practical wisdom or judgment, with a measure of self-control arising from self-understanding, is, he thinks, too often undermined by his tendency to "hoist up the mainsail to the wind and let her drive" (*Letters to Clough*, p. 110). The moral problem, as he sees it, is how to be free. To achieve both intellectual and poetical independence, he cannot merely follow his whims but must make reasoned choices. And he must, as man and poet, resist not only his own impulses but also the influence of the times.

He begins to feel that he has achieved some measure of independence, as he says at the beginning of the letter: "I am getting to feel more independent and unaffectible as to all intellectual and poetical performance the impatience at being faussé in which drove me some time since so strongly into myself, and more snuffing after a moral atmosphere to respire in than ever before in my life" (*Letters to Clough*, p. 109). The moral atmosphere for Arnold was the world in which he could be free; as he said in an often-quoted passage, the struggle to keep his independence required great determination in an age of great cities and small natures and of "moral desperadoes like Carlyle." This is the point at which he urges Clough, "Let us neither be fanatics nor yet chalf blown by the wind," and urges a reasoned choice of their own course of action (*Letters to Clough*, p. 111). The breathing space that Arnold needed for his own intellectual and poetical work was a "moral atmosphere" of a free activity.

As Arnold began to form his own theory of criticism, he continued to refer to Aristotle. This will be an important part of my analysis of the criticism. Here I will summarize some of the passages in other works that indicate Arnold's general view of Aristotle. Arnold thought Aristotle one of the great philosophical writers but not one of the great literary writers; and he saw Aristotle as coming after the great age of Greece, which Arnold here placed as the period from Simonides of Ceos to Plato. Aristotle's time, Arnold said, was marked mainly by scholarship and breadth of learning: "The Greek spirit, after its splendid hour of creative activity was gone, gave our race another precious lesson, by exhibiting, in the career of men like Aristotle and the great students of Alexandria, this idea of the correlation and equal dignity of the most different departments of human knowledge, and by showing the possibility of uniting them in a single mind's education" (*PW*, 4:291). Clearly the work of Aristotle was not literary or poetic; it was scientific and philosophic. The Greek genius, Arnold said in *St. Paul and Protestantism* (1870), has a "conscious and clear-marked division into a poetic side and a scientific side" (*PW,* 6:21). It would not be possible to take "from a chorus of Aeschylus one of his grand passages about guilt and destiny, just put the words straight into the formal and exact cast of a sentence of Aristotle, and [say] that here [is] the scientific teaching of Greek philosophy on these matters" (*PW,* 6:21). Even among philosophers, Arnold said in "Emerson" (1883), Aristotle belongs with Spinoza and Kant as a great philosophical writer but not with Plato as a great literary writer (*PW,* 10:174).

Yet it would be a mistake to think that Arnold saw Aristotle as only a dry, methodical logician. Arnold spoke of Aristotle as moralizing with a sense of sadness on human folly or philosophizing with a sense of joy in the capacities of the human mind. Thus, Arnold spoke about "the buoyant and immortal sentence with which Aristotle begins his Metaphysics, *All mankind naturally desire knowledge" (God and the Bible* [1874], in *PW,* 7:242). Earlier, referring to the *Ethics,* Arnold said that Aristotle has spoken "mournfully" of the unenlightened many (*PW,* 5:225). Else saw in these passages the ground of Aristotle's defense of the *Poetics,* the belief that everyone desires knowledge. Aristotle was not an authority to be followed without question. Arnold recalled that as an undergraduate he had found the discussion of the intellectual virtues quite unclear, and in spite of his tutor's easy resolution of the difficulties, Arnold thought the great philosopher might actually have been mistaken in his argument, "not right, not satisfactory" (*PW,* 8:11–12). Nonetheless, Arnold had thought, like the undergraduates in Clough's *Bothie,* about the virtues "moral and mental" and had understood how, in the *Ethics,* "the moral virtues . . . are with Aristotle but the porch and access to the intellectual, and with these last is blessedness" (*PW,* 5:167). From Aristotle's discussion of the moral virtues Arnold takes the idea that is the foundation of his practical criticism, quoting from the discourse a phrase that he used first in a letter to Clough and that in the lecture on Homer and in later essays he translated "as the judicious would determine" (*PW,* 1:99, 8:264, 11:98). The judicious, or the *phroni-*

mos, is the judge or the arbiter of taste, as Arnold said in the lecture on Homer, translating Aristotle, " 'as the judicious would determine,'—that is a test to which everyone professes himself willing to submit his works" (*PW*, 1:99).

This brief survey indicates that Arnold had a definite idea of Aristotle's place in the Greek world; it also indicates some of the Aristotelian precepts that Arnold was to develop in his criticism. Although the *Poetics* is important in the early essays, it is only when one reads Arnold's later criticism with an eye on the *Ethics* that one can fully perceive the Aristotelian cast of Arnold's central ideas. Yet—and this is the advantage of reading Arnold in the context of the Balliol group—Arnold's friends, although they may not have agreed with him, understood what he was doing.

Chapter Three

"Poetry as Such": Arnold's Early Criticism

In his letters to Clough, Arnold mused over his own poetics and politics. In 1853, after he had written the Preface, he brought the poetics and politics together in an effort to sum up his poetics. What, he asked, did his poems do for the audience? " 'The complaining millions of men / Darken in labour and pain'—what they want is something to *animate* and *ennoble* them—not merely to add zest to their melancholy or grace to their dreams.—I believe a feeling of this kind is the basis of my nature—and of my poetics."[1] The early letters reflected Arnold's struggle to find his nature and his poetics, not in isolation, but with a concern for humanity and especially for the many. Arnold's comments on poetry were often intermingled with his observations on politics. Writing about the revolution of 1848 and the Chartist agitation, Arnold showed that his sympathies were with the people, although at the same time he was apprehensive about a radical change in government that would give the people a power they were not trained to exercise. At times, however, Arnold entertained some revolutionary ideas of his own; writing to Clough, he speculated about a society of workers in "which an apostolic capitalist willing to live as a artisan among artisans may surely divide profits on a scale undreamed of" (*LC*, p. 69). When writing to his mother, he did not think the mob at Trafalgar Square was dangerous (*Letters*, 1:4). At a Chartist convention he was impressed by the "ability of the speakers" (*Letters*, 1:8), even though their message was that the enemies of the people were the aristocrats and "the large land and mill owners" (LC, pp. 74–75). Carlyle, Arnold thought, saw through the "din and whirl and brutality which envelop a movement of the masses" to "its ideal invisible character" (Letters, 1:4). To his sister "K," it is true, Arnold expressed a fear of "brutal plundering and destroying" where the middle and upper classes were themselves too ignorant to "train them [the masses] to conquer" (Letters, 1:6). Arnold believed that schools were important for "their future effects in civilising the next generation of the lower classes, who, as things are going, will have most of the political power of the country in their hands" (Letters, 1:20).

Arnold was impressed by the civilization of the French people, by "the *intelligence* of their idea-moved masses" (Letters, 1:6). He thought that the *Revue des deux mondes* was a guide to the current European opinion in "the *atmosphere* of the commonplace man as well as of the Genius" (LC, pp. 72–73). Indeed, he tried to persuade Clough that "amongst a people of readers the litterature is a greater engine than the philosophy" (LC, p. 74); *Figaro* was more influential than *Le Contrat social*. Popular literature was also influential: "Seditious songs have nourished the F[rench] people much more than the Socialist: philosophers: though they may formulize their wants through the mouths of these" (LC, p. 74). Convinced as he was of the importance of literature in shaping the ideas of the people, he was also concerned about the quality of that literature. As to whether, in a democracy, the individual was "lost in the crowd," as Mill was to say, Arnold in 1852, in a despondent mood, declared that the world had become "more comfortable for the mass, and more uncomfortable for those of any natural gift or distinction"; but he admitted that perhaps there was some justice in that, "for hitherto the gifted have astonished and delighted the world, but not trained or inspired or in any real way changed it" (LC, p. 123). Thus the early letters indicate Arnold's sympathy with the attempts of the people to gain greater control of their world and his sense of the responsibility of the poet to influence them in finding a more worthwhile life. In the letters to Clough, Arnold began to work out some of the aesthetic problems of a poetry in a new democratic age.

This early criticism by Arnold is informal and practical; Arnold mixes aesthetics with politics, especially during the events of 1848, with ethics, and with what he called generally "life." The letters are short—there are no extended essays on any subject—and were written in haste. Haste, as Arnold himself knew, does not guarantee either spontaneity or sincerity—effects that are gained, like others, by art. Furthermore, because the letters are not systematic essays in criticism, any attempt to find a coherent set of critical principles in them is bound to be somewhat tentative. Too much is missing to trace with any confidence a line of development, a definite shift in emphasis, a real change in ideas. Arnold does, however, touch on the subjects of his later criticism—the Romantic poets, Keats, Wordsworth; on Shakespeare and Milton; on Sophocles; on contemporary poets and the age; on the matter and form of poetry. His observations, which are rarely more than sentences or paragraphs in length, are properly explorations—insights or intuitions—about what poetry is or about the poetry that Arnold wanted to write. Certain positions are present from the first: the givens of the historians about the matter of all knowledge, which poetry has in common with history; and the givens of poetry—poetry as such—that which sets poetry apart from history, science, and religion. From the beginning, Arnold was struggling to sort out the claims of poetry from those of the other disciplines and to restore poetry to its own kingdom.

From the beginning, Arnold held that the poet's subjects are the world and the self. The clearest statement of the idea that the poet's materials are the life and the history of the world appears in a letter, or rather a fragment of one, dated about December, 1847, or early 1848, the sixth letter in Lowry's collection: "*The what you have to say* depends on your age. . . . The poet's matter being *the hitherto experience of the world*, and his own, increases with every century" (*LC*,

p. 65). Arnold did not advance this description of the poet's matter as anything new; it is something that he took for granted. What he was working out in the letter was the way in which the pressure of matter affects the form and style of poetry. But Arnold began from this position—namely, that the poetical life is lived in awareness of the experience of the world, of history. Thus the poet who is ignorant of the world, who is deficient in matter, is like Clough's collaborator in the volume of poems called *Ambarvalia*. As Arnold described him, "Burbidge lives quite beside the true poetical life, under a little gourd" (*LC*, p. 65). Arnold meant that Thomas Burbidge is like the prophet Jonah, who sat in the shade of the gourd vine, complacently indifferent both to the people of Nineveh and his own situation, unaware that the shelter of the vine is temporary. The poet's matter, Arnold held, is life; the question is not only how to know life but also how to find the poetic forms with which to treat life. Arnold felt that the burden of modern knowledge was a heavy weight for the poet. In his famous lament on the "damned times," Arnold despairs at "the height to which knowledge is come" (*LC*, p. 111). He gave the same lament to his character Empedocles and later identified Empedocles' complaint as his own (*LC*, p. 130). Nonetheless, it was the heroic task of the poet to uphold the burden of the world, like Atlas; and Arnold did not give up the struggle: "For me you may often hear my sinews cracking under the effort to unite matter" (*LC*, p. 65).

Arnold thought about various ways to "unite matter" in a poem; he often thought in metaphor. It is, I think, misleading to select any metaphor as central, or even as the key, to Arnold's early poetics. The metaphors are not always clear. In the letter to Clough in which Arnold spoke about cracking his sinews to unite matter, he described three ways in which poets deal with the Universe:

To *solve* the Universe as you try to do is as irritating as Tennyson's dawdling with its painted shell is fatiguing to me to witness: and yet I own that to *re-construct* the

Universe is not a satisfactory attempt either—I keep saying, Shakspeare, Shakspeare, you are as obscure as life is:
yet this unsatisfactoriness goes against the poetic office
in general: for this must I think certainly be its end. (LC,
p. 63).

The first part is clear enough: neither Clough's analytic nor
his philosophical poetry (solving the Universe) will do, nor
will the sensuous description of Tennyson's early poetry (looking at the painted shell). Arnold consistently held that poetry
was not philosophy, thinking aloud was not poetry, and mere
natural description was not good poetry. The second part of
this passage is more obscure, and I will attempt to give only
my own reading, which I think is consistent with Arnold's
general position in the letters and with his later formal criticism. Poetry, Arnold held, is art—a thing made, or constructed;
his own way in poetry is "to re-construct the Universe." The
rest of the passage is especially difficult. One possible reading
is that "to re-construct the Universe" was Shakespeare's way;
it was not a satisfactory way (for Shakespeare can be as obscure
as life is), yet his way must be the right way for poetry. Or
it may be that Arnold was saying his own way was to reconstruct the Universe but that his attempts were not satisfactory.
What is wrong is not the method (which was Shakespeare's),
but Arnold's own attempts. Because Arnold did not fully
understand Shakespeare's art, he could not see what was going
wrong in his own poetry.

    What Arnold meant by the phrase "to re-construct the
Universe" is not further explained, either in the letter or in
any later piece of criticism. Consistent with his classicism,
Arnold may have meant that poetry gives, not the actual
world, but an ideal world, a perfected Nature (or, as Aristotle
said, not Alcibiades as he was but as he ought to have been).
It is very possible that Arnold meant that the actual world
is somehow remade by the poetic imagination. Arnold did not
say that the poetic imagination creates a world but that it
reconstructs the world, implying that the imagination orders

the actual world. Froude, in his review of Arnold's poems, said that the imagination of the poet does not invent or fabricate plots; instead, it gives life and color to the actual. Later, Froude asserted that Shakespeare left the mysteries of life unsolved, that he was, in Arnold's phrase, as obscure as life is.[2] What Froude said illuminates Arnold's letter to Clough, but Arnold would allow more to the ordering power of the imagination.

The problem for Arnold was how to order his material, how to "unite matter" without falling back on the abstractions of philosophy or "solving the Universe." This appears to be the difficulty in the attempt to find order by having "an Idea of the World." Arnold advanced this notion in a letter that has not been dated with certainty but probably was written sometime in 1848 or 1849. Arnold had recently read Keats's letters, and he commented on what he saw as Keats's failure to order the "multitudinousness" of the world; Keats and Browning, he said, fail in the same way: "They will not be patient neither understand that they must begin with an Idea of the world in order not to be prevailed over by the world's multitudinousness: or if they cannot get that, at least with isolated ideas: and all other things shall (perhaps) be added unto them" (*LC*, p. 97). If Arnold was to be consistent with his later theory, an idea of the world was not for Arnold a philosophical or metaphysical concept or system, although his use of the word *idea* has an undeniably Platonic ring; and when Arnold later returned to Keats, he credited him with the Idea of Beauty. Certainly it is close to the appeal to reason, to the *phronimos*, by which Arnold himself hoped both to order his own life and to overcome the tendency to drift with the sensations of experience. Nonetheless, it is the world that Arnold spoke of here, and "the world's multitudinousness" suggests phrases that he had used earlier, the "hitherto experience of the world" or the history of the world.

Thomas Arnold's use of another Arnoldian word, *architectonice*, is helpful in understanding Matthew Arnold's "Idea." Dr. Arnold had written, "It were a strange world, if there were indeed in it no one *architektonikon eidos*."[3] Dr.

Arnold's *architectonice* is essentially a moral idea, a sense of
the Providence that orders and governs the world according
to a supreme idea of good, not merely by chance or expediency.
It is a good that appears in the events of the history of the
world and that is the historian's task to trace. In the 1857 lecture "On the Modern Element in Literature," Matthew Arnold
later spoke about the "intellectual deliverance" of the poet
or the historian who adequately comprehends his own world.
The idea was to appear again in Arnold's judgment that the
Romantic poets did not know enough, by which he meant that
they did not fully comprehend the events of the French Revolution. Whether or not the "Idea of the World" is a philosophical
or historical explanation, it does order the facts of the world,
as poetry reconstructs the universe according to a plan.

So far, then, Arnold was consistent in saying that the
poet's place is in what he called in the 1853 Preface "the empire of fact." The poet's matter is, in part, the life of the world,
its history, its experience. But Arnold has also said that the
poet's matter is his own experience; out of the poet's *individuality* comes the unique form, style, expression, that makes
poetry great art. This is how I understand the passages in
which Arnold took up the necessity of self-knowledge, his own
desperate attempts to protect his individuality within the
circle, and his struggle with the notion of "poetry as such."
Essentially he was struggling not only to keep intact his own
self and his own kind of poetry but also to keep poetry from
becoming rhetoric, metaphysics, theology, philosophy, science,
or even history. Although he succeeded early in writing his
own kind of poetry, his defense of the realm of poetry as such
was to occupy his entire critical life, not for the sake of defending his own poetry, but for the sake of poetry itself. The work
was not to end until his essay on "Literature and Science."

The importance of self-knowledge to a writer is evident
from the earliest letters. Writing about the growing popularity
of George Sand, Arnold predicted the reaction among his
friends who were "born-to-be-tight-laced," and he feared the
consequences: "the strong minded writer will lose his self-

knowledge" and will justify himself by an appeal to utilitarian principles and social reform (*LC*, p. 59). Over and over, Arnold expressed a desire to retreat from his friends, fearing to be drawn into controversy in which he would lose his sense of self. He imagined his character Empedocles' seeing the great flaw in his life, that he had "lived in wrath and gloom, / Fierce, disputatious, ever at war with man, / Far from my own soul, far from warmth and light."[4] In 1853, in a letter to Clough, Arnold spoke about the "unnatural and unhealthy attitude of contradiction and opposition" and asserted: "Only positive convictions and feeling are worth anything—and the glow of these one can never feel so long as one is pugnacious and out of temper. This is my firm belief" (*LC*, p. 142).

Arnold had felt the threat of an alien spirit most strongly five years earlier on the publication of Clough's *Bothie* in November, 1848; then, as Arnold had written, he sought refuge in Obermann from the "time-stream," where "Sellar and the rest of that clique who know neither life nor themselves" were raving about Clough's poem (*LC*, p. 95). That this was an honest confession of feeling is confirmed by Arnold's letter to Clough, written in February, 1853, when Arnold said that in 1848 he had needed "intellectual seclusion" to escape from "all influences that I felt troubled without advancing me" (*LC*, p. 129). This feeling he expressed in a letter from Thun in 1849, when he again spoke about a need to protect his own self; his "one natural craving is . . . a distinct seeing of my own way as far as my own nature is concerned" (*LC*, p. 110). Later, in a kind of apology to Clough, Arnold deprecated his own lack of intellectual and artistic strength, his lack of power. But Arnold's feeling was always one of a need for a retreat, a strong sense of the Epicurean need to "hide thy life."[5]

Within his circle of friends, Arnold had more and more to defend his own kind of poetry. The others were increasingly being drawn to the kind of poetry that Clough was writing in *The Bothie*, a poem that managed, by using a loose novelistic structure and a lively style, to combine a confessional and an autobiographical mode, dramatizing an agonizing personal choice with the "thinking aloud" and "solving the universe" of the philosophical hero and at the same time exalting the virtues of ordinary life. Moreover, Clough adopted for the poem a kind of mock-heroic version of the Homeric style, a rambling narrative dactylic hexameter with seriocomic imitations of Homeric epithets and similes. Arnold's friends distinctly preferred Clough's poetry to Arnold's classical imitations and subjects. In a letter to Clough on March 6, 1849, Froude, although he praised Arnold's "versifying" and "aesthetic power" and admitted that Arnold "shapes better" than Clough, nonetheless declared: "But you have marble to cut out—and he has only clay."[6] Some of the early differences arose over Arnold's preference for classical forms and subjects, perhaps entirely for things Greek; Shairp and Froude urged Arnold to give up the "old Greek forms," as early as *Empedocles* and as late as *Merope.* In late 1849, Arnold wrote with some annoyance, even personal spite, to Clough: "I said a lovely poem to the fool Shairp today which he was incapable of taking in. He is losing his hair" (*LC*, p. 113). Only Froude offered praise for some of the 1852 poems, as well as a fair review in the *Westminster*; and in a letter, Froude declared that *Sohrab and Rustum* was nearly perfect.[7] On the publication of *Merope*, Arnold remembered Froude's praise by writing that Froude was "one of the very few people who much liked my last vein" (*LC*, p. 136). But Froude, although he liked certain poems, was not on the whole on Arnold's side in the poetic controversy.

The question of the proper subject of poetry, which was important in the 1853 Preface, is in the letters only part of the question, What is Poetry? Arnold, almost alone among the early Victorian critics, held that poetry *as such* was art; it was distinguished from other forms of writing by form, style, and expression. Clough, on reading Arnold's letters, must have felt his own poetic self severely challenged. From the first, Arnold set down as the essential requirement that poetry be art, that it be beautiful. Then, in trying to find aesthetic reasons for his immediate response to Clough's poems, Arnold turned again to Shakespeare. Arnold had made only perfunctory comments in what he called in his next letter "a beastly vile note" (*LC*, p. 63). On further thought, Arnold acknowledged that Clough had achieved a kind of "individuality" in his poems, but as a thinker rather than as a poet, and a cranky and eccentric thinker at that; worse, Clough had expressed bitter and arbitrary opinions, without regard to his audience, by despising any appeal to the imagination. So, at any rate, I read the somewhat obscure reference to Shakespeare: "Shakspeare says that if imagination would apprehend some joy it comprehends some bringer of that joy: and this latter operation which makes palatable the bitterest or most arbitrary original apprehension you seem to me to despise" (*LC*, p. 63). Immediately afterward comes the famous passage, already discussed, in which Arnold said that Clough has attempted to solve the universe, rather than, like Shakespeare, to reconstruct the universe. That is, the dramatist makes a world in the play, a world in which the characters may have bitter or arbitrary "apprehensions" or dramatic thought and feeling that the audience, moved by the play's appeal to the imagination, can understand and accept. That Clough spoke too directly in his own voice, that he philosophized too openly, was clearly Arnold's view in the letters.

Arnold went on to separate poetry from related forms: "A growing sense of the deficiency of the *beautiful* in your poems, and of this alone being properly *poetical* as distinguished from rhetorical, devotional, or metaphysical, made me speak as I did" (*LC*, p. 66). Clough, Arnold went on to say, was not "an *artist*"; rather, he was like Novalis "in the way of direct communication, insight, and report" (*LC*, p. 66). What Arnold objected to in Clough's poetry was the lack of form; but he did not mean that "matter" was not also important. Arnold went on to draw an analogy between the matter of science and of poetry: "And there are the sciences: in which I think the passion for truth, not special curiosities about birds and beasts, makes the greater professor" (*LC*, p. 66). For Arnold, the man of science was Lucretius, who was also a poet. This fact may also account in part for Arnold's assertion, which is no doubt debatable; but the important point here is the idea that general truth, not an inquiry into the special problems of philosophy or theology, is proper to poetry. Clough took too little account of the poem as a whole, as Arnold pointed out in a letter defending Racine:

> Mithridate was a young man's effort—but you know you are a mere d—d depth hunter in poetry and therefore exclusive furiously. You might write a speech in Phèdre—Phedra loquitur—but you could not write Phèdre. And when you adopt this or that form you must sacrifice much to the ensemble, and that form in return for admirable effects demands immense sacrifices and precisely in that quarter where your nature will not allow you to make them. (*LC*, p. 81, May 24, 1848)

In general, Arnold was saying that in his poetry, Clough was self-indulgent, self-conscious; Clough thought aloud, spoke his thoughts in his own voice, made reports on the world, but made no appeal to the imagination through poetic or dramatic form. Yet, Clough followed his own nature in refusing to give in to the demands of form; and as might be expected, Clough did succeed in being sincere, as Arnold said two months later: "The good feature in all your poems is the sincerity that is evident in them: which always produces a powerful effect on the reader—and which most people with the best intentions lose totally when they sit down to write" (*LC*, p. 86, July 20, 1848). Two points are important here: sincerity was not, for Arnold, a primary value, although he acknowledged its effect on the reader; and perhaps more important, sincerity was not to be confused with artlessness but was an effect of art. The whole matter of sincerity has been given greater prominence in Arnold's criticism than it deserves, and it has often been misunderstood, especially in his later criticism. What he has said here is therefore significant.

In a letter written some months later, Arnold once more

considered the connection between form and matter, making explicit his argument that although both are important in great poetry, form is essential to poetry. First, Arnold said that Clough's poems were not "natural," which may seem inconsistent with his earlier judgment that the poems are sincere. What he meant here, however, was that the form was not natural: ". . . naturalness—i.e.—an absolute propriety—of form, as the sole *necessary* of Poetry *as such;* whereas the greatest wealth and depth of matter is merely a superfluity in the Poet *as such" (LC,* pp. 98–99). The qualification *as such* is important; Arnold had said and would say again that great poetry must have "wealth and depth of matter"; but what makes poetry is the shaping of matter into poetic form. The meaning of *form* was another question, and as Arnold recognized, the opposition of form and matter was to some extent misleading. Certainly no poem is without some form; and indeed, Clough, in his "formless" poems, used stanzas, verse forms, and diction that were relatively simple, and hence had an effect of sincerity—forms like the hymn. Whether these simple forms were appropriate for Clough's weighty matter was what Arnold was questioning; he was to discuss the question later in talking about the ballad form.

Here Arnold has borrowed the terms of the opposition and turned them to his own uses; Clough aimed exactly at "naturalness," at an effect of sincerity; it was Arnold who, using the old Greek forms, was supposed to be artificial. Arnold now went on to sort out some of the possible senses of form, something he would try to do in most of his major critical essays. Here he distinguished two forms, both natural to poets: "This lower form, of expression, is found from the beginning amongst all born poets, even feeble thinkers, and in an unpoetical age: as Collins, Green[e] and fifty more, in England only" (*LC,* p. 99). The higher, and presumably better, form belonged to the mature poet: "Form of Conception comes by nature certainly, but is generally developed late" (*LC,* p. 99). By "form of conception" Arnold evidently meant something like a form of thought, although not rhetorical or logical structure; the term is used about concepts of Aristotle that, Grant had said,

formed the basis of Aristotle's thought.⁸ The forms of conception I take to be the characteristic ideas or structures that give
a distinctive shape to a poet's thought.

Arnold thought that when the conception and the expression were poetical, the poet achieved his highest result. But
it was possible for thought to overwhelm poetic expression,
and especially in those who were not "born poets": "I often
think that even a slight gift of poetical expression which in
a common person might have developed itself easily and
naturally, is overlaid and crushed in a profound thinker so as
to be of no use to him to help him to express himself" (*LC*,
p. 99). Arnold has put the case rather oddly and in a way that
disparaged Clough's gifts as a poet while it praised his strength
as a thinker. Arnold might have said that a slight gift can develop easily and naturally in even a common person and that
even a powerful gift can be crushed in a profound thinker.
Arnold, however, who was uncertain of his own talent as a
poet and who did not want to deceive himself, was ready to
make severe judgments about himself; and he expected the
same kind of rigorous self-questioning of Clough. Certainly
Clough had the reputation among his friends of being a profound thinker but a doubtful poet.

Arnold continued to develop his conviction, which he
enunciated in an early letter, that a wealth of matter demands
a plain style. In the famous passage in which he sketched the
idea that poetry must be a *"magister vitae,"* he continued the
earlier analysis of the necessity for a plain style:

Modern poetry can only subsist by its *contents:* by becoming a complete magister vitae, as the poetry of the ancients did: by including, as theirs did, religion with poetry,
instead of existing as poetry only, and leaving religious
wants to be supplied by the Christian religion, as a power
existing independent of the poetical power. But the language, style, and general proceedings of a poetry which
has such an immense task to perform, must be very plain
direct and severe: and it must not lose itself in parts and

episodes and ornamental work, but must press forwards
to the whole. (*LC*, p. 124, October 28, 1852.)

No change in Arnold's aesthetics from an emphasis on form
to an emphasis on content can be deduced from this passage,
for there was a similar passage in 1847/48, as we have seen.
Nor did Arnold abandon the requirement that poetry must
be beautiful; he only looked for the severe beauty of a plain
style. In fact, Arnold was still hammering out the aesthetics
of poetry which combines great beauty of form with great
wealth and depth of matter. What he had not done hitherto
was to speak of religion as either part of matter or as, I think
here, the effect of poetry, for Arnold characteristically thought
of religion as being connected primarily with morality and
with emotion.

Arnold meant now to say, not that poetry should venture
into theology any more than into philosophy, but that poetry
produces effects as religion does, when it calms and ennobles
the soul or inspirits and rejoices the heart. Arnold was thinking again of drama, specifically of Greek drama, which moves
directly towards its end, unlike a poem such as *The Faerie
Queene*, which, for all its great beauty, loses itself in parts
and episodes and ornamental work. The examples are mine,
but I think they illustrate Arnold's meaning, and certainly the
drama of Sophocles was always for Arnold a model of dramatic
art. Another possibility is suggested by a scene from Froude's
novel *Shadows of the Clouds:* the hero on his deathbed is con-
soled, not by the reading of the Psalms or by traditional rites
or prayers, but by a passage read from Jean-Paul Richter.[9] Although Arnold never suggested this use of poetry, he was certainly aware of the way in which Victorians turned to poetry
for wisdom and consolation, and he was saying that if poetry
is to perform such an immense task, it had better not be trite
and sentimental; it must be direct, plain, and severe.

Finally, the question of form and feeling in poetry arises
from the idea that poetry is to be a *magister vitae.* Arnold
seemed, in general, to find in form the essential characteristic

of poetry—form as style, expression, conception, *architectonice*, form that in some way orders the "matter" of poetry. The matter so far considered has been "fact," the previous experience of mankind—that is, "things done," events, what we think of as history—and the experience of the individual, the world, and the self. The question is whether there is in Arnold's criticism any conflict between the form and the feeling of poetry—that is, the subjective emotions of the poet. The troublesome conflict, essentially a false one, between feeling and form, or emotion and reason, is a familiar topic in poetry and criticism, and it appears in Arnold's own early poetry, even in *Empedocles on Etna*. Arnold touched on a solution to the difficulty, at least in respect to lyric poetry. Arnold was discussing Burns, a poet to whom he would return in his great major essay on poetry: "Burns is certainly an artist *im*plicitly—fury is not incompatible with artistic form but it becomes *lyric* fury (Eh?) only when combined with the gift for this" (*LC*, p. 69). Far from seeing a conflict between form and feeling, Arnold here was saying that in poetry there cannot be any feeling without form. Arnold's early position, that art must have form, was clearly stated again. Burns was only an artist "implicitly," by virtue of his feeling; nevertheless, Arnold held that feeling (fury) was not incompatible with form but that the poet who has a gift for form transmutes feeling (fury) into lyric feeling. Beranger, he went on to say, "is an artist" both implicitly and explicitly—that is, in feeling and form: "They accuse him by his finisht classicality of having banished the old native French forms."

But Arnold would have none of the popular notion that associated feeling with the old popular forms and coldness with classical form. Arnold held, here as elsewhere, that poetry was not a direct transcription of reality or an expression of feeling or of thought; it was a thing made from the matter of life. Thus, poetry reconstructs the world, makes fury a lyric fury. Take, as an illustration, Arnold's "The Forsaken Merman." Froude anticipated recent criticism by saying that it "sounds right out from the heart." Yet if Arnold was speaking in the poem, it was through the art of the poem, through the characters and the dramatic situation and the technical virtuosity of the form, which elaborates the simple ballad verse and stanza and complicates the simple tale of the original story. In his later dramatic criticism, Arnold pursued the relation of form to feeling in poetry, but held, as in the Preface to *Merope*, that in poetry, form heightens feeling; also, Arnold would never have thought of drama or any kind of poetry as coldly formal. But—and this is equally clear—Arnold thought of feeling in poetry, not as a direct outpouring of personal or private emotion, but as an aesthetic feeling, a lyric fury, or a dramatic fury.

In this respect, Arnold was different from his friends, whose poetry and fiction approached a confessional mode. Froude's novel *Shadows of the Clouds* is largely autobiographical, and indeed his biographer quotes large sections from it to fill in the story of Froude's life.[10] Froude's *Nemesis of Faith*, if less true to the details of the author's personal history, is nonetheless an account of the author's ideas.[11] Clough's *Bothie*, with its recognizable characters and setting, has little of the epic form aside from the dactylic hexameter and the Homeric similes, which have an effect of mock heroics. In *Amours de Voyage*, Clough kept the loose hexameter as an approximation of colloquial discourse; he often succeeded in reproducing the tone of his own letters and adopted the form of the epistolary novel. Claude's letters describe the revolution in Italy very much as Clough did in his own letters. Even Shairp's poem "Balliol Scholars" has the form of a memoir, and it has been quoted in sketches of the lives of the group.[12] Arnold's poetry tends to be dramatic, not confessional. The Marguerite poems, at most veiled autobiography, are presented as dramatic lyrics. Attempts to read "Dover Beach" as a confession of doubt on the occasion of Arnold's own wedding journey have to be acknowledged as unsatisfactory; they contain unresolved contradictions between the gloomy Lucretian meditation and the supposed occasion. Moreover, Clough and others looked for forms to give an effect of the confessional, as he

used the letter in *Amours de Voyage* to give greater verisimili-
tude to the characters. Even in writing history, Froude uncov-
ered the "real" truth about Elizabeth's character in the letters
he found in the state archives in London and in Spain. Arnold
himself, in his criticism, examined the journals of Maurice
de Guérin and, in writing about Thomas Gray, gave as much
attention to the letters as to the poetry. But where Froude
thought that both drama and history are best when they come
as near as possible to reporting the actual words spoken by
people when they can be known, Arnold assumed, rather, that
poetry is not a report, but that art transforms fact into a poetic
reality or reconstructs the world. In his later criticism, Arnold
tried to separate the life and character of the poet from the
art of the poem.

To summarize Arnold's criticism in the letters to Clough,
Arnold attempted to make a place for the poet in what he
called in the 1853 Preface "the empire of fact." The poet's matter, he said, is the world, past, present, and to come, as well
as the self. The poet unites matter, intellectually, by an idea
of the world and, poetically, in a form that reconstructs the
universe. The art of poetry—poetry as such—begins in self-
knowledge, of a poet's nature, thought, and feeling, and
appears in a distinctive style. The form, style, and expression
must be beautiful, yet natural to the subject. The poet's greatest achievement lies in the uniting of form of conception and
form of expression, both poetical and in accord. Such poetry—
in which the form controls both thought and feeling—has the
effect of calming and composing the soul. Such poetry can
animate and ennoble, not by a direct teaching of moral truths
or by rhetorical discourse or by philosophical analysis, but
through the effect of the art.

Arnold seems to have found himself in a position where
he might be a great poet but could by no means reach the
people in a democratic age. Such, indeed, was the reaction of
Arnold's friends, who were themselves writing other kinds
of poetry, with Clough trying to catch the appeal of the novel
and Shairp preferring the ballad style. The letters, including

those by Froude, Palgrave, and Shairp, give a narrative and dramatic context to the reviews that stimulated Arnold's answer in the 1853 Preface. An exchange of letters while Arnold was writing *Empedocles on Etna* and Clough was writing *Amours de Voyage* was especially significant. Shairp was not pleased with either poem: about *Empedocles* he wrote, "I wish Matt would give up that old greek form" (*Correspondence*, 1:270). But he was no happier with Clough's poem, not because of the style, but because of the "conception." Clough had asked Shairp for criticism, but once he had received it, he attacked Shairp's tastes: "If one don't sing you a ballant or read you a philosophic sermonette, . . . you're not pleased" (*Correspondence*, 1:276). But Shairp persisted in finding the poem as not being "hearty and heart-whole" and as having "no strength except in its raillery at all men and things and in its keen, ceaseless self-introspection" (*Correspondence*, 1:277). Although Shairp denied that his tastes were so limited, he did like ballads; whereas Clough, as he wrote to Francis James Child, who had already begun his notable collection, was not "enthusiastic" about them (*Correspondence*, 2:515). Still, Clough and Shairp could agree on Arnold's poetry; Shairp wrote in 1853: "I fear Mat's last book has made no impression on the public mind." He thought that the poems rested on "a false and uninteresting (too) view of life" and that "Mat, as I told him, disowns man's natural feelings, and they will disown his poetry" (*Correspondence*, 2:401). They could also agree, if only briefly, on the poems of Alexander Smith. Palgrave, writing to Clough in America, reported on Smith as "the last poetical planet" (*Correspondence*, 2:412). Clough's first reaction was enthusiastic; as he wrote to Blanche Smith, his future wife, "I am very much taken with Alexander Smith's life-drama—it is really what I have had in my own mind" (*Correspondence*, 2:414). Although by the end of the month, Clough was advising Blanche not to read the poem, he was willing to praise Smith at the expense of Arnold in his review that appeared in the *North American* in July. When Shairp heard about the review, he thought there could be "no comparison between the two" poets, and he repeated his criticism of Arnold: "The terrible want of fresh heart spoils Mat. to my taste" (Correspondence, 2:437).

Clough set forth his views on the proper subjects of poetry in his review of Arnold's *The Strayed Reveller and Other Poems* (1849) and *Empedocles on Etna and Other Poems* (1852); this essay framed his criticism of Arnold's classical poems in a discussion of a modern domestic epic, Smith's *A Life-Drama* (1853).[13] In this astonishing performance, Clough seems to have tossed away any chance of being taken as a serious critic by preferring Smith's feeble verses over some of the great poems of his day. Yet Clough, because of his long association with Arnold and their discussion of poetry in the letters, was uniquely equipped to understand Arnold's poems; and Clough's brief summaries of *The Strayed Reveller* and of *Empedocles on Etna* show clear insights into the plan of the poems. Clough offered, however, only brief summaries of the major poems and longer summaries and quotations from the lesser poems, "The Forsaken Merman" and "Morality." Unwilling to perform for Arnold the kind of service his friend deserved at his hand, Clough preferred to preach a sermon on the text of Smith's *Life-Drama*.

Clough knew well enough that Smith was not a good poet and that Arnold was, although Clough professed to see the difference between the two only in diction and verse; but Smith came conveniently to hand in Clough's campaign for a poetry for the ordinary reader. To appeal to the "multitude," Clough said, "poetry should deal, more than at present it usually does, with general wants, ordinary feelings, the obvious rather than the rare facts of human nature" (PR, pp. 356–57). Like Froude, Clough followed Carlyle in seeing man's purpose, not as happiness, but as labor, work that is necessary but often "weary task-work" or "dirty, or at least dingy, work" (PR, p. 357). The poet was somehow to give "purpose," "significance," to this work; somehow he was to connect it to a "celestial," a "purer existence," a divine scheme. Clough did not say how this was to be done, whether on the plan of Soame Jenyns or some other; but he is clear that the poet must somehow reconcile the weary worker to his lot. Indeed, of all of Arnold's poems, Clough prefers "Morality," a poem addressed to those who perform the thankless tasks, assuring them that while Nature offers a way that is effortless and joyful, God's plan requires a stern self-control. Clough preferred this sermon to what he called Arnold's "dismal cycle of his rehabilitated Hindoo-Greek theosophy" (PR, p. 373) or, in *Empedocles on Etna*, "the pseudo Greek inflation of the philosopher musing above the crater, and the boy Callicles singing myths upon the mountain" (PR, p. 367). Clough praised "The Forsaken Merman" as a "beautiful poem" (PR, p. 370) and discussed at length "Tristam and Iseult," preferring what he saw as "the human passions and sorrows" of the Knight and the Queen to the cold philosophizing of Empedocles (PR, p. 367). Although these were not poems that had anything to say about the weary work of the world, they were poems that made use of the ballad or romance form and were at any rate not Greek.

Indeed, Froude, in his review of Arnold's poems, urged Arnold to find other subjects from other national literatures, from the Teutonic or Scandinavian, as well as the Greek.[14] Arnold apparently followed this advice in the 1853 *Poems* in choosing the Persian subject of *Sohrab and Rustum* and in 1854 in trying the Scandinavian myths in *Balder Dead*. In Homer, the place for the description of ordinary life is the long simile, but Arnold's similes belong to the heroic age of his epic poems. Arnold not only remained committed to the Greek forms and subjects, but in his criticism he continued to look for the foundation of his principles in the great democratic age of Greece.

In the Preface to his 1853 *Poems*, Arnold undertook to defend his use of subjects from the past, especially against his friends, who urged him to take contemporary subjects or to follow the lead of poets such as Alexander Smith. Arnold turned to Aristotle for his dramatic theory; the action, the plot, was the thing, rather than confession or thinking aloud or philosophizing. Arnold, indeed, withdrew his dramatic poem

Empedocles on Etna because he concluded that it lacked action and plot. By taking Aristotle as his mentor and by defending tragic drama, Arnold repeated Aristotle's defense of poetry against Plato. Aristotle argued for the place of drama in the city, as Arnold argued for its place in a democratic society.

Arnold followed Aristotle in centering the defense on the art of the drama, on plot and action, and on an art that is accessible, in theory, to all human beings. As Gerald Else argues in his recent book, Aristotle's *Poetics* was an answer to Plato's "intellectual elitism"; the basis of imitation *(mimesis)* is a "universal human tendency" that arises from "the desire to know, *which all men have.*"[15] Thus, Else argues, imitation is "a part of Aristotle's polemic against Plato's intellectual elitism (learning is most pleasurable not only to philosophers but to 'the others' as well" (48b13-15, *Plato*, p. 90). Imitation rests, as Else reads Aristotle, on a belief in the universals in human thought and action; imitation appeals to "the desire to know, *which all men have,*" through structures—plot and action—made "out of carefully observed 'universal' human tendencies to thought and action" (*Plato*, p. 75). Else says further that "the poet is a creator . . . just where he brings the universals to life most faithfully" (*Plato*, p. 113). Here, Else argues, Aristotle defended the poets against Plato's attack: the poet makes structures and characters; he is not an "impersonator" who is "deceiving us by pretending to be Agamemnon, Achilleus, and the rest" (*Plato*, p. 113). Similarly, Arnold argued that the poet makes plots and actions, rather than, as it were, "impersonating" himself or offering an allegory of the state of his own mind. Although the cases may seem to be the opposite, the "impersonator" or charlatan, as opposed to the "true" or sincere confession, both rest on the assumption that the poet can only speak in his own voice or reveal only his own thoughts and feelings—an assumption that both Arnold and Aristotle challenged when they defined the "truth" of poetry.

The advocates of the popular poets, such as Shairp, appeal to Plato (as Shairp read, or misread, the *Ion*) in the view that the "natural" poets sing spontaneously, without thought. Indeed, a basic assumption of many advocates of popular culture is that the people are warm-hearted, emotional, and sentimental but are incapable of thought. Aristotle, on the other hand, held not only that intellectual activity, a desire to know, is a basic human tendency but also that the "pleasure" of tragedy is intellectual in that, as Else says, "it is a pleasure based on our observation that the persons of the drama are well drawn: that their speeches and actions do grow plausibly or necessarily out of their characters" (*Plato*, p. 155). Else's argument throws light not only on Aristotle but also on Arnold's use of Aristotle and on his belief that Greek tragic drama might appeal to the many. So what seems on the surface to be an argument for a literature for the few turns out to be an argument for a literature for the many.

Thus Arnold begins his 1853 Preface: "We all naturally take pleasure, says Aristotle, in any imitation or representation whatever: this is the basis of our love of poetry; and we take pleasure in them, he adds, because all knowledge is naturally agreeable to us; not to the philosopher only, but to mankind at large" (*PW*, 1:1–2). Arnold began, then, with precisely the point that Else emphasizes in Aristotle— namely, that the theory of *mimesis* rests on the desire for knowledge, not of philosophers only, but of all humankind. This, Arnold implied, is the true basis not only for poetry but for a popular poetry.

Arnold went on to say that it is not enough for poets to "add to the knowledge of men"; they must also "add to their happiness." But the idea that happiness is an end of poetry is certainly Aristotle's idea as well. Arnold required that the "representation" be accurate, "particular, precise, and firm" in order to interest the reader and that it must also "inspirit and rejoice the reader; that it shall convey a charm, and infuse delight" (*PW*, 1:2). But like Aristotle, Arnold rested the theory of imitation on universal human traits; the actions that are interesting are those that appeal to the "great primary human affections: to those elementary feelings which subsist perma-

nently in the race, and are independent of time" (*PW,* 1:4).
Aristotle, as Else shows, rested the theory of *mimesis* on universals in human behavior; such knowledge as poetry possesses is knowledge of general truths about humanity (*Plato,*
p. 114).

Arnold pointed out that the "domestic epic," or "poems
representing modern personages in contact with the problems
of modern life, moral, intellectual, and social"—such poems
as *Hermann and Dorothea, Childe Harold, Jocelyn,* and *The
Excursion*—"leave the reader cold in comparison with the
effect produced upon him by the latter books of the *Iliad,* by
the *Oresteia,* or by the episode of *Dido*" (*PW,* 1:4). To the objec-
tion that the "externals" of past life cannot be known by
modern writers, Arnold replied that "his business is with their
inward man; with their feelings and behaviour in certain tragic
situations, which engage their passions as men; these have
in them nothing local and casual; they are as accessible to
the modern poet as to a contemporary" (*PW,* 1:5). Arnold, it
is clear, did not here see poetry as being inextricably attached
to the culture of a place and time. The "outward" man—the
houses, clothing, and details of ordinary life—did not seem
to him to determine the "consciousness" of the poet or the
audience; and he further assumed that the essentials of human
nature were universal. Universality, for both Aristotle and
Arnold, was part of their belief that tragic drama can make
an appeal to the people, because as *mimesis,* it is grounded
in the belief that all people desire to know and in the belief
that imitation is of universals in human action. Thus, class
or culture, time or place, are not barriers to the enjoyment
of Greek tragic drama.

For a contrast to Arnold's ideas, we may turn to Shairp's
review of Arnold's poems in 1854, wherein Shairp thought
that Arnold made an error in turning to Greek drama for
models and subjects. Shairp insisted that Arnold did not understand that the Greeks chose "subjects which were deeply
rooted in the hearts of their countrymen, and intertwined
with the very fibre of their national existence."[16] Although

the classical poets thus addressed their own people in their own time, Shairp implied, they could not reach beyond that time. Few modern readers, Shairp thought, were interested in the Greek poets, let alone modern imitations of Homer such as Arnold's *Sohrab and Rustum*. Indeed, few were any longer interested in ancient Greece: "No strength of imagination can turn back the world's sympathies to the shores of old Greece"; certainly no poet who used the old subjects and forms could "attain to thorough popularity" ("Poems by Matthew Arnold," p. 497). Shairp thus left Homer and the tragic writers to a scholarly few, an extreme position that was not shared by Froude or Sellar or, indeed, even Francis Newman and that Shairp himself later modified. Undoubtedly, at the time, Shairp was influenced by his own desire to write like Scott and Burns, using a northern English and celebrating the ordinary life as well as the great national events of the Scottish people. The core of Shairp's criticism was the division of poets into "natural" and "artistic" and the belief that art destroys life: "Where the sense of artistic beauty and power of expression predominate, their owner, intent on these, is ever ready to divorce himself from the warmth of life and human interests" (p. 503). Shairp found the greatest appeal in what he thought were the artless songs of the country folk and the natural singers, among whom he included Homer, Burns, Scott, and Wordsworth.

In his next essay on tragic drama, the Preface to *Merope*, Arnold clearly saw Greek drama as being played to an audience of the people of Athens and showed how the art of the Greek drama, the structures of plot and action, reached a large audience.

Arnold's belief that in a democratic society an audience could delight in a high art was based in part on his reading of the experience of the Greek theater. He put forth his reading in an analysis of Greek dramatic art in his Preface to *Merope* (1857).[17] Arnold intended his play to make available to the people who could not read Greek the idea of the beauty of the Greek forms; to do this, he preferred an original play in

English to a translation of a Greek tragedy. Greek tragic forms, Arnold thought, developed in a drama that was performed before a large audience; in the time of Sophocles, "the Greek theatres were vast, and open to the sky" (*PW*, 1:57). The plays were constructed to reach such a large audience in the great outdoor theaters: "Broad and simple effects were, under these conditions, above all to be aimed at; a profound and clear impression was to be effected" (*PW*, 1:57). In action, acting, and structure, Greek tragedy was developed to speak to a popular audience, an audience that responded to a drama that met "some of the most urgent demands of the human spirit" (*PW*, 1:58). One such demand was for "variety"; another was for "depth and concentration in its impressions" (*PW*, 1:58). In poetry, "powerful thought and emotion, flowing in strongly marked channels, make a stronger impression," an impression that was enhanced by the verse of Greek tragedy. Through the art of the drama the audience is drawn into a state of high thought and emotion (*PW*, 1:58–59).

Not only were the forms of tragedy—which were dictated by the outdoor theater—designed to reach a large audience through broad and simple effects, but the chorus also provided the audience with a guide to the action and ideas. Looking at various theories about the function of the chorus in Greek tragedy, Arnold expanded on the chorus as the ideal spectator, who guides the audience through the play. The chorus, as Arnold saw it, not only interpreted the action but also was "at each stage in the action, to collect and weigh the impressions which the action would at that stage naturally make on a pious and thoughtful mind" (*PW*, 1:60). At the end, the chorus summed up the action—it appeared on the stage "to strike the final balance." Furthermore, the chorus responded to the action in the play, looking to the past and to the future, and thus served to intensify the feelings of the audience. Arnold summarized the function of the chorus: "To combine, to harmonise, to deepen for the spectator the feeling naturally excited in him by the sight of what was passing upon the stage—this is one grand effect produced by the chorus in Greek tragedy" (*PW*, 1:61). Also, through lyrical song the chorus offered a release from the intense emotions of the action: "After tragic situations of the greatest intensity, a desire for relief and relaxation is no doubt natural, both to the poet and to the spectator" (*PW*, 1:61). Arnold thus saw the poet and the audience as sharing in the art of the drama, with the audience actively recreating the thought and the feeling of the poet.

In addition, the characters of the play, as Arnold observed in the lecture "On the Modern Element in Literature," which was delivered earlier in 1857, are representative of the times. The poetry of Sophocles "represents the highly developed human nature of that age—human nature developed in a number of directions, politically, socially, religiously, morally developed—in its completest and most harmonious development in all these directions" (*PW*, 1:28). The Athenians thus saw their own age reflected in the plays, for although the characters were drawn from the "old heroic world," they belonged to the new world and possessed "all the fulness of life and of thought which the new world had accumulated" (*PW*, 1:31). Because in the lecture Arnold had developed a theory of the modern that encompassed both the Periclean Age and the Victorian Age, it is likely that in his own play he intended the characters to interest a modern audience. Indeed, in *Merope*, the characters debate ideas that concerned the Victorians: the ethics of conquest, the rights of subject peoples, the rights of the people against a ruling class. Arnold, both in the Preface and in the drama, tried to show that Greek tragedy had developed techniques that would reach a large audience.

Arnold's attempt to reach a popular audience may be compared with other poems of the late 1850s. In the year or two before *Merope* appeared, Clough in his letters noted briefly the appearance of Tennyson's *Maud*, Longfellow's *Hiawatha*, Robert Browning's "Fra Lippo Lippi," and Whitman's *Leaves of Grass*. All of these were, in some way, attempts to reach a popular audience, and all have become "classics," although perhaps only *Hiawatha* would still be considered a popular poem. Clough liked *Hiawatha* and "Fra Lippo Lippi";

Whitman's poem he thought "rather a waste of power and observation" (*Correspondence*, 2:520). In late 1857, while Clough was preparing his *Amours de Voyage* for the press, he noted Arnold's announcement of *Merope*, which he described as "a tragedy (to rival Voltaire's)," and also the appearance of Alexander Smith's *City Poems*, of which Clough said he could not make anything (*Correspondence*, 2:534–35). But even though he was no longer taken by Smith's poetry, Clough was not drawn to Arnold's classicism: he had not liked the 1853 Preface (*Correspondence*, 1:470), and he saw little to admire in *Merope*. After *Merope* appeared, his letters contain some brief and perfunctory criticism of the play, on the contrast of characters, "skillfully executed"; on the choruses, which he thought long and tedious; and on the lack of any "unity of interest." Clearly he had in mind the contrast between his own poem and Arnold's drama; Clough said he found little "natural pleasure" in *Merope* and wondered whether anyone would find "natural pleasure" in his own "5 act epistolary tragi-comedy or comi-tragedy" (*Correspondence*, 2:540, 546). Emerson thought the joy of the first part was lost in the ending; he asked, "How can you waste such power on a broken dream?" (*Correspondence*, 2:548).

Neither Arnold nor Clough achieved the immediate popular success of *Hiawatha*; and neither of the poems would later be ranked with "Fra Lippo Lippi" or the *Leaves of Grass*. Clough's *Amours de Voyage* remains, with Tennyson's *Maud*, an interesting experiment; and *Merope*, which is seldom read, is generally dismissed as sterile classical imitation. Indeed, it may seem curious that Arnold supposed that his drama might have popular appeal; certainly he himself was disappointed by the reception of *Merope*, and he declared his intention to take up a new line altogether, which, as I understand his famous letter, was to be critical prose.[18] But it was to be a criticism in which he continued to advance the principles that he had worked out in his 1853 Preface and the Preface to *Merope*.

Chapter Four

Subjects from the Past

In his early criticism, Arnold had come to see that his conviction that poetry was an art was not inconsistent with a belief that in a democratic age, poetry had to reach a large audience. Rather, as Aristotle had shown, it was through the structures of drama that the poet could interest the many, because, as Aristotle held, all human beings desire to know. The theory of mimesis assumes that all people have the desire for knowledge. Now while, for Aristotle, this knowledge was a general truth about human character—and Arnold follows this in his discussion of drama—poetry might deal with "larger" truths, either philosophic or religious. Indeed, as Else has pointed out, there is a range in poetry beyond the vision of Aristotle, for whom Fate is the cause of human destiny. Although Arnold in his philosophical poem had made Empedocles struggle with "metaphysical" truths, he made the characters in *Merope*, however mythical in origin, very much of this world and mainly concerned with political ideas. "Fate," so far as it governs the lives of these characters, is something rather like history. Although Arnold did not talk about historical movements in the Preface to *Merope*, he clearly had these in mind in the lecture "On the Modern Element in Literature," which was given in 1857 to inaugurate his term as Oxford Professor of Poetry. This lecture is what gives support to critics who see Arnold's idea of history as central to his thought and to those who, like Trilling, take the view that Arnold's poetry for a democratic age was a poetry of ideas. Undeniably, Arnold

59

did lend support in this essay to such views; but I think it can be shown that this lecture, which was to a considerable extent drawn from the work of others, moved further towards a poetry of ideas, especially historical ideas, than Arnold really meant to go. While Arnold, even in this essay, finally made poetry superior to history or to other kinds of literature, this point tends to get overwhelmed by his talk of the "interpretation" of the age and of "adequate" ideas.

This lecture, which has been often taken as central to Arnold's thought, offers great temptations to those who are looking for a kind of cultural criticism and to those who are seeking keys to Arnold's thought. Terms are explained, defined, connected; bridges appear to be laid between the 1853 Preface and the later criticism. Yet the more that one looks at the lecture, the more one hesitates to trust the bridges. The explanations, the resolutions of difficulties, do not work well; little in the essay turns out to be original; and it looks finally as if Arnold was making great concessions to the historians.

In reading this lecture, one must be aware, first of all, of the influence of Dr. Thomas Arnold, once Regius Professor of Modern History. Matthew Arnold not only knew his father's theories about history, but in his first Oxford lecture, he consciously attempted to give due honor to his father. But the elder Arnold had in fact left poetry outside the new world he envisioned. What the younger Arnold was now attempting to do was to make a way for the poet by making the poet share the functions of the historian, who is able to comprehend both the past and the present, and to offer an adequate interpretation of the spectacle of life that is history. Arnold, however, found the place for poetry at a great cost to poetry, which in his theory now came so close to history that the poet must have not only a theory of history but also a philosophical system: he must have an adequate explanation of the times in which he lives, an explanation that takes account of the past and of the future as well. Arnold, having given so much to history, later reclaimed territory for poetry, and when he published the essay, he gave as his reason that it explained his idea of Hellenism in *Culture and Anarchy.* He did not, however, include this essay in his *Essays in Criticism;* indeed, he had abandoned the extreme positions of the essay.

Arnold, having given so much ground to an idea of history, shared with Dr. Arnold and others in the group some characteristic ideas: the existence of certain great ages, the idea of the modern, the importance of facts and of "laws," the poet and the historian as the interpreter of his own age. The piling up of borrowed academic opinions, often little changed in phraseology from the sources, has been mistaken for Arnold's subjective reading of the past, of classical poetry, and especially of Sophocles; but Arnold at best was grounding his argument on the best scholarship and critical opinion about the classical writers, and at worst he was getting up a lecture from various sources. Nonetheless, in silently drawing from Sellar on Thucydides and Lucretius, Arnold used his evidence to defend his own use of classical forms and subjects from the past. Sellar depicted Thucydides as the representative man of a great age, offering an interpretation of that age. Arnold took this as a major point to support his idea of adequacy, but he made Sophocles equal in his understanding of the age, here following K. O. Müller's literary history. What Arnold saw as the proper subject for the modern poet was the history of civilization—the present comprehended in its connections to the past. Clough had looked instead for contemporary subjects and everyday life, treated realistically in the novel or the verse-novel. Arnold was saying that if a poet is to interpret the age, a realistic description of ordinary life is not enough.

The ordinary life of the past had also become a subject for historians, poets, and novelists, and in the 1850s Arnold's quarrel with Clough, Froude, and Shairp took up the matter of ordinary life among the Greeks and Romans. Where Clough saw Plutarch as the historian who showed the ordinary life of the Romans in his time or where Froude sought to make history depict the particular scene, Arnold insisted once more that the classical poets had interpreted great ages and that though they had lived in times when democracy was triumphant, they had not taken ordinary life as their subject. Most important, finally, Arnold gave this answer to the scholars and the historians: the great democracies of the past—the Athens of Pericles, the great age of the Roman Republic—offered great subjects to the poet and the historian. Here, not in the depiction of ordinary life, lay the great subjects for the modern poet.

History belonged, certainly, to the "empire of fact," where in the 1853 Preface Arnold had placed drama—fact in the radical sense as things done, the events of history, and, in a more limited sense, the true report of what had happened or what might be constructed from such reports as had survived from the past. The sorting out of fact from legend, myth, and story, begun by Niebuhr in the history of Rome, had been continued by Dr. Arnold, who began his history of Rome by telling the legends in an archaic prose to separate the old stories from the facts of history.[1] Even in dealing with times that had been recorded more fully by the historians, it was necessary to sort out the facts from the "trash," as Matthew Arnold said in calling for a "judicious translation" of the Lives of Diogenes Laërtius.[2] Further, it was necessary to sort out the reliable historians of the past from the less trustworthy; Dr. Arnold early had announced his doubts about the Roman historians.[3] The historian not only sorted out the facts from the chaff, but, as Matthew Arnold put it in his Inaugural Lecture, "searched for their law" and offered an explanation that was adequate, not so much for particular or isolated events as for an age. This search for general laws tended to arrive at metaphysical heights, as the designs of Providence—or what Matthew Arnold called "the will of God"—were seen in the events of history, so that a single important event, such as the battle of Epipolae, was seen to affect the future course and welfare, not only of the Athenians, but of all nations.

The great ages of history were identified by Dr. Arnold, following Giovanni Battista Vico, as is thought; Matthew Arnold at various times saw the age of Pericles, the last days of the Roman Republic, the age of Elizabeth, and the Victorian age as great eras, subjects for history and for poetry. Following

Dr. Arnold, the Balliol group attempted in some form the great subject, the last days of the Roman Republic: Sellar in his essays on Lucretius in his history of Roman literature; Arnold in the unfinished play *Lucretius*; Shairp in an occasional essay; and Froude in his biography of Caesar. As historians, poets, or critics, they worked out theories of the relationship between the poet and the age or drew parallels between these ages and the modern world.

History came close to biography when the historian described the representative men, those whose characteristics were thought to embody the qualities of a nation, such as Pericles in the great days of Athens or Caesar in the last days of the Roman Republic. The dramatic art of the historian approached that of the tragic writer, for the characters of the drama were also seen as representative of their age. It was at this point that the dramatist was like the historian in his critical insight into the age. Thus, in his Inaugural Lecture, Arnold saw little difference between Thucydides and Sophocles except in art, the poetic form of the drama having the additional qualities of grace and beauty. Arnold intended finally to give the chief place to the poet, but to the poet qualified by his insight into the characteristics of the age and the people.

A great age and its representative writers or its leaders were also modern. For Matthew Arnold, the theory of the modern age, an advanced state of civilization in which people exhibited the intellectual maturity of the Athenians or the Romans, made history rather like comparative mythology. The theory may have owed something to the cyclical theories of Vico, as set out in the *Scienza Nuova* (1725); the third age of the cycle, the "age of men," saw the rise of popular commonwealths.[4] In the context of the great men of Greek and Roman history, however, the influence of Plutarch's *Parallel Lives* might be suggested. Clough spent a decade reworking Dryden's translation of Plutarch, and Arnold consulted Plutarch for his Roman play. Drawing parallels could lead to results that would rival such lists as the Nine Worthies. Alexander, Caesar, and Napoleon would make a modern set, and perhaps it is

significant that among the early favorites of Froude was the
Seven Champions of Christendom.[5] On the other hand, it was
thought that modern historians had an insight into the great
ages of the past, for only those who had had similar experiences could really know about revolutions and civil wars, as
Thomas Arnold said: "Our own experience has thrown a
bright light on the remoter past: much which our fathers could
not fully understand, from being accustomed to quieter times
. . . is to us perfectly familiar" (*History of Rome,* 1:vii). The
danger of such analogies between people who were so far removed from one another in place and time was later pointed
out by Richard C. Jebb in his review of Froude's *Caesar,*[6] but
Arnold thought the parallels were significant.

Because history was to educate a free and intelligent
people, it was not addressed only to historians or to a special
few; Dr. Thomas Arnold intended to be as widely read as Edward Gibbon. Furthermore, Arnold carried on the program of
the philosophes by publishing his early articles on the Roman
commonwealth in an encyclopedia designed to spread knowledge among the people. For his major work, which he did not
live to complete, Dr. Arnold planned "plain and popular histories of Greece and Rome . . . cleared of nonsense and un-
christian principles" (Stanley, *Life,* 1:73). In theory, the empire
of fact, like the great Roman Empire, was to offer citizenship
to all of its inhabitants; and with citizenship came freedom.
Practically, in the theory of Thomas Arnold, these citizens,
who would be free to explore thought within the limits of disciplined reason, would found a political society that would
perpetuate and transmit the institutions that, in turn, would
guarantee free inquiry. Thomas Arnold laid down the conditions under which this freedom would be won—a stern program that allowed no place for the poet, the orator, or the
moralist:

> For it is a most important truth, and one which requires
> at this day to be most earnestly enforced, that it is by the
> study of facts, whether relating to nature or to man, and

not by any pretended cultivation of the mind by poetry, oratory and moral or critical dissertations, that the understandings of mankind in general will be most improved, and their views of things rendered most accurate. (*LRC*, 2:454–55)

Dr. Arnold sketched the process by which, from the study of fact, by each person according to "taste" and "natural ability," the age of enlightenment would develop:

From the mass of varied knowledge thus possessed by several members of the community, arises the great characteristic of a really enlightened age, a sound and sensible judgment, a quality which can only be formed by the habit of regarding things in different lights, as they appear to intelligent men of different pursuits and in different classes of society, and by thus correcting the limited notions to which the greatest minds are liable, when left to indulge without a corrective their own peculiar strain of reflections. (*LRC*, 2:455)

Echoes of this program, essentially that of the philosophes, appear in Matthew Arnold's critical essays: the importance of judgment, trained by the observation of fact, in the 1853 Preface; the critical spirit as a characteristic of an enlightened age, in the 1857 lecture; criticism as leading to the growth of a great age, in "The Function of Criticism at the Present Time" in 1864; the insistence on the highest standards, in order to avoid provinciality, in "The Literary Influence of Academies" in 1864; culture as necessary in order to prevent a narrow view belonging to a class or an occupation, in *Culture and Anarchy*. This program, too, expressed Arnold's belief that the "intellectual maturity" of the people was essential in a democratic age. Indeed, the critic and the historian, in the widest sense of Arnold's use of criticism, are not far apart; but it was Arnold's task as a literary critic to make a place for poetry in this empire of fact, the empire from which Dr. Arnold, like Plato, had excluded the poet.

In the 1853 Preface, Arnold had claimed for the poet the subject given to the historians—the past—thus defending his choice of the subject of *Empedocles on Etna*, a dramatic poem that took as its principal character the Greek philosopher and that was set in the historical times of ancient Greece. The Athenian tragic poets, Arnold argued, had always taken subjects from the past, and so had Shakespeare.[7] Here Arnold countered the arguments of the critics among his friends and among the reviewers, those who called for modern poets to give up the old stories and turn to the problems of their own times. Arnold looked to the past for subjects partly because, as far as our literary experience goes, the great actions have been found in subjects from the past. He did not suppose, however, that the great mythic stories of the Greeks, although they are found in Homer and are attached to remote legendary figures or to mythical heroes, appealed to tragic writers as a retreat or a refuge from their own times. Arnold did not see Greek drama as being detached from the events of the age or from the political life of Greece.

Nor are we to suppose that Arnold thought that he had retreated from the world of nineteenth-century England in taking as his subject the Greek philosopher Empedocles. Even Arnold's friends thought they saw in Empedocles the reflection of Arnold himself.[8] Although they were mistaken in thinking that *Empedocles on Etna* was an allegory of the state of the poet's own mind, Arnold undoubtedly used the story and the characters to work out his own ideas about the function of the lyric and philosophic poets. But in his dramatic poem he was also treating the themes that were of absorbing interest to the people of the 1850s, as reflected in Tennyson's *In Memoriam*—the themes of death and immortality, the place of the individual in nature and of the mind in the cosmos, the destruction of genius in a hostile society. Arnold recalled his dramatic poem, not because it was either relevant or irrelevant to the issues of 1850s, but because of its deficiency, as he thought, in dramatic form. Indeed, in his appeal to the example of the ancient Greeks, Arnold found that they, more than any other people, were alive to experience; they were full citizens of the empire of fact.

In the Inaugural Lecture, when Matthew Arnold became Oxford Professor of Poetry, he took up the question of the poet's subject where he had left it in 1853. In this lecture, Arnold brought together in a formal essay the ideas that had appeared from the first in his letters, but now linked to the historians. The poet's matter is the "hitherto experience of the world"; the poet must have "an Idea of the world" in order to overcome the world's multitudinousness; and the poet's work is distinguished from the historian's by poetic art. In claiming a place for the poets in the empire of fact (from which Dr. Arnold had excluded them), Arnold's explanations and definitions were derived from the theoretical work of Dr. Arnold and from literary history.

In the letters, Arnold had said that the "poet's matter" includes the "hitherto experience of the world," or here, historical facts: "The facts consist of the events, the institutions, the sciences, the arts, the literatures, in which human life has manifested itself up to the present time: the spectacle is the collective life of humanity" (PW, 1:20). The poet (Arnold's example is Sophocles) and the historian (Thucydides) must offer an idea of the world, in order to bring about an "intellectual deliverance," which "begins when our mind begins to enter into possession of the general ideas which are the law of this vast multitude of facts" (PW, 1:20). The effect of the "intellectual deliverance" is like a calm of mind, a catharsis of the mind rather than the emotions:

> It is perfect when we have acquired that harmonious acquiescence of mind which we feel in contemplating a grand spectacle that is intelligible to us; when we have lost that impatient irritation of mind which we feel in [the] presence of an immense, moving, confused spectacle which, while it perpetually excites our curiosity, perpetually baffles our comprehension. (PW, 1:20)

Calm of mind follows when an idea is accepted as a sufficient explanation for the facts of history.

That Arnold had in mind a historical explanation is made clear by his examples: Thucydides in the ancient world, Niebuhr in the modern. To the idea of the intellectual deliverance, Arnold added another concept, from Baruch Spinoza, which is linked to the comprehension of the spectacle, the age, or human life. The explanation must be adequate, and an explanation that is adequate shows the "interpreting power, the illuminating and revealing intellect" (*PW*, 1:22). That Arnold had altered what Aristotle meant by catharsis in the *Poetics*— namely, the purging of pity and fear—is evident; the reason may be that he had studied Jakob Bernays on Aristotle, copying out some passages into his *Note-books.*[9] Bernays was influential in showing the medical theory underlying Aristotle's idea of catharsis—the health of the state guaranteed by the sound constitution of a populace that had been given a healthy imagination by the mediation of dramatic art. What Arnold did, however, was to follow Thomas Arnold in making the health of the state depend upon the enlightened understanding of the people—an understanding that is essential where the people are to govern.

Although thus far Arnold's theory in the lecture seemed to allow little to imaginative literature, it was in "poetical literature," he said, that we look for "the most perfect, the most adequate interpretation of that age,—for the performance of a work which demands the most energetic and harmonious activity of all the powers of the human mind" (*PW*, 1:22). Here Arnold turned to Samuel Johnson for the description of genius as " 'that energy which collects, combines, amplifies, and animates' " and which "is in poetry at its highest stretch and in its most energetic exertion" (*PW*, 1:22-23). In the empire of facts, Arnold finally gave the poet the highest place. The poet's genius both animates the imaginative work and offers an adequate interpretation of the age. Here was Arnold's answer to the historian Thomas Arnold, who had laid down a similar program but had excluded the poet. Matthew Arnold claimed that the poetic genius could both comprehend the age and represent it in a tragedy. Nonetheless, in this essay the emphasis falls, not on the art of the poet, but on the knowledge, on the "adequate interpretation," of the age.

Furthermore, the knowledge is largely that of a historical kind, presented under the categories of period and characteristics. Essential to the great poet is the great age or epoch; this central idea Arnold would hold to tenaciously, although he later changed in his estimate of the great ages. In this essay he identified the great periods as the time of Pericles and the last days of the Roman Republic, although in a letter written at the same time he included the Renaissance and the eighteenth century, and later, perhaps influenced by Froude's history, he added the Elizabethan Age.[10] Arnold here advanced a formula for identifying a modern age: the "supreme characteristic" of such an age is "the intellectual maturity of man himself, the tendency to observe facts with a critical spirit; to search for their law, not to wander among them at random; to judge by the rule of reason, not by the impulse of prejudice or caprice" (PW, 1:24).

In the formula, Arnold followed his father, and in the particulars of the great ages of Athens and of Rome, Arnold relied on such authorities as Karl Otfried Müller and on his old friend Sellar, especially Sellar's essays on Thucydides and the Roman Republic. Arnold set forth the characteristics of the great age of Athens: "There was the utmost energy of life there, public and private; the most entire freedom, the most unprejudiced and intelligent observation of human affairs" (PW, 1:23); Müller had said that Sophocles "possessed in perfection that free Attic training which rests upon an unprejudiced observation of human affairs; his thoughts had entire freedom."[11] The echoes of key phrases such as "entire freedom" and "unprejudiced observation of human affairs" clearly point to Arnold's reading of Müller. For both Müller and Arnold, Sophocles was a representative man of his age.

For the description of the age—the civil peace, the "tolerant spirit," the "refinement of taste," and the "intellectual maturity"—which Thucydides, Arnold said, found in Athens, Arnold was following Sellar, whose essay "Characteristics of Thucydides" appeared in the *Oxford Essays for 1857*.[12] Sellar, in his conclusion, summed up the history of Thucydides as "the most complete and vivid picture of political life that the world possesses; a [permanent possession] which can never lose its meaning or its interest, so long as free institutions and national independence continue among men" (*1857 Essays*, p. 313). The greatness of the individuals depended upon their political freedom, Sellar thought. Characteristic too, of the Athenian democracy was "energy, intelligence"; Thucydides "appears to admire the energy, intelligence, and patriotism of democracies, their enjoyment of equal rights, their strong regard for law, and the development of individuality to which they give rise" (*1857 Essays*, p. 301). Arnold, Sellar, and Müller were agreed on the "fact" that in a great democratic age the people have energy, intelligence, and the utmost freedom. Sellar went further in arguing that Thucydides traced general laws from facts: "He traces particular facts to their causes; from these facts he forms general conceptions of human affairs, and he shows how certain tendencies and characteristics of men are related to one another, and are operative on events" (*1857 Essays*, p. 309). Arnold also depicted Thucydides as the interpreter of his age, selecting the Peloponnesian War as the "most instructive" or the "dominant" event in the history of mankind, and as being able to sort out the facts from the records of the past and the present and "to examine them critically." Moreover, Arnold saw Thucydides as "no isolated thinker, speaking far over the heads of his hearers to a future age"; Thucydides spoke to the people, as one like them, sharing "the general intelligence of his age and nation; of a nation the meanest citizens of which could follow with comprehension the profoundly thoughtful speeches of Pericles" (*PW*, 1:25–26). No doubt, Arnold saw a brighter glory in Greece than actually existed, and he described, not Athens, but the ideal democracy of his own imagination. But he did not invent the idea of Athens, an idea that, for his literary theory, is significant. For Arnold, democracy was the rule, not of the mob, the uneducated, but of an energetic and intelligent and, above all, free people.

The same ideal underlay Arnold's analysis of the great age of Rome, the last days of the Roman Republic. This period might well be "the greatest, the fullest, the most significant period on record" (PW, 1:32); it offered a great subject for the poet: "Think of the varied, the abundant, the wide spectacle of the Roman life . . . ; think of its fulness of occupation, its energy of effort" (PW, 1:33). Here he may have been recalling that Dr. Arnold had attempted this great subject; writing in 1824, as he prepared to write the later history of the Civil Wars, he had spoken of the period as " 'a subject so glorious that I groan beforehand when I think how certainly I shall fail in doing it justice' " (Life, 1:213). Stanley, in his Life, regretted that Dr. Arnold had not lived to complete his later History of Rome; Stanley wondered how Dr. Arnold

> would have represented the pure character and military genius of his favourite hero, Pompey—or expressed his mingled admiration and abhorrence of the intellectual power and moral degradation of Caesar;—how he would have done justice to the coarseness and cruelty of Marius, "the lowest of the democrats"—or amidst all his crimes, to the views of "the most sincere of aristocrats," Sylla. (1:213)

It was his father's earlier work on Roman history that Matthew Arnold read in 1855, when he was preparing to write his Roman play, "a tragedy of the time of the end of the Roman Republic—one of the most colossal times of the world," as Arnold put it. In his play, which Arnold called Lucretius, the characters were to be the same Caesar, Pompey, and Sulla about whom Dr. Arnold had written in his articles, as well as Cicero, Lucretius, and such minor figures as Clodius and Milo.[13] The conflict between the aristocrats and the democrats in the Roman Republic was complex, and as the view about

Caesar changed during the Victorian age, it became more difficult to accept the elder Arnold's condemnation of Caesar.

In Sellar's 1855 essay on Lucretius and his age, Caesar emerged as the representative man of a great age. Whatever Arnold may have planned to do in his unfinished play, in his 1857 lecture he followed Sellar. Sellar anticipated Arnold in his description of the great age of the Roman Republic: "an epoch of unexampled power, freedom, and activity, productive of the greatest variety of individual character, calculated by its occupations, its excitement, its struggles, its acquisitions, to brace the energies, to impress the imagination, to enlarge the sphere of thought, and to kindle the capacities of enjoyment."[14]

As the representative of the age, Caesar had not so much the old Roman virtues as the energy of the great age: "Julius Caesar combines many of the most striking, and some of the best, characteristics of that age in his wonderful variety of powers and accomplishments, all subordinate in him to a commanding will, in his independence, reality, and simplicity, in his energy and daring, in his keen sense of enjoyment, his liberal culture, his enlarged humanity" (1855 Essays, p. 6). As Arnold was to say in his lecture, Sellar thought that Lucretius withdrew from the excitement and the struggles of Rome. But Caesar controlled events because only he understood the events of the Civil Wars and the political movements of the age and because he had the new ideas to bring order to Rome in the Civil Wars: " 'The Cloud Compeller' of this storm, who alone was able to reduce its elements to order and tranquillity, was Julius Caesar" (1855 Essays, p. 21). Sellar moved nearer to the idealization of Caesar found in Theodor Mommsen; it was already appearing in England in the history by Charles Merivale, who took up the history of Rome where Thomas Arnold had left off, and later in Froude's sketch of Caesar.[15]

Matthew Arnold had little to say about Caesar in his lecture, but he did include him among the moderns in saying that "Caesar did not write history like Sir Walter Ralegh" (PW, 1:32). Arnold had, in 1848, seen the later Caesar—Napoleon—

as a leader who comprehended the future of Europe better than his enemies had, and Arnold had then outlined his idea as a subject for a play:

> The inability of the English of that time in any way to comprehend him, and yet their triumph over him—and the sense of this contrast in his own mind—there lies the point of the tragedy. The number of ideas in his head which "were not dreamed of in their philosophy," on government and the *future of Europe,* and yet their crushing him, really with *the best intentions,* but a total ignorance of him—what a subject![16]

Clearly, Matthew Arnold felt none of the sentiment that made Thomas Arnold in his lectures on modern history assign to Providence the defeat of Napoleon in Russia, for no other power was strong enough to save Europe.[17] Although here Matthew Arnold seems to share Sellar's view of the leader as one who comprehends the age, Arnold did not develop this idea in his lecture. Rather, he took another question; he argued that the great poets of Rome—Lucretius, Vergil, and Horace—did not offer an adequate interpretation of the great age of Rome, but that unable to comprehend the vast spectacle, they had sunk into melancholy.

What Arnold had done in the Inaugural Lecture was to turn back against his critics their idea of interpreting the age, but with a difference. He did not mean, as they generally did, that the poet, in a democratic age, was to take subjects from ordinary life. Rather, Arnold said, an adequate interpretation of an age demands far more than domestic realism or sentimental tales about the poor. The present time, Arnold insisted, can truly be understood only in relation to the past, and even to the future. The poet must, like the historian, understand what are the important events in a great age, as Thucydides grasped the importance of the Peloponnesian War, and must be able to deal with them intelligently. Moreover, the poet, or the dramatist, whether inventing stories and characters or taking them from the great stories of myth and legend, nonetheless draws the representative men of the age or the individuals that exhibit characteristics of a great age. Thus Arnold described the art of Sophocles:

> Aeschylus and Sophocles represent an age as interesting as themselves; the names, indeed, in their dramas are the names of the old heroic world, from which they were far separated; but these names are taken, because the use of them permits to the poet that free and ideal treatment of his characters which the highest tragedy demands; and into these figures of the old world is poured all the fulness of life and of thought which the new world had accumulated. (*PW*, 1:31)

Arnold went on to add, significantly, "This new world in its maturity of reason resembles our own"; this is another reason why modern drama may follow the models of ancient drama, as Arnold had said in the 1853 Preface and would say later in the Preface to *Merope*. In the unfinished play *Lucretius* and in *Merope*, Arnold took subjects from the past and figures from the old world; but Arnold intended, by using those figures, to show the life and thought of the new world, of his own time. Although in some ways Arnold's historical theory required parallels between the great ages of the world, there was nothing in his dramatic theory that required a "modern" subject taken from the Periclean age or the last days of the Roman Republic. The story of Merope, from the edge of historical times, provided a vehicle for Arnold's analysis of the thought and feeling of his own time.

The 1857 lecture in part explains the principles by which Arnold had written *Merope*, insofar as the subject of that play was a historical one, connected to great movements in history and to the rise of political freedom in Greece. Arnold's discussion in the Preface to *Merope* of the earlier plays on that subject indicated that it was the political theme that had interested Alfieri and Voltaire. As Clough had said, Arnold's play was to rival Voltaire's. Furthermore, the discussion of the events of Dorian history in Connop Thirlwall's history of Greece shows the historical importance of the Dorian conquest in Messenia, as well as the parallels to the Norman Conquest of England, a topic that Dr. Arnold had touched upon briefly in his edition of Thucydides.[18] The conflict between the Dorian aristocrats in Messenia and the native population—between conquerors and conquered—is the theme that runs through the action of the play and the political set speeches, even the choruses that Clough found long and tedious. Matthew Arnold thus drew, in a general pattern, the recurring problems of ancient Greece, the Roman Republic, and modern Europe.

Although in the Inaugural Lecture, Arnold brought tragedy very close to history, by saying that both must offer an adequate interpretation of the age, he nonetheless had clearly distinguished between the art of the poet and the work of the historian. In the early letters, the problem of the difference between the two appears somewhat casually in a letter to Clough in August or September, 1849: "But the difference between Herodotus and Sophocles is that the former sought over all the world's surface for that interest the latter found within man" (*Letters to Clough*, p. 90). Arnold, as the letter shows, was at the time composing the sonnet "To a Friend," from which he quotes three lines. The sonnet begins with a tribute to Epictetus, whom, as he told Clough, he had been reading, and closes with the tribute to Sophocles.

Arnold apparently had already begun his reading in Müller's history of Greek literature, for Müller compared the poet and the historian in a similar way:

They both scrutinized the knowledge of human affairs with calm and comprehensive vision; but the Samian [Herodotus], with a more boyish disposition, sought out the traditions of many nations and many lands, while the Athenian [Sophocles] had applied his riper and more searching intellect to that which was immediately before him—the secret workings of power and passion in the breast of every man. *(History of Literature,* 1:447–48)

In the letter on matter and form dated February, 1849, which I discussed in the preceding chapter, Arnold seemed to reverse this position in regard to the poet's vision, when he quoted from his poem "Resignation": " 'Not deep the Poet sees, but wide': think of this as you gaze from the Cumner Hill toward Cirencester and Cheltenham" *(Letters to Clough,* p. 99). In the sonnet, however, Arnold suggested that the poet must see both "deep" and "wide." Arnold took from the sonnet the phrase he used to describe Sophocles, "who saw life steadily and saw it whole." This phrase restated Müller's description of Sophocles: "calm and comprehensive vision." Neither Arnold nor Müller has made Sophocles the Romantic introspective poet who analyzes or lays bare his own heart. Rather, as Müller said, Sophocles analyzed "the secret workings of power and passion in the breast of every man." In a sense, the poet sees deeply into human nature yet also takes a wide view of the spectacle of life.

When Arnold did refer to the introspective poet in this letter, he said that Clough's best poetry was the hymn "where man, his deepest personal feelings being in play, finds poetical expression as *man* only, not as artist" *(Letters to Clough,* p. 99). What Arnold said here was consistent with the point that he developed in his earlier criticism, on the difference between poetry as an art and as the direct expression of feeling. Sophocles, in the earlier letter, was the observer of the life of Athens, and in his poetry he analyzed, not his own heart and feeling, but that of the Athenians.

Indeed, Arnold was fairly consistent in his view of Sophocles in the letters, in the sonnet "To a Friend," in the 1857 lecture, and in "Dover Beach." It has been argued that Arnold invented Sophocles' poetic character to accord with his own preconceived ideas of a poet.[19] No doubt here he has brought Sophocles nearer to the historians than anyone else had done. Yet Arnold's invention, if such it was,

was remarkably close to Müller's portrait of Sophocles. Arnold, in working out the relation between poetry and history, relied on Müller's account of the poet in his literary history. During the nineteenth century, the historian undeniably dominated the empire of fact, and Arnold especially felt the power of the new discipline, as he had felt the influence of one of the early enthusiasts, Dr. Arnold. Yet Arnold would not have turned to history in order to work out his poetics at this time had he not felt strongly the need to find an alternative to the kind of poetry that his friends were advocating and a way to defend his own belief about the kind of poetry that was necessary in the age of democracy. He was sure that poetry was not to be a personal confession or a hymn or an outpouring of the poet's spontaneous emotion. Neither a self-conscious introspection nor a sincere expression of feeling was what Arnold had in mind when he tried to find his individuality as a poet. Rather, he tried to find his individual voice in a poetry that comprehended the great facts of the age and was addressed to all the people. Arnold turned to Sophocles for a model not only because Sophocles was a great dramatic poet but also because he spoke to the people of the Athenian democracy. Arnold was trying to find a way back to a great public poetry, and for this reason he turned to the classical poets in the age of democracy. At the same time, because he thought that the poet must know the age, he turned also to the historians, working out in his 1857 lecture and in his experimental drama *Merope* a strong though temporary union between the historians and the poets.

As Arnold read the great ages of the past as modern in intellectual maturity, the others were looking to the past for analogues to the domestic epic or the tales of ordinary life. Although this distinction became especially significant in Arnold's Homeric criticism, which I will take up in the next chapter, I will here look at Clough's idea of the age of Plutarch.

In the decade when Arnold and Sellar were planning works on the great age of Rome, Clough was revising the so-called Dryden translation of Plutarch. Plutarch is important in English literature as the primary source of the "matter of Greece and Rome," notably in the Roman plays of Shakespeare; Plutarch was among the classical prose writers whose works continued to be read and translated for the reading public. Throughout the decade, Clough worked his way through the lives of the men of the age of Pericles and of the last days of the Roman Republic, the ages that Matthew Arnold in 1857 said were the great ages of the world. Plutarch, in his *Parallel Lives*, had compared the great men of Greece and Rome, and without any theory of a modern age, he nonetheless had paired the great men of similar periods, such as Theseus and Romulus, Demosthenes and Cicero, Caesar and Alexander.

Clough, in his brief introductions to his two editions of Plutarch, said nothing about these great ages or about their representative men; instead, he considered Plutarch and his age.[20] Clough clearly subscribed to the idea of the great age and its representative figures, but he did not adopt Arnold's idea about the modern and the adequate interpretation of the age. Clough was aware that Plutarch's stock had fallen during a period of critical and comprehensive history, and in the introduction to the complete *Lives*, Clough made his defense of Plutarch as "a moralist rather than an historian." But he also saw Plutarch as a representative man living in one of the great ages of the world, the time of "Nerva, Trajan, and Hadrian; the commencement of the best and happiest age of the great Roman imperial period" (pp. xv–xvi). Plutarch, because he was "a simple Boeotian provincial," better represented "the general spirit and character of the time" than did the Latin metropolitan writers Tacitus and Juvenal. Plutarch was actually less provincial in thought than the Romans were, because he wrote in "a more universal language, and [was] unwarped by the strong local reminiscences of the old home of the Senate and the Republic" (*Lives*, p. xvi).

Clough described Plutarch as the happy man:

It is . . . the serener aspect and the better era that the life and writings of Plutarch reflect. His language is that of a man happy in himself and in what is around him. His

natural cheerfulness is undiminished, his easy and joyous
simplicity is unimpaired, his satisfactions are not sad-
dened or imbittered by any overpowering recollections of
years passed under the immediate present terrors of imperial wickedness. (*Lives*, p. xvi)

Yet Plutarch's was not a naïve but an "instructed happiness,"
that of "one who had lived into good times out of evil" (*Lives*,
p. xvii). Clough saw Plutarch as living the ideal life of retirement from the world, a man "passing a happy, domestic literary life in a little Boeotian town," as he put it in the preface
to the little edition of Plutarch (*Greek History*, p. ix).

Clough made no claims for Plutarch as the adequate historian of the Periclean age or of the last days of the Roman
Republic, nor did he attempt to show that the *Lives* provide
useful examples for modern political life. Clough recognized
that Plutarch had little standing as a historical writer in a time
when the evidence of "co-temporaries" was sought and when
the chief interest was in the politics of the ancient world. Yet
Clough suggested that although the modern historians can
reconstruct the political life of the past, such "restorations"
are at best uncertain and (agreeing with Sellar) are likely to
be distorted by "new thoughts and views" (*Lives*, xvii). Plutarch, on the other hand, let us see how the Romans of the
Imperial Age saw their own history and how they thought
about certain universal moral problems:

> As a picture, at least, of the best Greek and Roman moral
> views and moral judgments, as a presentation of the re-
> sults of Greek and Roman moral thought, delivered not
> under the pressure of calamity, but as they existed in ordi-
> nary times, and actuated plain-living people in country
> places in their daily life, Plutarch's writings are of indis-
> putable value. (*Lives*, pp. xvii–xviii)

Ordinary times and plain-living people in country places—
these are the opposite of what Matthew Arnold had under-

stood to be the great subject; they constitute, however, the kind of subject that Clough had taken in poems such as *The Bothie*. Clough's defense of Plutarch had little to do with the principles that Arnold had laid down in the 1857 lecture; although Clough presented Plutarch as a representative man in a great age, he made no claims that the age was modern or that Plutarch was an intellectual deliverer. Admitting that Plutarch was a Boeotian provincial, Clough held that in fact Plutarch was less provincial in his outlook that were the Romans of his time. Finally, Clough questioned the absolute value of the modern critical historians, pointing out the uncertainty of their "restorations" of ancient political life and the likelihood that their interpretations had been distorted by modern views.

Clough ended his defense of Plutarch at the point where Thomas Arnold had asked: "But is our work now done? Is this full and distinct impression of the events, characters, institutions, manners, and ways of thinking of any period, that true historical knowledge which we require?" (*ILMH*, pp. 83–84). Dr. Arnold's answer was that such knowledge of the past was only "antiquarianism" unless it was connected to the present. Matthew Arnold took the view of the elder Arnold when in 1863, in the essay on Marcus Aurelius, he praised George Long's *Roman Lives*, an edition of Plutarch that is comparable to Clough's selection from the Greek lives. Long's commentary, Arnold observed, brought out the modern aspect of the life of ancient Rome: "In his notes on Plutarch's Roman Lives he deals with the modern epoch of Caesar and Cicero, not as food for schoolboys, but as food for men, and men engaged in the current of contemporary life and action" (*PW*, 3:136). Arnold clearly had the requirements of Thomas Arnold in mind, for he went on to compare George Long to Dr. Arnold "in this lively and fruitful way of considering the men and affairs of ancient Greece and Rome"(*PW*, 3:136).

Matthew Arnold asserted that the great epochs of the past had "a side of modern applicability and living interest," and he said about Long's work on Marcus Aurelius that Long "treats this truly modern striver and thinker not as a Classical

Dictionary hero, but as a present source from which to draw 'example of life, and instruction of manners' " (PW, 3:136). Clough had said that the modern world might find moral instruction in Plutarch, but he had based that conclusion on the universality of moral truths, rather than on evidence of Plutarch's modernity. Clough's notes on Plutarch did not, like Long's, attempt to illuminate the political life of the ancient Greeks and Romans. Arnold seems to have been referring obliquely to Clough in his reference to "Classical Dictionary" heroes and the phrase "food for schoolboys." Clough had written seventy-seven brief sketches for Sir William Smith's *Dictionary of Greek and Roman Biographies*, and Clough's selection of Greek lives from Plutarch was intended as a school text. Clough had discussed this plan with Arnold, who listed the book as "Clough's Select lives from Plutarch" on his reading list for 1860 (*Note-Books*, p. 565). Clough, in letters to Charles E. Norton, had in fact said that his revision of the old translation would not interest scholars but would do for boys.[21] Arnold may have heard from Clough directly some such estimate of Clough's Plutarch.

By 1863, when Arnold wrote the essay on Marcus Aurelius, he had begun to turn over in his mind ideas for his elegy on Clough and, in the process, had begun to review Clough's career. Arnold may have felt regret at the waste of Clough's energies in the minor pieces for Smith's *Dictionary* and in the revision of the old translation of Plutarch. As a critic, however, Arnold would not let pass Clough's defense of Plutarch on the ground that the Roman political life was not important to the Victorian political world. Arnold, in the essays to be introduced in the following year by "The Function of Criticism at the Present Time," was developing his literary criticism to include the idea of the modern in contemporary life and thought, the modern to include the ancient Greeks and Romans, an idea to be most fully developed in *Culture and Anarchy* but never to be lost sight of in Arnold's criticism.

Arnold had attempted to get Froude to review Clough's Plutarch, but Froude had declined because he was too busy.[22] Early in 1864, however, Froude gave a lecture that appeared to take a view of critical history much like that found in Clough's defense of Plutarch. Froude by this time had taken as his subject his own great age, the Elizabethan. By this time, Arnold had also changed his opinion, given in 1857, that the Elizabethan was not a modern age. Froude's lecture, "The Science of History," was given on February 5, 1864.[23] Froude began by denying that a science of history was possible, for "the phenomena never repeat themselves" (*SSGS*, p. 16), the records are never entirely trustworthy, and historians cannot make any useful predictions. Nor can any lesson be learned from history, except the old one "that the world is somehow built on moral foundations," and eventually good will be rewarded and evil punished (*SSGS*, p. 21). Another reason why there can be no science of history is that men's motives are too mixed, whether noble or selfish, to draw up any laws of human action (*SSGS*, pp. 23–25). Here Froude's view coincided with that of Sellar, who had pointed out that Thucydides recognized the individuality of human beings and their mixed motives. One use of history, Froude said, is to show that "justice and truth alone endure and live" (*SSGS*, p. 27). Froude cast doubt on the possibility of any theory of historical pattern or progress: "Hegel falls out of date, Schlegel falls out of date, and Comte in good time will fall out of date" (*SSGS*, p. 35). Thus Froude agreed with the historians who emphasize the particulars rather than the general laws of history.

From this point, Froude moved to a consideration of history as drama. Whereas Aristotle had argued that poetry is truer than history because it is more "philosophical," that is, it relies on general truths, Froude insisted that both history and drama rely on particular facts: "Even literal facts, exactly as they were, a great poet will prefer whenever he can get them" (*SSGS*, p. 33). Froude offered the example of Shakespeare's having used Wolsey's speeches from George Cavendish's *Life of Cardinal Wolsey*, and he might have pointed to Shakespeare's use of Plutarch. Poetry, Froude said, may complete a picture, or unify an action in time and place, "but it may not alter the real conditions of things, or represent life as other than it is. The greatness of a poet depends on his being true to nature, without insisting that nature should theorize with him, without making her more just, more philosophical, more moral than reality, and, in difficult matters, leaving much to reflection which cannot be explained" (*SSGS*, p. 34). As Arnold had said in the letters to Clough, Shakespeare can be as obscure as life is. Froude, however, differed radically from Arnold in holding that the poet reports the facts as he finds them, rather than reconstructing the universe. But if Froude restricted drama to a direct reporting of facts, so even more did he restrict the historian:

> If the drama is grandest when action is least explicable by laws, because it best resembles life, then history will be grandest also under the same conditions. "Macbeth," were it literally true, would be perfect history; and so far as the historian can approach to that kind of model, so far as he can let his story tell itself in the deeds and words of those who act it out, so far is he most successful. (*SSGS*, p. 35)

Froude pointed to Gibbon as the example both of the narrative technique and the theory: "The splendid intellect of Gibbon for the most part kept him true to the right course in this; yet the philosophical chapters for which he has been most admired or censured may hereafter be thought the least interesting in his work" (*SSGS*, p. 35). Froude, then, made drama like history, not because history can be said to have a tragic plot and design, but because both ought to tell a story directly and simply. Unlike both Sellar and Arnold, Froude argued here that history does not look for general laws or explanation, nor does drama.

Froude seems to have chosen to report the particulars, not shaped by any theory of history or even of drama. He took a naïve view of Shakespeare in order to support his idea of how history should be written: Shakespeare represents in his play "real life," is "true to real experience," and does not attempt to explain life: "The mystery of life he leaves as he finds it; and, in his most tremendous positions, he is addressing rather the intellectual emotions than the understanding,—knowing well that the understanding in such things is at fault, and the sage as ignorant as the child" (*SSGS*, p. 291). Froude thus tended to rely on particulars and to distrust any interpretation of history, such as Arnold sought in the 1857 lecture.

In general, Froude, Sellar, and Arnold were breaking down the distinctions between the poet and the historians, but with different purposes. Arnold was defending the claims that poetry has intellectual weight and significance; Froude and Sellar were enlarging on the claims of history as art. On the other hand, when Froude went on to outline how history is to be written, he adopted the idea of a great period, the actors being representative of their time:

> Mind can be seen matched against mind, and the great passions of the epoch not simply be described as existing, but be exhibited at their white heat in the souls and hearts possessed by them. There are all the elements of the drama—drama of the highest order—where the huge forces of the times are as the Grecian destiny, and the power of the man is seen either stemming the stream till it overwhelms him, or ruling while he seems to yield to it. (*SSGS*, p. 36)

But though the historian should understand the dominant forces of the times, "We should no more ask for a theory of this or that period of history, than we should ask for a theory of 'Macbeth' or 'Hamlet' " (*SSGS*, p. 36).

Like Clough, Froude looked in history and in drama for an artless record of an age; Clough, in Plutarch's history for a record of ordinary life; Froude, in Shakespeare for a representation of "real" life. Arnold, for the moment, had allied himself rather with the classicist Sellar, finding in the drama and history of Athens not only parallels to the modern age but also the evidence of an intelligent and democratic people, in a time when even the greatest historians and tragic writers could speak to an audience of intelligent and mature people—not the few, but the entire people of Athens. Another battle was being waged over the great poet of the heroic age, whether Homer was a ballad poet and whether a modern poet who used the old forms, such as Scott, was a modern Homer. In this debate Arnold laid the foundations for his great period of criticism, and he established the principles for poetry in a democratic age.

Chapter Five

"That Natural Heart
of Humanity":
Homer and the Ballad Poets

In the essays on translating Homer, Arnold engaged the criticism that not only made extravagant claims for the merits of folk poetry but also tried to claim the classical poet for the folk. Arnold began by criticizing Francis Newman's claim that Homer's poetry is like ballad poetry, to be translated into the form and style of the English border ballads; Arnold ended by examining Clough's epic meter in *The Bothie.* The larger question is the one that Arnold had debated with the Balliol scholars: the place of classical poetry in a society that was moving towards democracy. In these essays, Arnold looked at the folk and their place in literature, as subject, source, poet, and audience. Shairp had urged Arnold to give up the old classical form; Clough had used the epic meter in the way of Longfellow's *Evangeline,* to tell a modern tale of the people. As a classical scholar, Shairp tried to make the classical poets accessible by looking for the common touch and by seeing Vergil as a poet of the country. On the theory that the Homeric epics were made up of shorter "lays," perhaps by a collector such as Scott, Shairp suggested that Scott was a modern Homer. Arnold, who had written a few poems in the ballad style, including one of this best poems, "The Forsaken Merman," and who admired the "lyrical ballads" of Wordsworth, did not merely dismiss the question of whether ballad poetry or the poetry of Scott is Homeric and whether Homeric poetry has anything in common with the English traditional ballad. Indeed, Arnold gave due consideration both to the traditional ballads and to Scott's poems before he decided that they fell short of Homer's grand style.

Arnold first dealt with the question of how to translate Homer. Arnold began by noticing Francis Newman's assertion that "the translator's 'first duty . . . is a historical one: to be *faithful.*' "[1] Arnold asked what it meant to be faithful to Homer. Newman, believing that Homer addressed a popular audience, had argued that Homer's "natural hearers" were equivalent to the unlearned English readers; thus, the ordinary reader becomes the judge of the translation. Arnold, however, denied that anyone could now tell "how Homer affected the Greeks," least of all those who know no Greek (*PW*, 1:98–99). There were, however, those who could tell how Homer affected them; and the "only competent tribunal" of the faithfulness of a translation were the scholars "who possess, at the same time with knowledge of Greek, adequate poetical taste and feeling" (*PW*, 1:99). Here Arnold announced the appeal to the judicious, which would become the standard in his formal criticism: " 'as the judicious would determine' " (*PW*, 1:99). This appeal to the scholar who has poetical taste would coincide, in Arnold's later criticism, with his setting up tests for poetry which depend, not on any body of rules or codes, but entirely on the taste or "tact" of instructed critics.

Now Arnold warned against letting "modern sentiment" intrude on any judgment of Homer: "Modern sentiment tries to make the ancient not less than the modern world its own; but against modern sentiment in its applications to Homer the translator, if he would feel Homer truly—and unless he feels him truly, how can he render him truly?—cannot be too much on his guard" (*PW*, 1:101). What Arnold regarded as modern sentimentality was Ruskin's comment on Homer's "life-giving" in the famous lines from Helen's speech in the *Iliad* (iii.243): "So she spoke; but the life-giving earth already held them in Lacedaemon, in their dear native land" (*PW*, 1:101). Ruskin's commentary, quoted by Arnold, was this: " 'The poet . . . has to speak of the earth in sadness; but he will not let that sadness affect or change his thought of it. No; though

Castor and Pollux be dead, yet the earth is our mother still,—
fruitful, life-giving' " (*PW*, 1:102). False criticism, Arnold said,
because Homer did not use the adjective *physizoos* for those
sentimental reasons: "It is not true, as a matter of general criticism, that this kind of sentimentality, eminently modern,
inspires Homer at all" (*PW*, 1:102). A better clue to Homer
than the "tender pantheism" of Ruskin, Arnold said, is Goethe's
tragic view, " 'that in our life here above ground we have, properly speaking, to enact Hell' " (*PW*, 1:102). Arnold did not go
on to explain how, with Goethe's clue, the passage might be
read; but certainly he did not mean that translation was impossible. We can know what Homer means; we can also know
the Homeric style.

Arnold's attack on Francis Newman's theories about
Homer seems disproportionate to the importance of this
minor writer; what Arnold really aimed at was the movement
to exalt folk poetry and to claim Homer for the folk. Arnold's
criticism, although in some points it was directed at Newman,
in general aimed at the criticism that reduced Homer to a ballad poet or raised the ballad poet to the rank of Homer. Arnold,
using Newman's translation as an example, had to try to show
the difference between English ballad poetry and Homer. What
gave Arnold, theoretically, the most difficulty was the question, raised by Newman, of Homeric Greek. Newman took
the skeptical view that Homer's language would have seemed
"quaint and antiquated" to Sophocles, as Chaucer's language
seems antiquated, and as Shakespeare's at times seems one
or the other or both (*PW*, 1:119–20). Arnold appears to have
wanted to argue that a great poet is never quaint or antiquated
in style, as if, as Huntington Brown used to tell us, the great
poet does not mistake language, does not use words that will
later seem quaint. Shakespeare, Arnold said, could write in
a language "perfectly simple, perfectly intelligible," though
he did not always do so (*PW*, 1:120). Arnold's argument did
not adequately account for the natural and inevitable changes
in language, and Newman, as critics have pointed out, was
better aware than was Arnold of such changes in Greek.[2] In

the first essays, Arnold more or less dismissed the question, denying that we can know how Homer affected Sophocles or the Greeks of the Periclean Age. In his "Last Words," however, Arnold argued for the familiarity of the Homeric language, not as the everyday speech of Athens, but as a poetic language familiar to those who had heard Homer from their childhood (*PW*, 1:178–80). Both arguments about Homeric style may now seem irrelevant in view of the prevailing theories of oral-form-ulaic style, although Arnold's grasp of a traditional poetic language has fared better than Newman's notion of an antiquated Homer. Arnold, furthermore, rightly discerned that these questions were primarily historical or philological and that the aesthetic effect of the translation was the question for literary criticism.

Arnold had no doubt that the style of Homer could be known by an English Victorian critic and that it was plain, direct, rapid, and noble, that it was a grand style. The English ballad style, Arnold thought, was none of these things. The ballad manner can be found, Arnold said, also in the *Nibelungen Lay*, a poem that he said was composed by a "very ordinary mortal" and therefore was often prosy, "anything rather than a grand poem" (*PW*, 1:128–29). The modern imitations of "heroic lays" equally fell short of the grand style: for example, "the pinchbeck *Roman Ballads* of Lord Macaulay" (*PW*, 1:131). On the other hand, the reproduction of Homer's dactylic hexameter and similes did not necessarily produce the grand style in English, as Arnold saw when he turned to consider Clough's style in *The Bothie*. Clough had made Homer serve the cause of the people by following Longfellow in telling a tale of ordinary life in epic style. The grand style that is used to relate events of ordinary life is a standard device of mock epic, and although Clough intended rather to dignify the common people, the poem often had a comic effect: Arnold described it as a "serio-comic poem" (*PW*, 1:150). Judging by the criteria of the grand style, Arnold concluded that the poem failed to be plain and direct in thought and diction: "The thought in this poem is often curious and subtle, and that is not Homeric; the diction is often grotesque, and that is not Homeric" (*PW*, 1:150). Judged as a comic poem, however, it may be grotesque; it is rapid in movement and plain and direct in manner if not in thought. The scope of the poem, its rapidity, and its directness produced in the reader "the sense of having, within short limits of time, a large portion of human life presented to him, instead of a small portion" (*PW*, 1:151). *Evangeline*, on the other hand, was "tenderly elegant," even "lumbering" at times. Arnold's judgment of the domestic epics was definite: he would not call them Homer.

In insisting that the grand style of Homer was marked by grace and civility, unlike the rude style of the folk ballad, Arnold was in conflict with his friends, who held strong sentiments about the poetry of the folk. Although Arnold did seriously consider the claims of the traditional ballad and the modern imitations, especially those of Wordsworth and Scott, his position was indicated when he said, "The old English balladist may stir Sir Philip Sidney's heart like a trumpet, and this is much; but Homer, but the few artists in the grand style, can do more; they can refine the raw natural man, they can transmute him" (*PW*, 1:138-39).[3] Although the criticism of the border ballads as poetry that is suited to the capacities and tastes of the people seems democratic, such criticism actually rested on a distrust of the people, on a belief that Homer, Shakespeare, and Greek drama are beyond the folk, whether they be peasants or "workfolk," who, however, may follow the simple forms and ideas of poetry in a ballad style or a Homer translated into a ballad style. Matthew Arnold, on the other hand, thought that a result of the French revolution was the spread of general culture in France, so that the ordinary person, even the peasant, was on the whole capable and intelligent. Arnold thought that democracy could succeed only where the people were influenced by genuine learning, and his criticism, as he worked it out in the 1860s, did not offer the people something suited to their limited circumstances and tastes, nor did his literary criticism offer them a lesser literature.

Only the great poets would "refine the raw natural man," and the great poets were Homer, Sophocles, Dante, Shakespeare, and Milton. Homer appealed both to the reason and to the "natural heart of humanity." Arnold, perhaps surprisingly unless one sees that he is taking his stand on the beliefs of the Enlightenment, said that Homer was like Voltaire:

> Homer, indeed, has actually an affinity with Voltaire in the unrivalled clearness and straightforwardness of his thinking; in the way in which he keeps to one thought at a time, and puts that thought forth in its complete natural plainness, instead of being led away from it by some fancy striking him in connection with it, and being beguiled to wander off with this fancy till his original thought, in its natural reality, knows him no more. (*PW*, 1:114)

Homer went beyond Voltaire, however, for Homer had "the power of profoundly touching that natural heart of humanity which it is Voltaire's weakness that he cannot reach, but can also address the understanding with all Voltaire's admirable simplicity and rationality" (*PW*, 1:114). What Arnold was saying here was that Homer speaks plainly to any person of adult reason and that he speaks as well to the natural human heart; there is no need to try to appeal to the ordinary reader through a translation into a false ballad style or modern sentimentality.

Arnold's criticism, then, was aimed at two positions he considered false: (1) that Homer was a ballad poet and that English ballad poetry was Homeric and (2) that the untutored folk were a source of wisdom and poetry. The Balliol scholars had fostered both ideas in their criticism: the classicists, even more than the others, tended to see in the epic poets Homer and Vergil the depiction either of daily, ordinary life or of rural, primitive life.

Froude, in an essay on Homer in 1851, at about the time that Clough and Arnold were busy with Homeric imitations, wrote an enthusiastic account of Homer as the observer of

the ordinary life of the Ionians. Froude's essay is worth examining in some detail, because it raised some of the questions
that Arnold considered about the universality of epic poetry,
yet with a difference. Granting that historical characters are
absent from Homer's poems, Froude found another kind of
history:

> . . . a picture not of the times of which he sang, but of
> the men among whom he lived. How they acted; how they
> thought, talked, and felt; what they made of this earth,
> and of their place in it; their private life and their public
> life; men and women; masters and servants; rich and
> poor—we have it all delineated in the marvellous verse
> of a poet who, be he what he may, was in this respect the
> greatest which the earth has ever seen.[4]

Froude, the future historian of England, made a distinction
between the prose historian and the poet, in that the poet can
give a distinct impression of actual events and human actions,
so that the poem seems to give actual life: "Poetry has this
life-giving power, and prose has it not; and thus the poet is
the truest historian" (*SSGS*, 1:506). Thus, although Homer
did not give accurate facts, events, and names, he gave us his
world, even in the episode of Odysseus among the Phaeacians:

> Though Phoeacia was a dreamland, or a symbol of the
> Elysian fields, yet Homer drew his material, his island,
> his palaces, his harbour, his gardens of perennial beauty,
> from those fair cities which lay along the shores of his
> own Ionia; and like his blind Demodocus, Homer doubt-
> less himself sang those very hymns which now delight
> us so, in the halls of many a princely Alcinous. (*SSGS*,
> 1:507)

Although Froude devoted a paragraph or two to an argument
that only poetry, not prose, can give us great men, such as
Caesar and Alexander, not ordinary men (*SSGS*, 1:507-8),

in arguing that the Homeric age was neither barbaric nor primitive (*SSGS*, 1:508–10), much of his essay was devoted to showing Homer as the poet of everyday life. Having established the premise that people in the Homeric Age were much like those of the Victorian Age, so that "child would meet child without sense of strangeness in common games and common pleasures," he illustrated the Victorian world of Homer: "The little Ulysses, climbing on the knees of his father's guest, coaxing for a taste of the red wine, and spilling it as he starts at the unusual taste" (*SSGS*, 1:510). Like Elizabeth Barrett Browning in *Aurora Leigh*,[5] Froude saw in Homer touching Victorian vignettes of little children or family life: Laertes is "a calm, kind father of the nineteenth century" (*SSGS*, 1:510). Where Arnold looked for universals in great subjects—permanent affections in which all could share— Froude looked for universals in the ordinary life, even in children's games, in a kind of common sentimentality.

Froude set aside differences in religion, laws, and social life. As a matter for belief, the mythology and religion of the ancient Greeks might seem strange and alien to a Victorian, but Froude denied that "theogonies" and "theologies" were essential to religion, and he looked for "real belief" in the intuitions of the poem, "the natural expressions which burst out spontaneously—expressions of opinion on Providence, on the relation of man to God, on the eternal laws by which this world is governed" (*SSGS*, 1:512). Froude offered, not a special notion of Homeric justice, but a universal idea, that the gods honor the righteous and punish the wrongdoers (*SSGS*, 1:514–15). The laws and social arrangements of the Homeric poems, Froude acknowledged, are not the same as those of the Victorians (*SSGS*, 1:521–22). But in daily life, in the life of nature, there were universal elements. In the similes and metaphors of Homer, "scene[s] of daily life [are] worked out with elaborate beauty" (*SSGS*, 1:523). "The designs on the shield of Achilles are, together, a complete picture of Homer's microcosm"; these depict scenes from daily life, especially the harvest scenes and festivals (*SSGS*, 1:524). "Homer had seen these things," Froude said, "or he would not have sung of them" (*SSGS*, 1:525). Froude thus included Homer with Shakespeare as among the poets of reality.

Like Clough writing about Plutarch in Boeotia, Froude saw Homer's daily world as a cheerful, idyllic world, very different from Arnold's view of the *Iliad*. Froude wrote, "It is difficult to point to a time when life in general was happier, and the character of man set in a more noble form" (*SSGS*, 1:533). Froude acknowledged that the lot of women was not so happy then for the women who were slaves, having been taken as prisoners in war; yet women held a relatively high place, and "the relation between wife and husband was of . . . a free and honourable kind" (*SSGS*, 1:535). Indeed, Penelope is the hero of the *Odyssey*; comparing Penelope to Clytemnestra, Froude concluded, "Women, therefore, according to Homer, were as capable of heroic virtue as men were, and the ideal of this heroism is one to which we have scarcely added" (*SSGS*, 1:536). As for work, however, "their chief occupations were household matters, care of clothes and linen, and other domestic arrangements" (*SSGS*, 1:536–37)—even, one might add, in the ideal world of Phaeacia. Here, too, Froude saw Homeric women in the light of Victorian ideals of domestic virtue; and undeniably the intrusion of modern sentiment, which Arnold deplored in his Homeric essays, informs Froude's account of the Homeric poems as reports on an age much like the Victorian one.

In his poetry, Clough attempted another task, to adapt Homeric style to Victorian themes, to make ordinary life into an epic poem. Although Clough did not write about the world of Homer, one can assume that he held ideas much like those of Froude about the similarity between the Homeric world and the Victorian one and that he thought using Homeric style for a modern verse novel was therefore appropriate. Clough had very early fallen into what Arnold thought was the error of linking modern ballad poetry with Homer, in remarks that Clough had made about Macaulay's "Battle of Ivry," which appeared in the *Rugby Magazine* in October, 1835.[6] Clough then attempted to make a rather ponderous distinction between the subjective and the objective poet, which he evidently had learned from Coleridge, here meaning simply that Homer said nothing of his own self or his feelings. Clough's labored analysis of the old fourteeners of Macaulay's poem and the ideas about French character do not reveal a sensitive ear or a fine discrimination in the young critic; but it does indicate the path that Clough's interest in Homer would take, largely in adapting the Homeric line to modern poetry. This interest appeared in Clough's piece on translating Homer.[7] This, one of the "letters of Parepidemus," was chiefly concerned with the use of the English hexameter in translation; it offered a few examples that recall the style of *The Bothie* and anticipate *Amours de Voyage*. He discussed the matter of English stress and quantity, or "our forward-rushing, consonant-crushing Anglo-savage enunciation" (*PR*, p. 394). Clough's attempt to invent an English dactylic hexameter interested Arnold, who examined Clough's verse in the lectures on Homer and found them "too rough and irregular" (*PW*, 1:151), although possessing some Homeric qualities. But it seems clear that Arnold, unlike Froude and Clough, saw no similarity between the heroic age and the Victorian one, did not think that the Homeric style had been used to depict ordinary life in Ionia, and did not think that it could be used for a modern domestic epic.

The debate continued in reviews of Clough's poems that were collected and published after his death. Sellar's review touched on the accepted view that Clough was a profound thinker, working out his own doubts in his poetry. Sellar praised Clough as a modern poet who expressed with "desperate sincerity and intensity of feeling" his need for certainty in matters of faith.[8] Sellar saw the poems as a kind of autobiography: "His [Clough's] book is the sincere and real expression of the various phases through which his mind passed, and of the great emotions and affections which filled his heart" ("Poems," p. 327). Clough's modernism was soundly based, Sellar thought. "Intensely modern" in his use of poetic forms and materials, Clough knew the ancient literature as well as the modern Europeans, the most influential "original thinkers and imaginative writers" ("Poems," p. 328).

Sellar's recognition of Clough's classicism, however, led to a surprising criticism; while Clough's strength lay in his ability to express his own feelings and to describe his own times, his range was limited. Unlike "our two greatest living poets," Clough could not give "life, substance, and personality to the modes of thought and feeling of other ages" but only of "what he had felt, seen, and sympathized with in actual life" ("Poems," p. 336). Sellar could praise *Mari Magno*, Clough's series of tales of ordinary life in modern times, which had been "written with great ease and simplicity" ("Poems," p. 342), but he held that the greatest poets could also bring to life, by the power of their imagination, the life and thought of other times. Sellar, more than anyone else in the Balliol group, came increasingly to agree with Arnold about the poetry of Homer and the Greek tragic writers.

Shairp, on the other hand, from the first had combined his attack on Arnold's poetry with claims that Homer was a ballad poet and that Scott and Scottish songs and ballads were Homeric. In his review of Arnold's poems in 1854, Shairp had included Homer among those whom he called "natural poets," along with Scott, Burns, and Wordsworth. These poets were "unlearned" and sang "straight from their own heart, in the native dialect, to a self-taught tune, in whatever form [came] readiest to hand."[9] Shairp continued his argument in an 1861 article, "The Songs of Scotland before Burns," an essay containing a statement of his position that he was to repeat later in an Oxford lecture and in "Scottish Song, and Burns" in *Aspects of Poetry.*[10] Here Shairp made a plea for seeing the songs of Scotland as "the poetry of the people," possessing "literary excellence" but able to "thrill the simplest, most untutored bosoms, as no book-poetry can" ("Songs," p. 399). Such poetry was "the creation and the property of the people":

The productions, many of them, not of book-learned men, but of country people, with country life, cottage characters and incidents, for their subjects, they utter the very feelings which poor men have known, in the very words and phrases which poor men have used. No wonder the Scottish people love them; for never was the heart of any people more fully rendered in poetry than Scotland's heart in these songs. . . . Every way you take them—in authorship, in sentiment, in tone, in language,—they are the creation and property of the people. (*AP*, pp. 208–9)

For Shairp the "poetry of the people" was not the poetry of the great age of Greece; it was a ballad poetry arising from the creative power of the folk. This was the argument that Shairp announced in his review of Arnold's 1853 *Poems* and was to repeat in the article in 1861 on Scottish poets and again in his Oxford lecture. This argument was what Arnold answered in his Homeric essays, the first essays in criticism, and again in "The Study of Poetry." In respect to Homer, however, it is Shairp's essay on Scott that offers an illuminating contrast to Arnold's criticism of Homer.

In "The Homeric Spirit in Walter Scott," Shairp called Scott a "truly great" poet, and compared him to Homer: Shairp did not claim that Scott was an epic poet, but he did assert that Scott's poems "contain more of the Homeric or epic element than any other poems in the English language."[11] For a definition of an epic poem, Shairp referred briefly to Aristotle, as summarized by Thomas Arnold the Younger in his *Manual of English Literature* (1862), and to Matthew Arnold on Homer's style. But Shairp's principal attention was given to Friedrich August Wolf's distinction between literary and popular epic, as summarized by John Stuart Blackie in his *Homeric Dissertations*. Matthew Arnold, in his essays on Homer, had noticed Blackie's articles in *Macmillan's*.[12] Shairp's enumeration of four points describing the popular epic included the assumption that epics were composed in "an early and primitive age," when "the songs or ballads of the people were still preserved in memory" or were transmitted orally (*AP*, p. 381). Shairp made a distinction between the ballad and the epic style, emphasizing the nobility and grandeur of the epic, much as Arnold had; nonetheless, Shairp thought that the Homeric epics "grew out of a ballad literature" and that the *Iliad* was a popular epic of the heroic age, composed somewhere near the end of the age (*AP*, pp. 382–83). The *Aeneid* and *Paradise Lost*, on the other hand, were literary epics, "not singing unconsciously and spontaneously as native passion dictated" (*AP*, p. 383). Homer was, in Shairp's view, not the conscious literary artist or the clear thinker that Arnold saw, but was a primitive bard.

Shairp saw that Scott was like Homer in having lived at the end of a heroic age and in having taken his material from times that were passing away. In his poetry, Scott "revived the Homeric inspiration, and exhibited, even in this late day, something of the primitive spirit of Homer" (*AP*, p. 384). True, Shairp realized that in the Scotland of Scott's youth, there was culture and civilization in Edinburgh. But in the country, "the traditions of former times still prevailed, and formed the intellectual atmosphere which they breathed" of the Covenanters, still earlier "Border feuds and battles," and in "the wilder Highlands" as well as in the Lowlands, memories of the Fifteen and the Forty-five, of Flodden Field and Culloden Moor (*AP*, p. 385). Shairp thought that Scott, who grew up at his grandfather's place at Sandyknowe, had heard the old tales from his grandmother, ballads from his aunt, and stories from the old shepherds and that Scott had collected legends and ballads in the Highlands for the *Border Minstrelsy.* Scott's experience, Shairp implied, was like that of Homer—at the end of a heroic age, Scott had gathered up the old tales, legends, songs, and ballads and had created out of this stock his own epic poems.

Scott's poetry is in fact like the popular epic in its "spontaneity" or the "absence of all artistic consciousness" and in its "naturalness of treatment" or "absence of effort" (*AP*, p. 394). In *Marmion*, Scott took "a national and truly heroic action" in "the battle of Flodden"; "no other event, not even Culloden, ever equalled it" (*AP*, p. 395). Scott's treatment of the theme was not always epic, for the style varied, "now high, now low, spirited or tame, in stately or in homely strain" (*AP*, p. 396), but Scott reached epic grandeur in the battle scenes. Arnold had looked at the famous battle scenes but had denied to them epic grandeur: "Scott is certainly at his best in his battles. Of Homer you could not say this; he is not better in his battles than elsewhere; but even between the battle-pieces of the two there exists all the difference which there is between an able work and a masterpiece" (*PW*, 1:138). Shairp, however, claimed that Scott was an epic poet, at least, "He is the only Homer who has been vouchsafed to Scotland—I might almost say to modern Europe" (*AP*, p. 406). The novels, too, Shairp declared to be Homeric, especially in scenes like "the romantic adventures and beautiful home-pictures of the *Odyssey*" (*AP*, p. 402). Froude had found a detailed picture of everyday Ionian life in the Homeric epics, which thus became like the novel in rendering ordinary life.

Shairp, too, could see Scott as a Homeric poet only by making Homer into either a ballad poet or a novelist. Arnold, who admired Scott as a poet, did not include him among the ballad poets. Scott indeed used the ballad style,

but, being a man of far greater powers than the ballad-poets, he has tried to give to their instrument a compass and an elevation which it does not naturally possess, in order to enable him to come nearer to the effect of the instrument used by the great epic poets,—an instrument which he felt he could not truly use,—and in this attempt he has but imperfectly succeeded. (*PW*, 1:137)

Arnold thought, not of the mystical notion of a folk creating a poetry, but of the art of the ballad form.

The ballad form, Arnold argued, defeated Scott in his attempt to forge it into an epic style; nor could Wordsworth use the ballad for anything but the simplest narrative. "Let us but observe," Arnold said, "how a great poet, having to deliver a narrative very weighty and serious, instinctively shrinks from the ballad-form as from a form not commensurate with his subject-matter, a form too narrow and shallow for it, and seeks for a form which has more amplitude and impressiveness" (PW, 1:207–8). Wordsworth, Arnold said, "strove to be simple; it was his mission to be simple; he loved the ballad-form, he clung to it, because it was simple"; and for the "unpretending simplicity" of "Lucy Gray," he said, the form is "quite adequate." In "Ruth," however, "the gravity of his matter is too much for this somewhat slight form; he is obliged to give to his form more amplitude, more augustness, to shake out its folds" (PW, 1:208).

Arnold did not say absolutely that great poetry may not be written in the ballad form or that even the grand style could not be achieved in that form, but he thought it more likely to succeed in the lyric: "When there comes in poetry what I may call the *lyrical cry*, this transfigures everything, makes everything grand; the simplest form may be here even an advantage, because the flame of the emotion glows through and through it more easily" (PW, 1:209). Arnold found such a grand style in Wordsworth's "To the Cuckoo," comparing a stanza to a line from "Ruth" and another from "Michael." Arnold acknowledged that "by the occurrence of this lyrical cry, the ballad-poets themselves rise sometimes, though not so often as one might perhaps have hoped, to the grand style," quoting as illustration two stanzas from "Sir Patrick Spence." But only in the stanzas that are lyrical, not in the narrative, did Arnold see the ballad style as rising to the grand style. In this judgment, Arnold looked ahead to "The Study of Poetry," in which he found that Burns approached the classic only in his lyrics. Yet, recalling Arnold's earlier comments on Burns in the letters to Clough, this lyrical cry was not the spontaneous outpouring of emotion—not a cry, but a lyrical cry—as fury had to become a lyrical fury.

Style or form for Arnold did not exist for its own sake, nor was it independent of the emotions or the ideas of the poet. Homer, Arnold said, found a style answerable to his ideas; the ballad poets were chiefly storytellers:

In the ballad-poets in general, as in men of a rude and early stage of the world, in whom their humanity is not yet variously and fully developed, the stock of these ideas is scanty, and the ideas themselves not very effective or profound. [For] them the narrative itself is the great matter, not the spirit and significance which underlies the narrative. (*PW*, 1:210)

Later poets may, however, have "a *balladist's mind*"; they have "a fresh and lively curiosity for the outward spectacle of the world" but little for the "inward significance of that spectacle." Such poets, when they stop to comment on the narrative, often fall into trite or banal comments; Arnold found painful the banality of Macaulay's Horatius: " 'To all the men upon this earth / Death cometh soon or late' " (*PW*, 1:210-11). Homer, on the other hand, shared with Milton "the noble and profound application of ideas to life—[which] is the most essential part of poetic greatness" (*PW*, 1:211-12). Although Arnold may here seem to have been giving a great deal of ground to philosophy in making ideas the essential part of poetry, or at least great poetry, he was actually trying to work out the basis of the grand style. Form and matter were not in practice separable; a grand style cannot exist independently of great thought and emotion. Arnold, in his later criticism, would attempt to separate what he would call "poetic truth" from philosophy, and he would refine his distinctions by making use of his distinctive term, used in the lectures on translating Homer, "criticism of life." Arnold no longer would expect of the poet an adequate explanation of the age, a historical explanation. In the succeeding lectures, which were collected in his first *Essays in Criticism*, he would attempt to work out a connection between criticism and ideas. But the Homeric "criticism of life" suggested primarily the observations on life of an intelligent, disciplined, and cultivated mind.

Although Arnold continued to insist that the great poems of the great civilizations were, to use his later term, classics, he never denied his early taste for the ballads or for Scott.

Arnold's poetry shows how well he knew the poetry of Scott and Coleridge that was written in the old ballad style. Among Arnold's narrative poems, there are echoes of Coleridge's meter in *Tristram and Iseult* and "The Forsaken Merman." Even when Arnold wrote the drama *Merope*, in which he tried to recreate a Greek classical form, he still drew scenes of mountain life that borrowed from Scott's *Lady of the Lake*.[13] Arnold was flexible enough to give serious consideration to the old ballad poems and to Scott and to recognize that at times, poets could achieve the very best poetry using the old forms. But he did not accept the premise that the ballad poems, because they were the creation of the people, were the kind of poetry needed in a new democratic age; Homer could best refine the raw natural man. In his next lectures, Arnold set out to define the functions of a criticism that both judged by the highest standards and remained disinterested—a criticism for the present time and for the coming democratic age, which needed, above all, a great poetry.

Chapter Six

The Great Work of Criticism

When Arnold collected the best of his articles for *Essays in Criticism* (1865), he wrote an introductory essay that in its general theory sought to explain his own recent criticism and to work out new answers to the old questions. "The Function of Criticism at the Present Time" asserted once more his faith that the intellectual movements of the Enlightenment were returning to full vigor and that free inquiry in all branches of human knowledge was promising once more to sweep away the old and false ideas. In this essay, however, in setting out a theoretic basis for his criticism, Arnold no longer emphasized the power of criticism to destroy the encumbrances on human thought. Now he showed the power of criticism not only to discover or to recognize worthy ideas but also to preserve what was true or good in the past. Emphasizing the work that criticism was to perform, he also began to see criticism as an activity performed, not so much for a further end, social or aesthetic, but as an activity worthwhile in itself. In the "present time" to which Arnold was speaking in the essay, the revival of romanticism—with a renewed enthusiasm for creative genius and the power of the imagination, the poetic temperament, and the ordinary life—was met by the rigorous inquiry that Arnold had begun in the essays. What Arnold now tried to show was not only that the criticism or examination of these notions indicated the limits of poetry and criticism but also that the activity of criticism—in its broadest sense the examination of ideas and of life itself—is a productive work. Arnold now answered Wordsworth's claim for the superiority of poetry over criticism and Shairp's assertion that the new spirit of imagination had led to the great age of Romantic poetry. Arnold sets out to show the defects of this argument and to find a theoretical basis for his criticism of the Romantic poets in the earlier essays, which were collected in this volume and formed the bulk of his first major criticism. Arnold found his theoretical basis in ideas suggested by Aristotle's *Ethics;* he developed the notion of criticism as an activity, as in his essays on the Romantic poets he had turned to Aristotle for his analysis of the Romantic temperament and the provincial mind.

Arnold did not intend so much to show the deficiencies of the Romantics as poets as to show the inadequacy of their criticism, above all the danger of elevating the folk as the standard of taste and reason. Arnold's insistence on the function of criticism in finding the best that is thought and said was meant for the coming age of the people: the people were not, in his view, to be cheated by being handed ideas or poetry that were thought to be good enough for them. Arnold, it may be said, was offering a new declaration of the rights of human-kind—the right to know the best that is thought and said. Arnold's declaration of an equality of such rights did not mean that Arnold naïvely supposed that the best was necessarily within the reach of all people. One must also keep in mind here his practical work for an improved public education. In practice, he tended to aim at an educated middle class rather than at the populace or at an aristocracy that was indifferent, or so he thought, to ideas. But there is nothing in Arnold's thought that assumed that the common people were by nature incapable of intelligent reflection and comprehension. Preceding Arnold's insistence on the work of criticism in finding and making known the best that is thought and said was his criticism of Homer, in which he had insisted that Homer was not a ballad poet and that the ballad poets were not Homer; Arnold's essay on the modern, in which he held that the contemporary was not always new or fresh, let alone the best; and his essay on the discoveries of Bishop Colenso, which was essentially naïve and uninformed Biblical criticism. Arnold's praise of the Romantic poets was reserved for Shelley and Byron, who neither lost their faith in the democratic revolution nor fell into a sentimental view of the folk.

In emphasizing criticism as work or activity, I should say at the outset that Arnold did not have in mind Carlyle's notion of work as duty or an economic or utilitarian view of work as useful labor. Arnold's emphasis was on the activity itself as the end, on the happiness found in the performance. Arnold insisted, in opposition to Emerson and Carlyle, that the end of human life was happiness, and he located happiness in performing an activity well. Moreover, Arnold, like Aristotle, was to find the highest human activity in thinking—*theoria*, or theoretical activity, and this aspect of Arnold's criticism explains his emphasis in these essays on ideas, on the best that is thought and said, and his lack of interest in judging the value of literary works—his eye was on the activity, on the question of whether the activity of criticism was one in which the critic might find the good life, or happiness—on what criticism does when it is done well. Although he thought about theoretical more than practical criticism, he did not neglect practical criticism, nor did he neglect the effect that criticism could have on society. He saw that the effect was not different from the activity but extended its scope—that is, made it possible for more, if not all, to share in the activity of knowing the best that was being thought and said.

In spite of Arnold's emphasis on thought in the activity of criticism—on judgment and theory—it would be wrong to think of Arnold's idea of literary criticism as severely "intellectualist," a criticism that was rigorously logical or that relied on the application of unvarying principles. The "free play of mind" was the phrase that best indicated the kind of inquiry that criticism undertakes; the qualities of flexibility and "sweet reasonableness" that Arnold later would develop and define were necessary to the best criticism, the best that is written. Arnold's own critical essays did not offer a body of abstract ideas or principles; they were literary essays, nearer to art than to scientific treatises. At its best, Arnold's own criticism exemplified his own description of criticism as "ardent" and "flexible." If one compares, for example, an essay by Arnold with one by Shairp on a similar theme, one can see how often Shairp fell back on critical abstractions, how often he relied on a numerical order of points in a way that is alien to art and how he made his way, in rather plodding fashion, through the life and works of his subjects. Arnold, on the other hand, conveyed always the sense of a curious mind that was observing and exploring the life and work of his subjects, a mind that was responding in various ways to what he saw, perceiving, ordering, and judging, not according to a plan, but as his subject led him to fresh and original ideas.

In inquiring into the function of criticism in the introductory essay, Arnold consciously set out on the kind of inquiry that Aristotle had undertaken in the *Nicomachean Ethics.* Thinking about the function of criticism, Arnold adapted for his own purpose certain terms and ideas from the *Ethics.* Arnold did not appeal to Aristotle as an authority, but he kept in mind Aristotle's discussion of the moral and intellectual virtues and the appeal to the "judicious" in determining the best. Arnold's inquiry into the activity of criticism, especially into the relation of criticism to creation, appears to go beyond the *Ethics,* but Arnold did begin with the idea of the activity that is proper to a human being, in order to find the correct place for criticism in the good life.

Throughout the essay, Arnold kept the emphasis on criticism as an activity. When Arnold spoke of the "function" of criticism, he was asking what the essential *work (ergon)* of criticism should be. By means of various synonyms for *function,* he kept before his readers this essential idea of criticism as an activity: thus "a critical effort" is " 'the endeavor, in all branches of knowledge, theology, philosophy, history, art, science, to see the object as in itself it really is' " (*PW,* 3:258, 261). Again, "a great critical *effort* is necessary for a creative epoch": "Goethe's [poetry] was nourished by a great critical *effort* providing the true materials for it" (*PW*, 3:262; emphasis added). Arnold predicted that "a time of true creative *activity*" would come "when criticism has done its *work*" (*PW*, 3:269). By such words as *function, effort,* and *endeavor,* Arnold kept the focus on the *work* of criticism.

Although the idea of work or function was important to Aristotle, what is distinctive in his thought is *energeia,* activity—roughly, the performance of the work—as Clough said in *The Bothie,* to find and to *do* the *ergon.* For a human being, Aristotle concluded in his inquiry in the *Ethics,* the highest activity is contemplation, or theoretical activity: at the highest level, the level of *arete* or excellence, this is the good for mankind, and in this activity is to be found the greatest happiness.[1] While it is now generally agreed that by *theoria* Aristotle meant mathematics, physics, and metaphysics, earlier commentators in the nineteenth century included aesthetic and divine thought.[2] Arnold included in critical thought nearly all branches of knowledge; it is likely that Arnold at this point would have seen *theoria* as inclusive. Criticism, certainly, is a mode of inquiry that is not restricted to any discipline.

Arnold went on to connect thought or inquiry with disinterestedness. Criticism, he said, follows "the law of its own nature, which is to be a free play of mind on all subjects which it touches" (*PW*, 3:270), and the definition of criticism at which Arnold ultimately arrived is that criticism is *"a disinterested endeavor to learn and propagate the best that is known and thought in the world"* (*PW*, 3:283). To what extent Aristotle's idea of *energeia* implied either what Arnold called "a free play of mind" or *disinterestedness* is a question. Alexander Grant, in a note on individuality, saw in *energeia* "a sense of life and free action," and later he used the phrase "play of mind" in commenting on *energeia.*[3] Arnold made a similar connection when he said that criticism requires a "disinterested love of a free play of the mind on all subjects, for its own sake" (*PW*, 3:268). In saying that the activity is pursued for its own sake, Arnold was keeping in mind what Aristotle had said on theoretical activity: "And this activity alone would seem to be loved for its own sake; for nothing arises from it apart from the contemplating, while from practical activities we gain more or less apart from the action" (*NE*, x.7.1177b1–4, trans. Ross). Arnold also defined the proper end of criticism as being essentially theoretical, "to create a current of true and fresh ideas" (*PW*, 3:270). In this respect, criticism has no end beyond itself. Arnold was here especially concerned to show that criticism does not aim at the practical application of the ideas that it examines but that it belongs in the "pure intellectual sphere" (*PW*, 3:271). As a theoretical activity, criticism cannot leave the intellectual sphere for practical action without becoming another kind of activity; otherwise it would cease to be free, and it would no longer be disinterested.

When Arnold asserted that criticism has the end of "creating a current of true and fresh ideas," he indicated still the activity of criticism as he had defined it, and the result or product of criticism is more or less the same as the activity. When, however, Arnold said that criticism provides the materials for poetry, he seems to have been saying that criticism exists, not for itself, but for the sake of poetry. When he spoke earlier about the effect of a current of ideas, he seems to have been suggesting a further end, for, according to Arnold, as criticism does its work, ideas stimulate in society "a stir and growth," and out of this growth develop "the creative epochs of literature" (*PW*, 3:261). Certainly, Arnold wanted to argue that criticism has an effect, and indeed his apology for criticism depends largely on the argument that criticism does have this particular effect.[4] One may suggest, however, that criticism may have an effect without aiming at any end beyond its own activity—the disinterested endeavor to know the best that is thought and said. Thus, so far as criticism is an intellectual activity, it is free.

Clearly, Arnold was trying to include the work of the critic in theoretical activity. Therefore he distinguished between theory and practical criticism, again following Aristotle's distinctions. Indeed, Arnold's idea that criticism is knowing and communicating the best that is thought and said takes no account of what is considered the usual business of criticism, as Arnold recognized: criticism as the "mere judgment and application of principles," whether to literary works of other kinds of work, is, he said, not "the most satisfactory work to the critic" (PW, 3:283). But here, too, Arnold turned to Aristotle. The literary criticism that sorts out the good from the bad depends, Arnold thought, on what Aristotle called *phronesis*, now generally translated as "practical wisdom," but what Arnold called "judgment." As Arnold had said in *On Translating Homer*, after quoting the passage from the *Ethics*, " 'As the judicious would determine'—that is a test to which every one professes himself willing to submit his works" (PW, 1:99).[5] Arnold referred such questions to the instructed human reason.

As a young poet struggling for self-discipline, Arnold had hoped to get some measure of judgment; now, Arnold, in his analysis of such poets as Maurice de Guérin and Keats, argued essentially that the nature poets lack practical wisdom and, unable to keep in bounds either their emotions or their fancies, fall into melancholy. Nature poets, Arnold theorized, have a certain temperament which is related to "a faculty of naturalistic, not of moral interpretation"; such poets have "an extraordinary delicacy of organization and susceptibility to impressions" (PW, 3:30). Arnold moreover saw an opposition between this temperament and moral activity: "Assuredly it is not in this temperament that the active virtues have their rise" (PW, 3:32). In this analysis Arnold drew on Aristotle's discussion of melancholy, on the melancholics who are among those who lack practical wisdom: "It is keen and excitable people [melancholics] that suffer especially from the impetuous form of incontinence; for the former by reason of their quickness and the latter by reason of the violence of their passions do not await the argument, because they are apt to follow their imagination."[6] That this passage was considered a locus for the theory of melancholy is indicated by Grant's comment on Aristotle's treatment of melancholy; Grant showed that the classical account attributed melancholy to an excess of passion, and he cited Tennyson's *Maud:* " 'The passionate heart of the poet is whirl'd into folly and vice.'"[7] What the melancholics lack is judgment, and Arnold found that the nature poets and the critics alike could fall into this Greek kind of melancholy—a passionate and impetuous excitability.

In the essay on academies, Arnold pointed out that the absence of a high standard is evident in what he called provinciality; the provincials are also those who lack judgment; they are indeed melancholics: "The provincial spirit . . . exaggerates the value of its ideas for want of a high standard at hand by which to try them. Or rather, for want of such a standard, it gives one idea too much prominence at the expense of others; it orders its ideas amiss; it is hurried away by fancies; it likes and dislikes too passionately, too exclusively" (*PW,* 3:249). Thus Aristotle's melancholics, Arnold's nature poets, and Arnold's provincial critics have these characteristics in common: they are too passionate, they follow their fancies, they are impetuous, they cannot order their ideas—they lack, in short, judgment. Judgment is also what the practical critic must have; and literary work, in Arnold's theory, is to be referred to the judicious critic.

Neither Aristotle's *phronimos* nor Arnold's critic are, perhaps, entirely satisfactory solutions to the way in which the good or the best is to be determined. Grant pointed out that Aristotle's ethics was saved from relativism by the concept of the *phronimos,* as his idea of justice is by the *epieikes* or the equitable man (1857 ed., 2:118; 4th ed., 2:91). Arnold would continue to think about the question in "The Study of Poetry," but his solution would remain much the same—the standard found in human reason and experience, practically, in a critic.

In saying that in discovery of fresh knowledge lies "the sense of creative activity" (*PW,* 3:283), Arnold addressed another question—the relative importance of critical and creative activity. He began the essay on the function of criticism by acknowledging the Romantic claim of the superiority of genius, creative genius, or original genius. Arnold offered

the Romantic claim, however, in the form of the classical definition, putting "creative power" in the place of theoretical
activity as the proper activity for humankind. Whether Arnold
meant to raise creative power to the level of *theoria* or whether
he meant ironically to note the magnitude of the Romantic
claim are questions that can best be answered by noting first
that all such questions are subordinate to the main question—namely, whether criticism can be as important as
poetry or even whether it is in some ways the same kind of
activity.

Arnold began by answering Wordsworth's assertion that
poetry is of higher worth than literary criticism. It is evident,
however, that Arnold had in mind not only Wordsworth but
also current revivals of Romantic thought and criticism, particularly those of Shairp. Arnold said in this essay that it was
Shairp's essay on Wordsworth that had drawn his own attention once more to Wordsworth; and while there may be some
truth in this, it is more important to see that Shairp had attacked some of the major positions that Arnold had taken.
Shairp had begun by tracing the operation of the "new birth
of imagination" in Europe and its flowering in the English
Romantic poets.[8] Shairp's emphasis on the new spirit of imagination was exactly the opposite of Arnold's emphasis on the
new critical spirit in "On the Modern Element in Literature"
and such later essays as "Heinrich Heine."

Because Arnold in "The Function of Criticism" was clarifying the theoretic basis of the earlier essays, he had to make
a case for criticism. Thus Arnold, although he praised the essay on Wordsworth, actually set out to show that Shairp was
mistaken in his estimate of the Romantic poets and in his view
that the "new birth of imagination" alone could bring about
a new age of poetry. Shairp had assumed that the Romantic
imagination, as a kind of inspired intuition, was sufficient
for great poetry. Arnold, although advancing no theory of the
imagination, intended to show the necessity of criticism to
poetry, to say that the poets, including Wordsworth, had failed
because they did not know enough. In a subsequent essay,

Shairp defended the polymath Coleridge against this charge but did not fully answer Arnold's arguments until his own Oxford lecture, "Criticism and Creation" (1878). In Plato's *Ion*, Shairp found authority for a theory that the poet is "inspired and possessed": "Plato's few words on this in the *Ion* are worth all Aristotle's methodical treatise on Poetry."[9] Shairp went on to describe Plato's metaphor of the chain of rings suspended from a magnet, from which inspiration flashes out from the magnet—or the muse—to the poet, the actors, and the spectators. Shairp missed the irony in Plato's satire of the "inspired" or irrational poet and his audience. Shairp made explicit, correctly, what Arnold himself had not claimed—namely, that his criticism was based on Aristotle. Shairp, on the other hand, aligned himself with Plato, as Shairp understood the *Ion*, and asserted not only that creation was superior to criticism, because it had the spark of divine truth received by the inspired poet, but also that it was independent of criticism. Indeed, the so-called Arnoldian Concordat, which Geoffrey Hartman has found in "The Function of Criticism at the Present Time," described the work of Shairp, rather than that of Arnold, insofar as this "concordat," as Hartman has said, "assigns to criticism a specific, delimited sphere detached from the creative (which remains superior and the object of millenial hopes)."[10] But it was Shairp, not Arnold, who separated criticism and creation and who argued most strongly for the supremacy of poetic creation. Arnold's problem, in "The Function of Criticism," was, rather, to defend criticism against those who argued for the supremacy of poetry and to claim for criticism, at its best, a share in creative activity.

Arnold began the essay by agreeing that the creative power was higher than the critical power, ostensibly accepting the proposition offered by Wordsworth; but Arnold then looked for reasons why criticism might be considered a creative activity. First he took the high Romantic notion of creation, with its implications of inspiration, prophecy, and visionary power, and confined it within the Aristotelian formula for theoretical activity, putting "free creative power" in the place of *theoria* as the activity or *energeia* that leads to happiness: "It is undeniable that the exercise of a creative power, that a free creative activity, is the highest function of man; it is proved to be so by man's finding in it his true happiness" (*PW*, 3:260). Whatever Arnold intended to say in this passage, whether to go beyond Aristotle and to say that the proper activity for human kind is creative, not theoretical, or to extend *theoria* to include creative activity, he put the question in the Aristotelian form. In what follows, Arnold made the terms inclusive, when he said that creative power may be exercised in several ways. And he followed Aristotle in the emphasis on "well-doing," when he said that creative power may be exercised in "well-doing . . . in learning, . . . even in criticising" (*PW*, 3:260). In adding well-doing to the list of creative activities, Arnold was showing that he understood that well-doing was not the same thing as doing good or even doing well but that the Greek *eudaimonia* or happiness carried the sense of living the life of a good person, or living a good life, in the sense that the person was performing an activity that was satisfying. Arnold thus seems to have included criticism among the other kinds of activities that belong to the general category that he called creative activity.

When Arnold said that the critic may have "the sense of exercising this free creative activity" (*PW*, 3:260), it should be made clear that by "sense" he was referring, not to an illusory sensation, but to something like an awareness. Aristotle had argued that pleasure in friendship lay not only in being engaged in an activity but in being aware that one is engaged in the activity. Grant extended this notion to make *energeia* not only the activity but also the consciousness of the activity; he saw consciousness as something like the inspired visionary moment of the Romantics.[11] Although Arnold was not thinking of the critic as a visionary, he acknowledged that the awareness of an activity was necessary if one were to be happy in performing it. So far, then, Arnold did claim that the critic could exercise free creative power; the question then became one of the limits or conditions under which this power may be exercised.

At the end of the essay, Arnold set up, not so much definite limits, as a scale in which criticism may share in creative
activity and be "genuine" creation. Criticism could be creative, he said, when it was "sincere, simple, flexible, ardent,
ever widening its knowledge"; then the critic could have "a
joyful sense of creative activity" (*PW*, 3:285). Since Arnold had
defined criticism as knowing the best that is thought and said,
it would follow that such criticism was, as he said, "ever widening its knowledge" as was thus far creative. In the last paragraph of the essay, however, Arnold qualified what he had said
earlier: "in full measure, the sense of creative activity belongs
only to genuine creation" (*PW*, 3:285). Arnold did not, however,
draw a clear boundary line between the two activities.

When Arnold spoke here of "genuine creation," he was
clearly referring to literary creation—more narrowly, poetry.
Furthermore, Arnold distinguished between creative literary
genius and philosophy and, significantly, did not assign to
creation the discovery of new ideas:

> . . . creative literary genius does not principally show it-
> self in discovering new ideas, that is rather the business
> of the philosopher. The grand work of literary genius is
> a work of synthesis and exposition, not of analysis and
> discovery; its gift lies in the faculty of being happily in-
> spired by a certain intellectual and spiritual atmosphere,
> by a certain order of ideas, when it finds itself in them;
> of dealing divinely with these ideas, presenting them in
> the most effective and attractive combinations,—making
> beautiful works with them, in short. (*PW*, 3:260-61)

The work of literary genius is making a work of art, as Aristotle had made clear in the *Poetics* and as Arnold had argued
earlier in his letters to Clough and in the 1853 Preface. Originality, so important to the Romantic idea of genius, does not
figure in Arnold's definition; indeed, much of his criticism
had insisted instead on the importance of tradition and imitation in poetry. Nor does the poet have the function of the seer
or the philosopher; the materials of literary art, Arnold said,

are ideas. But the creative literary genius does not discover ideas; the genius makes works of art with them. The philosopher does discover ideas, but it is not evident that Arnold was thinking of philosophic thought as belonging to what he called creative activity. Originality, then, was not for Arnold a defining characteristic of creativity. Creativity belonged, rather, to making, to "poetics" in the radical sense. Thus, if criticism was to aspire to being a creative activity, it must do so, not by approaching philosophy, but by becoming a work of art.

Whether creative activity included more than poetry and critical thought was another question; Arnold did not ordinarily speak of philosophy as being creative, but in the essays he did talk about the "inventive power" of science. In "The Literary Influence of Academies," Arnold discussed energy and genius: "Genius is mainly an affair of energy, and poetry is mainly an affair of genius; . . . Again, the highest reach of science is, one may say, an inventive power, a faculty of divination, akin to the highest power exercised in poetry" (*PW*, 3:238). By *energy*, Arnold here was implying the ordinary meaning of power or force. Indeed, "inventive power" in Arnold's criticism was much the same as creative power, and Arnold used both in "The Function of Criticism" (*PW*, 3:259) and further equated energy with "creative force" (*PW*, 3:262).

If creative and inventive power are more or less synonymous, then Arnold thought that both the poet and the scientist were engaged in creative activity; he implied the same thing by attributing to both "the faculty of divination." While we may more readily have opposed the poet to the scientist, Arnold tended to think of the scientist as one like Lucretius, who was also a poet.

As a critic, however, Arnold was engaged not so much in synthesis as in analysis, in sorting out the functions of the poet and the critic. In this essay, Arnold set the intellectual, including the critical, power below the genius of the poet and of the scientist. He acknowledged, in response to Wordsworth's ranking of criticism, the superiority of creative or inventive genius: "Everybody, too, would be willing to admit, as a general proposition, that the critical faculty is lower than the inventive" (PW, 3:259). Thus in "The Function of Criticism," Arnold, although he was primarily arguing that the critic could have a sense of creative activity, separated the poet from the critic in that the poets had a power of "divination" and the critic had intellectual power. Arnold did not resolve the Romantic idea that creation is inspiration, which in some degree is suggested by "divination," and the classical idea of poetry as art, a thing made.

Certainly Arnold did not find a solution in imaginative reason, a phrase that he used at the end of the essay on "Pagan and Medieval Religious Sentiment" (1864). Some have found a key to Arnold's poetry and even to his criticism in the phrase; others have looked for the origins of the phrase.[12] In this essay, Arnold used "imaginative reason" to suggest his idea of Hellenism, the particular quality of Greek thought that would renew the "modern spirit" in the nineteenth century:

But the main element of the modern spirit's life is neither the senses and understanding, nor the heart and imagination; it is the imaginative reason. And there is a century in Greek life,—the century preceding the Peloponnesian War, from about the year 530 to the year 430 B.C.,—in which poetry made, it seems to me, the noblest, the most successful effort she has ever made as the priestess of the imaginative reason, of the elements by which the modern spirit, if it would live right, has chiefly to live. (PW, 3:230)

The limits of meaning that Arnold assigned to "imaginative reason" are suggested when he went on to say that "no other poets, who have so well satisfied the thinking-power, have so well satisfied the religious sense" (PW, 3:231). Arnold's "thinking-power" seems to be close to scientific, logical, or analytic reason, and what satisfies the "religious sense" is most likely to have to do with intuition, or what Arnold called "divination" (which both poets and scientists have).

Certainly, in the two lectures, which were given three months apart, Arnold was clearly thinking about the connection between knowledge and intuition and between imagination and reason. It is even possible that Arnold was again following Aristotle and that "imaginative reason" corresponded to *sophia* (wisdom), which combines scientific knowledge *(episteme)* and intuitive reason *(nous) (NE* 1139a15–20).[13] Arnold took his illustration of "imaginative reason" from Sophocles' chorus on divine law in *Oedipus Tyrannos.* Arnold had used Sophocles as the ideal poet from the 1853 Preface to the essay on "Pagan and Medieval Religious Sentiment" and had seen Sophocles as the ideal poet of the age of Pericles. Arnold had seen in the age of Pericles the critical spirit in 1857; now he saw in it imaginative reason; and in 1868 he would see in the age the great example of creative activity. Either the shifting emphasis marks only Arnold's particular concern at the moment, or else these terms are closely related in his thought and there is a close connection between the critical spirit and imaginative reason.

At this point in the development of his criticism, Arnold was arguing for the importance of criticism, of the "critical spirit," which he made the chief characteristic of a modern age. Because throughout the *Essays in Criticism,* Arnold was arguing for the revival of a critical method in dealing with ideas, the emphasis in the phrase "imaginative reason" surely has to be kept on *reason;* it may even be a synthesis of two kinds of reason, as in Aristotle—intuition and scientific knowledge. One may follow Grant in noting that Aristotle had no theory of the imagination (1857 ed., 2:255, on VI. 4 and 5). But this, too, is evidence that Arnold was identifying a kind of reason.

In any case, Arnold was answering Shairp's claims for the imagination—namely, that imagination can bring about a new age; not imagination, Arnold replied, but imaginative reason. It will be useful, in exploring further the sense of the term, to place it in the context of the writing of the Balliol scholars. Grant said that "with Plato, philosophy was a higher kind of poetry, in which reason and imagination both found their scope" (1857 ed., 1:89). Conceivably Grant was influenced on this point by Jowett, but clearly it was a standard reading of Plato. According to Müller's literary history, which Arnold had consulted on Greek drama, "In Plato the powers of the imagination were just as conspicuous as those of reasoning and reflexion; he had all the chief characteristics of a poet, especially of a dramatic poet."[14] On the side of science and poetry, Lucretius also had a claim to imaginative reason.

Sellar, in his discussion of Lucretius in *The Roman Poets of the Republic* (1863) spoke about the imaginative power of Lucretius in the invocation to Venus, in the association of Venus and Mars, which achieved "a symbolical representation of the philosophical idea of Nature, as creating and sustaining the harmonious process of life, by destruction and dissolution in union with a productive and restoring principle."[15] Lucretius, through his "conception of Nature," was able, Sellar thought, to bring his "abstract philosophical system" into "complete harmony with his poetical feelings and his moral convictions. . . . The contemplation of Nature satisfies the imagination of Lucretius by her aspects of power and life, order, immensity, and beauty"; Sellar also said that there was a difference between what the understanding (or analytical reason) and the "higher speculative faculty" could see:

> Though the mechanical view of the universe may be accepted by the understanding, it has never been acquiesced in by the higher speculative faculty which combines the feeling of the imagination with the insight of the reason. The imagination, which recognizes the presence of infinite life and harmony in the world, rises to the recognition of a creative and governing Power, which it cannot help endowing with consciousness and will. (*Roman Poets*, pp. 279–80)

Although Sellar did not use the term "imaginative reason" here—instead he used the "higher speculative faculty"—in some ways he was very close to Arnold in the distinctions that he made; the "higher speculative faculty" was separated from the understanding, or analytical reason; this faculty combined imagination and reason; and it was in some sense a faculty of "divination" which satisfied the religious sense, to use Arnold's terms, in the contemplation of Nature.

It is another question whether Arnold meant that to associate poetical feeling or feeling with imagination and insight with reason, as Sellar did, is to achieve imaginative reason. Arnold had read Sellar's *Roman Poets of the Republic*, because he had been asked to recommend Sellar for the professorship of Latin at Edinburgh.[16] Both men may, however, have been drawing from a shared knowledge of the group.

Certainly Sellar later attributed to Lucretius the quality of imaginative reason when, in comparing Vergil to Lucretius, he described the analogies of Lucretius: "The apprehension of these analogies between great things in different spheres proceeds from the inventive and intellectual faculty in the imagination,—that by which intuitions of vast discoveries are obtained before observation of reason can verify them."[17] Here Sellar clearly was connecting what he called "the faculty of imaginative reason" to the "inventive faculty," as it seems that Arnold may have done, and to "intuition"; Sellar distinguished between "imaginative reason" and the analytic reason connected with "observation." Even more clearly, Sellar thought of several kinds of reason—imaginative, scientific, inventive, intuitive—and connected "imaginative reason" to what would nowadays be called the creative imagination, as the faculty by which, through metaphor and symbol, scientific theories are grasped before they can be described and proved by scientific method. Sellar's linking of the poet and the scientist is very close to what Arnold had done in "The Literary Influence of Academies," as we have seen, in assigning to the scientist "an inventive power, a faculty of divination, akin to the highest power exercised in poetry" (*PW*, 3:238). Yet Arnold's discussion of the great Romantic concepts of the creative imagination, original genius, and inspiration was, like Sellar's, grounded in Aristotelian ideas of reason and was illustrated by the example, not of Wordsworth, but of Lucretius.

The principal idea in Arnold's theory of creation was not that criticism is creative but that the critic knows the best that is thought and said and that he makes this known. Further, given the idea that criticism is an activity, the critic, the poet, and the reader may share in the activity, so that the kind of happiness to be found in the discovery of new ideas or in theoretical activity is open to everybody. Practically, in his own criticism, Arnold illustrated how ideas were to be shared, not so much by the rigor of his arguments or the difficulty of his exposition as by the grace of his prose. Arnold used all the art of his magnificent prose—which is supple, ingenious, witty, graceful—to elucidate the kinds of questions that Shairp, in his somewhat heavy-handed way, made abstract, or "philosophical." Arnold was vivid, particular, varied, interesting; he seems lightweight, but he touches difficult problems with his clarifying intellect. Again, practically, the subjects that Arnold touched upon in these essays were not exclusively literary; they further draw attention to writers who were distinguished for their literary as well as for their social importance. The list of writers has caused some to question Arnold's own judgment: Are these the best that have written in modern Europe? But that was not Arnold's intention; others could write on Goethe, Kant, Voltaire; on Shakespeare and Milton; on Lucretius and Thucydides; on Sophocles and Plato. Arnold, in these essays, turned to the little-known writers or to those who had lived ordinary lives. Thus he wrote about the brother and sister Maurice and Eugénie de Guérin, about Joseph Joubert, about Marcus Aurelius, but also about Epictetus. In other essays he wrote about those who had taken up the cause of the people, such as Heinrich Heine; and in an essay on a classical writer, not about Sophocles but about Theocritus, not so much about Theocritus as about the ordinary people of the Hellenistic age. Further, his subjects included not only these particular writers but also the common subjects—of nature, man, and society; of the nature poets; of the French Revolution; even of the ordinary life of ancient Rome. This is not to say that Arnold had now accepted the criticism of his friends and turned his prose to the illumination of ordinary life in modern times. Rather, his intention was to show the deficiency of the contemporary, the mistake of relying upon the inspired but uninstructed imagination; he showed that the critical intelligence is needed everywhere.

Although the essays that Arnold collected for *Essays in Criticism* do not deal directly with democracy, Arnold had once intended to include his essay "Democracy" (1861) in the collection. Certainly, the theme winds in and out of the essays as a connecting thread. So far as there is any visible plan for the whole, it is in the idea of the modern which was the subject of the lectures from about 1857 to 1863, an idea that is certainly attached to Arnold's idea of democracy. Although the chronological order shows to some extent the development of Arnold's aesthetic ideas (as we have seen), the arrangement of the essays in the collection, beginning with "The Literary Influence of Academies" and ending with "Marcus Aurelius," shows how Arnold presented his theme of poetry in a democratic age. Arnold was here concerned with the question, which is central for literature in a democracy, of how to keep to a high standard of art yet reach the many. Thus, Arnold began with an examination of an academy in a democratic society and ended with the emperor who, although he thought about the idea of a democracy, attempted to crush the "new spirit" of his own time.

The first essay, "The Literary Influence of Academies," takes up the question of setting a high standard for a national literature. At first glance, Arnold seems to have set aside his essay "Democracy" and declared instead for an authoritarian society or at least for a society of artists ruled by a national academy, a high tribunal of artists. An academy, Arnold suggested, is not necessarily inconsistent with a democratic society, and he pointed out that the French Academy had continued to exercise a beneficial influence on the national literature of a people who possessed some of the characteristics of the ancient Athenians, "openness of mind and flexibility of intelligence" (*PW*, 3:233–35, 237).[18] These qualities of mind are especially necessary in a democracy, as Arnold pointed out in the essay "Democracy": "democracy has readiness for new ideas, and ardour for what ideas it possesses"; but ancient Athens was also the model for a great popular culture: "the spectacle of ancient Athens has such profound interest for a rational man [because] it is the spectacle of the culture of a *people*" (*PW*, 2:25).[19] As Arnold said, "It was the *many* who relished those arts, who were not satisfied with less than those monuments" (*PW*, 2:25). Although Arnold did not always use the terms *democracy* and *people* as synonymous and although he sometimes meant by *democracy* the lower classes, here by *people* he clearly meant both the middle and the lower classes of Athens. Thus, Arnold found no inherent conflict between a democratic society and a high standard of art or literature.

Thus, in looking at the French Academy, Arnold considered whether an academy could work in a modern democratic society. Arnold began by showing the difficulty of the critic in England, who must speak from "the critic's isolated position." Citing as an example Palgrave's *Handbook to the Fine Arts Collection of the International Exhibition of 1862*, Arnold noted that Palgrave had adopted a style that was intended to reach the multitude:

> Mr. Palgrave . . . feels himself to be speaking before a promiscuous multitude, with the few good judges so scattered through it as to be powerless; therefore, he has no calm confidence and no self-control; he relies on the strength of his lungs; he knows that big words impose on the mob, and that, even if he is outrageous, most of his audience are apt to be a great deal more so. (*PW*, 3:254–55)

There are other ways to reach the multitudes, Arnold implied, than by impressing them with big words. An academy that enforces a high standard in intellectual work, as Arnold thought the French Academy did, encourages good prose, prose without the note of "provinciality" that is the mark of the lonely critic speaking to the crowd. Arnold's ideal was of a classical prose: "the problem is to express new and profound ideas in a perfectly sound and classical style" (PW, 3:247–48). But as Arnold showed in a complex argument, this was true for prose, for intellectual work, but not for poetry.

Poetry—and here Arnold was true to his earliest critical principles—required freedom, the free activity of genius: "And what that energy, which is the life of genius, above everything demands and insists upon, is freedom; entire independence of all authority, prescription, and routine,—the fullest room to expand as it will." And this energy, "the life of genius," which naturally resists authority, also reaches "splendid heights in poetry and science" (PW, 3:238). Thus, poetry and science require freedom; prose, an intellectual work that depends upon flexibility and quickness of mind, profits from the authority both of a form and of an academy (although even the best poetry requires the structure of form). Arnold, with an unexpected chauvinism in a critic who had deplored provinciality, declared that the English were greater in poetry than were the French. His problem then became whether democracy would in fact nourish poetry. If freedom or liberty was necessary to poetry and to the free activity of genius, then the question was whether democracy would allow such freedom or whether democracy (as John Stuart Mill later thought) would restrict individual liberty or stifle individual genius. Arnold had already examined this question in "Democracy," where he had argued that political freedom could be established as well by an aristocracy as by a democracy; here Arnold was thinking about the English barons (PW, 2:7–8). Arnold argued that what democracy certainly established was social freedom: "Social freedom,—equality,—that is rather the field of the conquests of democracy" (PW, 2:8). The effect of living amidst a society of equals was liberating:

Can it be denied, that to live in a society of equals tends in general to make a man's spirits expand, and his faculties work easily and actively; while, to live in a society of superiors, although it may occasionally be a very good discipline, yet in general tends to tame the spirits and to make the play of the faculties less secure and active? (*PW*, 2:8)

Arnold, following Alexis de Tocqueville, thought that equality in France had "given to the lower classes, to the body of the common people, a self-respect, an enlargement of spirit, a consciousness of counting for something in their country's action, which has raised them in the scale of humanity" (*PW*, 2:9). Still, Arnold was not sure about the changes that would take place as the English lower class became part of a democratic society. The class, which Arnold saw as remarkable for individualism and self-reliance, would give up something to a sense of community or cooperation, though it would gain, as others had, an increased self-respect through belonging to a class that would now have greater importance and through losing a sense of deference to superiors. Certainly, Arnold concluded that although an academy had worked well in France, it would not work so well in England, and it would not encourage poetry, which indeed required individual freedom. Arnold did not, in this essay, answer the question of how one can assure, without an academy, a high standard of art and literature in a democratic society.

Nonetheless, the example of the French Academy, which is set before us in the first essay, is followed by essays on French writers of the nineteenth century. Arnold's two essays on Maurice de Guérin and Eugénie de Guérin serve as examples of the influence of the French Academy; they also illustrate the distinction achieved by almost-ordinary writers working in minor forms—the journal and the letter. Arnold's further purpose was to make these two authors known to English readers through his own lively and vivid translations and through quoting at length from their works. Arnold, then, was making known to the common reader the works of two rather ordinary writers, but ones who were working in a country in which a high standard prevailed. Indeed, commenting on Maurice de Guérin's sure taste in his reading, Arnold observed, "His literary tact is beautifully fine and true" (PW, 3:20).[20] Although what now seems most interesting about Arnold's criticism is the comparison to Keats and the analysis of the romantic or poetic sensibility, in the context of the democratic society one must keep in mind that the Tory reviewers had attacked Keats as an apothecary who was trying to be a poet. Arnold's criticism was disinterested. Like the Romantics, Arnold said, Maurice de Guérin withdrew from society to contemplate Nature: "So he lived like a man possessed; with his eye not on his own career, not on the public, not on fame, but on the Isis whose veil he had uplifted" (PW, 3:34). Yet Guérin had held to a high standard, because of "his passion for perfection, his disdain for all poetical work not perfectly adequate and felicitous" (PW, 3:35). Through his style, Maurice de Guérin had achieved distinction: "The magic of expression, to which by the force of this passion he won his way, will make the name of Maurice de Guérin remembered in literature" (PW, 3:35).

Turning to Eugénie de Guérin, Arnold again showed what could be done in the minor forms of the journal and the letter by a woman who was like Blaise Pascal mainly in "the clearness and firmness of her intelligence, going straight and instinctively to the bottom of any matter she is dealing with" (PW, 3:89).[21] The only essay in which Arnold dealt with the writing of a woman, he, much like the feminists of the present time, did not leave out of account "femininity" and the difference that this made to her writing. Unhappily, at least to those of us who are too Americanized or just plainly too American (as we have lately been reminded by an eminent historian) and who are looking for something like equality, the "difference" that Arnold saw lay mainly on the side of inferiority of talent. Thus, in natural description, Maurice reached the sublime but Eugénie only the picturesque; Eugénie suffered from an ennui that arose from her situation and thus differed from Pascal: "Pascal is a man, and the inexhaustible power and activity of his mind leave him no leisure for ennui. . . . Eugénie de Guérin is a woman, and longs for a state of firm happiness, for an affection in which she may repose" (*PW*, 3:89). Arnold found in Eugénie's prose "a feminine ease and grace, a flowing facility" (*PW*, 3:89). Arnold noted in Eugénie's journal a perennial concern of women, the conflict between " 'a life of household business' " and "this life of reading, thinking, and writing" (*PW*, 3:92, 93). Arnold noted her resolution to do her household tasks without complaining, to keep "in her proper sphere"; " 'I feel that I cannot go beyond my needlework and my spinning without going too far' " (*PW*, 3:94). As Arnold compared Maurice to the English Romantic Keats, so he might have compared Eugénie to the Romantic Emily Brontë, especially when he saw "something primitive, indomitable in her, which she governs, indeed, but which chafes, which revolts" (*PW*, 3:88). Instead, Arnold brought in for comparison the poet Emma Tatham, the better to make a point about the narrowness of Philistinism in England (*PW*, 3:97) and, by implication, the limits placed in such a society on the genius of women as well as men.

Arnold ended the essay by noting the quality of distinction in the work of Maurice and Eugénie de Guérin: "It procures that the popular poet shall not finally pass for a Pindar, nor the popular historian for a Tacitus, nor the popular preacher for a Bossuet" (*PW*, 3:106). Arnold's use of intrusive alliteration had a function here. As in a heroic couplet, it showed that he had assumed the role of the heroic satirist: the "popular poet" and the "preacher" are contrasted to Pindar and are measured against the great writers who set the standard. Thus, Arnold at the end brought his essay around to his central theme, the high standard set by criticism; at the same time he showed that distinction could be achieved by writers like the isolated brother and sister even in the minor forms.

The essay "Heinrich Heine" seems to stand at the center of the collection, announcing the central theme of the age of democracy and defining the task of literature in the new age.

Certainly the idea of democracy is central: Heine was "a most effective soldier in the Liberation War of humanity (*PW*, 3:107).[22] The essay carried on Arnold's speculation about the modern, which he had begun in "On the Modern Element in Literature." As there he had asserted that poetry must offer an adequate interpretation of life, so here he said that poetry in the "main current" must "apply modern ideas to life" (*PW*, 3:122). Although "modern ideas" may have a wide reference, as in the opening of "The Function of Criticism at the Present Time," where all branches of knowledge were included, actually Arnold seems here to be thinking of political ideas, of democracy, literally "the liberation of humanity" by the ideas of 1789. Thus he said that Byron and Shelley, the great revolutionary poets, though they failed as artists, did apply "modern ideas" to life, whereas the other Romantic poets retreated from life—Wordsworth to "the inward life," Scott to the feudalism of the past (*PW*, 3:121–22). It could not be said that either Coleridge or Wordsworth were not aware of modern philosophical ideas, but they did turn away from their early enthusiasm for democratic ideas.

Although Arnold denied that poetry aims at "direct political action" (*PW*, 3:118) and would develop in the later essays the principle of disinterestedness, still he continued to say that poetry must offer an "intellectual deliverance"—that is, an adequate interpretation of the age. Equally, the critic must "ascertain the master current in the literature of an epoch" (*PW*, 3:107). And in the modern times (whether past or present) both poets and critics were alive to what Arnold called the "modern spirit," were aware that inherited institutions were not rational and no longer worked. True, as in the essay on the French Academy, Arnold noted the limits of living by reason: the English Revolution, which had been practical rather than theoretical and had made no appeal to reason or to principles, did gain for England a remarkable degree of liberty and prosperity (*PW*, 3:114). But the future, Arnold warned, would require something more. All of Arnold's talk about a modern spirit, about adequate interpretation of an age, about master-currents, really amounted to saying that this was the age of democracy or that it was coming and that it was the task of the critic to make ready for it.

The essay is the source of some remarkable and striking images, definitions, and epigrams of the sort that work well for a lecture but later prove to be more baffling than clarifying. There is the great metaphor about the prison of Puritanism: "the great English middle class . . . entered the prison of Puritanism, and had the key turned on its spirit there for two hundred years" (PW, 3:121). Although the image is striking, the history seems suspect. Some definitions are remarkable for their simplicity: "Poetry is simply the most beautiful, impressive, and widely effective mode of saying things, and hence its importance" (PW, 3:110). There are also firm pronouncements: "Direct political action is not the true function of literature" (PW, 3:118). There are sweeping profundities, as on the great religious poets: "These spirits reach the infinite, which is the true goal of all poetry and all art,—the Greek spirit by beauty, the Hebrew spirit by sublimity" (PW, 3:128). In effect, the essay aimed at a "thoroughly modern" criticism, with neat definitions and usable phrases such as "mainstream" and "main-currents" to supply critics and literary historians for another fifty years.

Yet the statements cannot be put together into a coherent theory. If poetry is saying things effectively, why may it not be used for propaganda or for direct political action? Or why should poetry reach for the infinite? And if it does so, then why are not Keats and Wordsworth the great poets of the Romantic age, rather than the Revolutionary poets Byron and Shelley? Arnold would return to each of these points in his later essays on the Romantic poets and would modify these definitions of poetry.

Here what gave Arnold the greatest difficulty was the practical or the political use of literature, especially of poetry. As in all of his essays on the "modern," beginning with the lecture "On the Modern Element in Literature," Arnold wanted to say that the *modern* lies, not in the contemporary or the new, but in a critical or a rational habit of mind. To some extent Arnold also wanted to say that a truly modern literature responds in some way to *modern ideas;* indeed it may offer a historical or a philosophical interpretation of events. Not until "The Study of Poetry" did Arnold successfully disentangle poetry from philosophy and from history. Because a democratic people had to respond to ideas, poetry had in some way to satisfy this need. Arnold tended at times to imply that a poetry of ideas was what democracy needed, yet he realized that poetry could not aim at direct political action.

In the following essays, the emphasis shifts from what might seem to be the necessity of the intellectual appeal of poetry to its emotional appeal, the question now being how poetry can reach and move the people. Strictly speaking, Arnold held to the idea that people in a fully developed democracy would be like the Athenians—that is, lively, open-minded, flexible, and demanding the very greatest art and poetry. Nevertheless, this remained an ideal to be attained in the future; and for the present, Arnold thought that the lower classes in England were nearer to the state of the populace in the late Hellenistic Age or the early Middle Ages. Thus, in the essay "Pagan and Medieval Religious Sentiment," the question was how poetry in each age could reach the people.[23] Arnold's method was to compare a popular (religious) poem by Theocritus to a poem written by Saint Francis, choosing these as typical. Arnold offered the hymn to Adonis in the "Fifteenth Idyll" by Theocritus as "a representative religious poem of paganism" (*PW,* 3:216). Setting the hymn in the context of its audience—the chattering housewives—Arnold translated the idyll and the hymn and offered his own commentary. He contrasted the treatment of the Adonis story in the popular hymn to the symbolic treatment that would have been found in the Eleusinian mysteries: the hymn presents a "story as prepared for popular religious use, as presented to the multitude in a popular religious ceremony" (*PW,* 3:222). Arnold found that the poem made its appeal to the senses; it was not consoling but was wearying.

From Theocritus, Arnold turned to Saint Francis, the saint who "brought religion to the people": "Poverty and suffering are the condition of the people, the multitude, the immense majority of mankind; and it was towards this *people* that his soul yearned" (*PW*, 3:223). Saint Francis's *Canticle of the Sun* was "designed for popular use" (*PW*, 3:224). Arnold found, however, that neither poem appealed to the whole human mind: "Now, the poetry of Theocritus's hymn is poetry treating the world according to the demand of the senses; the poetry of St. Francis's hymn is poetry treating the world according to the demand of the heart and imagination" (*PW*, 3:225). Nonetheless, the appeal to the heart was preferable to the appeal to the senses. Returning once more to Heine, the subject of an earlier essay, Arnold reflected now on what he saw as Heine's own religion of pleasure, a religion that gave no comfort to "the mass of mankind" (*PW*, 3:229). In contrast, Arnold now decided that "a religion of sorrow" had the power to reach the "many millions"; it had the "power to be a general, popular, religious sentiment, a stay for the mass of mankind, whose lives are full of hardship" (*PW*, 3:229–30). Not entirely satisfied with the idea of a religion of sorrow, Arnold reflected that Christianity was also a religion of joy, "drawing from the spiritual world a source of joy so abundant that it ran over upon the material world and transfigured it" (*PW*, 3:230). The appeal of such poetry as that by Saint Francis was, in any case, to the emotions, and this was an appeal that could be made to the "many millions."

In a modern age, as in the Athenian age of Pericles or in an age of democracy, poetry must make yet another appeal, which Arnold here specified as the appeal to the "imaginative reason." Beyond the popular poetry that speaks to the heart and the imagination, such as the *Canticle of the Sun*, or the poetry that speaks to the senses and the imagination, such as the hymn to Adonis, was the poetry of Simonides, Pindar, Aeschylus, and Sophocles, which speaks to the imaginative reason. Here Arnold tried to discover the appeal that popular poetry makes in a democratic age, to people such as the Athenians. Arnold did not, I think, try to offer a synthesis of the heart and the senses, the imagination and the understanding. Rather, he tried to define another faculty—the imaginative reason—a reason, as I have suggested, of the kind that poetry and science use in reaching for an analogy or a metaphor as a way of explaining an insight. He developed this idea in his next essay, on the French Academy. Such a poetry, which makes an appeal both to reason and to feeling, may be the best poetry for a democratic age.

In the following essay, "Joubert," Arnold advanced another theory of the way in which poetry reaches the reader, using still the Romantic idea of creative genius: "And yet what is really precious and inspiring, in all that we get from literature, except this sense of an immediate contact with genius itself, and the stimulus towards what is true and excellent which we derive from it?" (PW, 3:183)[24] The idea of sharing, in a sense, the inspiration of the genius corresponds to Arnold's theory of the way in which an audience delights in the "high art" of the drama. To Aristotle's principle that all men desire to know, Arnold added the delight in novelty: "from what is new to us we in general learn most"—his argument for noticing a minor author. Arnold, near the end of the essay, defended his choice of Joubert. Arnold had asserted that "a criticism of life" was "the end and aim of all literature" (PW, 3:209). He went on to note the difference between the criticism of "men of ability" and that of "men of genius." Here, again, is Arnold's defense of the "modern" as against the merely contemporary: his "modern" is what "is permanently acceptable to mankind"; it possesses "inherent truth" (PW, 3:209), in contrast to the ideas that make a great appeal in their time. "But the taste and ideas of one generation are not those of the next" (PW, 3:209)—and here Arnold sketched the energetic march of the leaders of the new generation as it sweeps away the old, saving the great men—the Homers and the Shakespeares—and those of their family—the Jouberts—protecting them from the destroying hordes that follow. Arnold commented on those who spoke to their age alone, "What a fate, . . . to be an oracle

for one generation, and then of little or no account for ever"
(PW, 3:211). Arnold's paradoxical definition of *modern* was an
answer to those who held that the writer could only speak
to his own age.

Although Arnold abandoned his series of lectures on the
modern element before he wrote the essay "Joubert," he had
not abandoned the idea of the modern, which is central in
"The Function of Criticism at the Present Time." Nor had
Arnold changed in finding the "modern" in ancient Greece,
whether in the "critical spirit," in "imaginative reason," or
in a "criticism of life." Rather, Arnold dramatized once more
his defense of what he would later call the classic against
Shairp and others who had declared that the classical poet was
irrelevant to the Victorian world. Arnold's "modern" meant
what is permanently true, whether this be an idea discovered
in ancient Greece or in the nineteenth century. On the other
hand, as he had said in the essay "On the Modern Element
in Literature," the historian or the poet must have an adequate
understanding of his own age and of new ideas, which might
include radically different ways of looking at the world.

In taking up the works of Marcus Aurelius, Arnold in fact
considered the consequence of failing to grasp a radical "new
spirit" in the history of the world. The essays of the Roman
emperor had always had a popular appeal, and in translation,
they continued to make an appeal to the common reader, like
the essays of Epictetus. True, Arnold here expressed doubt that
moral ideas as such could reach the many: "The mass of mankind have neither force of intellect enough to apprehend them
clearly as ideas, nor force of character enough to follow them
strictly as laws. The mass of mankind can be carried along
a course full of hardship for the natural man, can be borne
over the thousand impediments of the narrow way, only by
the tide of a joyful and bounding emotion" (PW, 3:134).[25] Like
religious poetry, moral discourse must appeal to emotion: and
Arnold here included pagan with Christian, Empedocles with
Paul, as those who "have insisted on the necessity of an inspiration, a joyful emotion, to make moral action perfect" (PW,

3:134]. Once more, Arnold saw in religion the clue to reaching the multitude; here Arnold compared the wisdom of Epictetus and that of the Old Testament to the "warmth" of the New Testament. Again, it appears that Arnold had forgotten the "idea-moved" masses; he saw the multitudes as being nearer to those of the Middle Ages than to the Athenians of the Age of Pericles.

Yet, when Arnold took up the modernity of the Roman emperor Marcus Aurelius, he saw him as "a man like ourselves, a man in all things tempted as we are" (PW, 3:140); indeed, Arnold made a strong case for seeing parallels between the age of Marcus Aurelius and the Victorian. Indeed, Arnold's interest lay in just this parallel. Discussing the mistakes for which the Roman emperor had been criticized, the worst being his persecution of the Christians, Arnold clearly kept before him the modern parallel. The new spirit in Rome at the time of Marcus Aurelius was Christianity, the new "dissolvent" of the old order: "It was inevitable that Christianity in the Roman world, like democracy in the modern world, like every new spirit with a similar mission assigned to it, should at its first appearance occasion an instinctive shrinking and repugnance in the world which it was to dissolve" (PW, 3:144). The modern sage, Arnold implied, must take warning from the example of Marcus Aurelius and therefore not impede the new spirit of democracy. Marcus Aurelius, according to Arnold's account, meditated on the idea of equality and freedom: " 'The idea of a polity in which there is the same law for all, a polity administered with regard to equal rights and equal freedom of speech, and the idea of a kingly government which respects most of all the freedom of the governed' " (PW, 3:147). Arnold saw Marcus Aurelius as the Roman emperor who could imagine equality and freedom in an ideal state yet who dealt with the new spirit of Christianity as others in later times would deal with the new spirit of democracy.

As to whether the emperor in his own writing could move the reader, whether he could, like the Christian moralist, reach the emotions, Arnold finally said that the emperor could, although not so powerfully, with something "less than joy and more than resignation"; "the sentences of Marcus Aurelius find their way to the soul" (PW, 3:149). Although Marcus Aurelius was not a poet, Arnold did deal with the question of how literature reached the multitudes. Certainly in writing about the late Roman Empire, the age of Trajan, Arnold could see the division (as Sellar was to show) between the aristocrats and the populace in Rome. Marcus Aurelius, in suppressing a popular religion, could not cross this division—to the greater loss of Rome and to European civilization, which would have benefited from a Christianity that learned from Roman culture. This is the parallel, and this is the lesson: the Victorians had to recognize that the new spirit of democracy was inevitable, and in order to assist its development, they must make available the best of the old civilization. Thus, Arnold ended his collection of essays with the example of Rome, as he had begun it with the example of Greece in "Democracy."

Chapter Seven

The Activity of Poetry

Arnold's general theory of poetry was set forth in "The Study of Poetry" (1880), in which he explored the question of the activity of poetry: that is, whether in poetry, or in what kind of poetry, one could find the good for the poet and for society, especially for the new democratic society. Once more, Arnold turned, not to the *Poetics* of Aristotle, but to the *Ethics*. And although Arnold was now primarily concerned with the English poets, for in effect the essay served as an introduction to Thomas H. Ward's *English Poets* (1880), he set out to define the quality of greatness in poetry. Later the essay was used as an introductory one for the posthumous collection *Essays in Criticism*, second series (1888). But whereas the essay on criticism followed the essays written over a period of years and drew together certain assumptions about poetry into a coherent theory of criticism, this essay on poetry was followed by a series of articles on the Romantic poets in which Arnold tested and expanded his theory. Some earlier essays, notably the essay on Wordsworth, set the problems, problems that continued the debate in the earlier essays with the Balliol group, now chiefly represented by Shairp. Once more Arnold found the standard of criticism in the judicious critic; once more he pointed out the error of provincialism, in the critical fallacies of a national or a personal bias. Arnold's problem was now to find a standard of excellence for poetry, corresponding to the *phronimos* for criticism. This standard he found in what he called high seriousness, a term developed from Aristotle's

135

spoudaios, or the serious man. What Arnold took as the test of great poetry was, for Aristotle, the test of excellence. Thus, Arnold's test of poetry was ethical, but was based on a Greek ethics in which the aesthetic and the moral are not rigidly separated. In Arnold, nobility, sweet reasonableness, and high seriousness were not rigorously differentiated; they were aspects of character that appeared most clearly in their appropriate activity.

In thinking about criticism as an activity, Arnold had followed Aristotle, but in suggesting that the highest activity is creative, he had followed the Romantics. Although Arnold seemed to be concerned in part with the comparative value of critical and creative activity, he was also attempting to separate poetry from philosophy and science. In the essay on Wordsworth, Arnold attempted to separate poetry from philosophy; in this essay he began with Aristotle's observation that poetry is superior to history. And because Arnold, in his own poetry, had aspired to both philosophy and history and in the 1857 lecture had seen no great difference between the poet and the historian, the wrenching of poetry away from its connections to both history and philosophy was not an easy thing for Arnold to do. Arnold had still to separate poetry from science; whether he ever separated poetry from politics remains an open question.

The place of poetry in the state had always concerned Arnold, who had feared that his early poetry had done nothing for the suffering millions; it did not animate and ennoble. In the political thought of *Culture and Anarchy,* Arnold had sketched an idea of human perfection that was essentially Greek in that he thought of what was necessary not only for the development of the solitary individual but also for those who lived in society. The qualities of character that Arnold examined in various essays were those that particularly make social life possible—the notions of flexibility, sweet reasonableness, and seriousness. Thus, high seriousness, as the test of great poetry, belonged to this complex of ideas and not to the earnestness of a lonely seer or a visionary. Arnold, like

Aristotle, intended to keep a high place for the poet in society, in the state, and not, like Plato, to move him out of the republic into the desert.

Arnold, in defending this position, was continuing a debate with Shairp, whose attack on Arnold's criticism had begun in his essay on Wordsworth in 1864 and had been renewed in "Criticism and Creation" (1878), a long-delayed answer to Arnold's "The Function of Criticism at the Present Time." In Shairp, Arnold saw the provincial critic and the Victorian moralist; it is instructive to see how Arnold disengaged himself from Shairp's moralism and, in so doing, defined more clearly the ethical basis of his own thought. At the same time, in seeking to establish the right basis for an appreciation of the Romantic poets, Arnold attacked the positions that Shairp had taken as the champion of the early poets of the century. Of these positions, the most significant is the importance of sincerity. Many critics see in sincerity the essential idea of Arnold's criticism by taking sincerity as Arnold's test of great poetry. Although Arnold did wrestle with the notion of sincerity, he tried to confine it within his classical poetics, and he never abandoned the idea of high seriousness as the standard. The highest excellence in performance is the test of great poetry.

In showing the development during this final stage of Arnold's criticism, I center my discussion on three problems in the second *Essays in Criticism:* the development of the criterion of high seriousness; the separation of the activity of poetry from that of philosophy and science; and the redefinition of sincerity. As Arnold solved each of these problems, he defined a poetry for the new age of democracy, and he rescued for the people the great revolutionary poets.

Arnold had always held that great poetry must be serious in subject, genre, and style. In the 1853 Preface he urged the importance of a great action, and in the essays on Homer he said that the grand style required *"a serious subject."*[1] Now, in "The Study of Poetry," Arnold examined the idea of seriousness and established it as the test of excellence in the activity of poetry.

The genesis of the term, which he now connected to the *spoudaios*, was in the immediate context from the *Poetics*, although Arnold kept in mind the larger context of the *Ethics* that informed his thought in "The Function of Criticism at the Present Time" and in *Culture and Anarchy*. Further, although the idea of seriousness had appeared in his earliest criticism as a measure of greatness in poetry, he now used the term "high seriousness" for the first time. As we look at the texts in which Arnold tried out various translations of the famous passage in the *Poetics*, we become aware that Arnold was not only looking for a memorable phrase but was also trying to find an expression for *spoudaios* as well as for his sense of the proper activity of poetry.

Arnold first tried his hand at translating the phrase in a minor essay "On Poetry." Trying to define the "superior adequacy" of poetry to other forms of art, Arnold offered a plain rendering of the phrase in which Aristotle defined the difference between poetry and history: "Aristotle declared poetry to be more philosophical and of more serious worth than history, because poetry deals with generals, history with particulars" (*PW,* 9:61–63).[2] This standard translation was the base from which Arnold moved toward his idea of "high seriousness" and the activity of poetry. In this essay he moved a little forward in changing "more philosophical" to a "higher wisdom": "Poetry . . . has a higher wisdom and a more serious worth than history" (*PW,* 9:62). When Arnold revised the conclusion of "On Poetry" for the opening paragraph of "The Study of Poetry," he revised his earlier translations in order to emphasize the autonomy of poetry. Early in the major essay, to indicate the "mark and accent" of "a high quality of poetry," Arnold offered as a guide his new translation: "Aristotle's profound observation that the superiority of poetry over history consists in its possessing a higher truth and a higher seriousness [*philosophóteron kai spoudaíoteron*]" (*PW,* 9:171). The changes that Arnold has made show the development of his thought up to the time when he wrote his major essay. When he dropped the phrase "more philosophical," he struck out the phrase that might imply a notion that poetry was a form of philosophy, a position that he had taken in his essay on Wordsworth. For this same reason, Arnold was not satisfied with his next attempt, "a higher wisdom," because *wisdom*—a standard translation of *sophia*—would still have kept the emphasis on philosophy. By adopting finally "a higher truth," Arnold was leaving room for poetic truth by taking truth out of the province of logic, or away from Aristotle's point—namely, that history deals more with individuals while poetry deals more with general character.

The steps by which Arnold arrived at "high seriousness" are still more instructive. The earliest phrase, "of more serious worth," implies little more than a ranking. Arnold kept this meaning, but he also stressed the notion of excellence in "high and excellent seriousness" (*PW*, 9:176) and finally arrived, in the criticism first of Chaucer and then of Pope and Dryden, at the condensed phrase "high seriousness" (*PW*, 9:177, 180). No longer a comparative term, "high seriousness" assumes a meaning that is derived from *spoudaios*. This term indicates not just the difference between poetry and history but also the positive quality of poetry as an activity performed at the level of excellence, an activity in which human beings may find their good.

When Arnold took high seriousness as the mark of great poetry, he clearly saw the poet as being among the good men of the state, those who live the good life. In Aristotle's *Ethics*, the *spoudaios* is connected not only with the *phronimos* but also with the *epieikes*. And Arnold had seen the critic as the *phronimos* who possesses judgment, and in his Biblical criticism, he had made much of *epieikeia*, or what he called "sweet reasonableness."[3] Arnold's reading of *epieikeia* as a Greek philosophical term is not surprising, since in 1867 Arnold had read Aristotle and Plato with the New Testament and had remarked that Thomas Arnold had insisted that there was a connection between Greek culture and the doctrines of the New Testament.[4] *Epieikeia* is thus among the Hellenic qualities of sweetness and light that Arnold found to be part of the ideal human character, like the *spoudaios*, or good man.[5]

Arnold may have had an idea that there were several roads to the good life, the poet's being one, along with that of the good or fair-minded man. Just as likely, Arnold may have had in mind a balance of several qualities, so that the good poet has the qualities of the just man, the wise man, or the open-minded man. Arnold's treatment of *eutrapelia*, or flexibility, suggests, as in *Culture and Anarchy*, such a balance or harmony of the qualities. Arnold annotated the term in "A Speech at Eton," given in April, 1879, by tracing through Greek history the changes in the meaning and connotation of the word.[6] Arnold was, as he said, following the clue of *eutrapelia* to find the order and sense of the Greek world and to clarify his own ideal of human perfection, which here he defined as a harmonious balance of the "powers" of human life: "the lines of conduct, of intellect and knowledge, of beauty, of social life and manners" (*PW*, 9:27).[7] In tracing the history of the Western World in its journey towards perfection, Arnold held that people never get the balance quite right, although the Athenians came close (*PW*, 9:29).

In other essays, in working out the moral, social, aesthetic, and intellectual "powers," Arnold suggested that a harmonious character would imply the balance of flexibility, sweet reasonableness, and seriousness. Arnold implies that it is not only the social person who has flexibility, or aerial ease; nor is it only the practical critic who is judicious; nor is it only the artist who has aesthetic charm. Rather, judgment must be tempered by sweet reasonableness and by aesthetic charm. Restricting the point to the art of poetry, high seriousness or the pursuit of excellence in both character and art, gives us the art of a Milton. In his prose, however, Milton lacked flexibility, or sweet reasonableness. Shelley, on the other hand, had these qualities, and even high seriousness, yet he lacked still another quality—a sense of humor. For Arnold, no one thing was needful, in art or in life, and seriousness, although it was of great importance in "The Study of

Poetry," was nonetheless not a single quality of great poetry but one of a complex of qualities.

Arnold's taking of the term high seriousness as the key term in "The Study of Poetry" was, then, not a casual or a chance reaching out for a useful rhetorical term; it was a natural development of his thought. I shall now try to limit the meaning of the term as it applies to poetry and to rule out any casual reading of the term as *sobriety* or *solemnity* or even *earnestness*. As we have seen, in "The Function of Criticism at the Present Time," Arnold had made the "judicious" the standard of practical criticism ("as the judicious would determine"). At the same time, as part of an inquiry into the kind of activity in which human beings are to seek happiness, he had tried to define the nature of critical activity. Now in inquiring into the nature of poetry, as the highest and best activity, Arnold needed to find the measure of the best. He took from the *Poetics* the term *spoudaios*. In the *Ethics*, however, the meaning of *spoudaios* is not simply good but excellence in the performance of an activity.

Although *spoudaios*, in the passage that Arnold quoted in "The Study of Poetry," could have either aesthetic or moral senses.[8] Arnold, in translating the phrase, kept the emphasis on excellence ("high and excellent seriousness"); he never translated the word as simply *good* or *goodness*. In general, Arnold kept moral goodness distinct from aesthetic excellence, although to do so would require, in his criticism of the Romantic poets, considerable subtlety. This line of argument is indicated by some earlier essays on Edmond Scherer and the English poets. In reviewing Scherer's work on John Milton, Arnold pondered once more the connection between moral and aesthetic choices that determine character and style—the subject of his early letters to Clough. Clough had privately questioned the notion that character forming was a matter merely of choice and of habit governed by reason.[9] But Arnold had held, in the letters and again in the essay on Maurice de Guérin, that the judicious could make choices guided by reason but that undisciplined people act hastily, impulsively, without thought, in art and in life. This argument, which was derived from Aristotle, was the basis of what Arnold had to say on the character and style of Milton. Arnold considered whether the sense of style and qualities of moral goodness are "part of our natural constitution." But allowing that style may be "a gift of nature," Arnold argued that moral habits may certainly be strengthened by practice and concluded: "Certain high moral dispositions Milton had from nature, and he sedulously trained and developed them until they became habits of great power" (PW, 8:184). By making a distinction between style and moral character, Arnold avoided saying that style was derived from character or that a good style was derived from a good character.

So far as Arnold made any connection between the "purity" of Milton's character and the beauty of his style, it was that both were perfected through discipline, but discipline of two kinds, one of art, the other of character. Clough and Shairp had tended to muddle this distinction. Rejecting the discipline of judgment as mechanical, certainly in poetry, they depended rather upon sincerity, upon the expression in style of character, or upon the inspiration of the manic poet—the visionary—or on the sympathy of heart and feeling. Arnold, from his earliest life as a poet and embryonic critic in the letters, had claimed that poetry was art, and now he found in seriousness an expression of the criterion of excellence. Before seeing how he made use of the idea in his poetics, it is first necessary to see how Arnold detached poetry from philosophy.

In defining the activity of poetry, Arnold was making a claim for poetic truth, but he separated poetry from philosophy. Here Arnold continued what he had begun in the essay on Wordsworth, when he made a distinction between the "powers" of the human character as they are exercised in the writing of poetry. What Arnold did in the essay on Wordsworth was to make clear that the greatness of Wordsworth's poetry had nothing to do with the supposed worth of the philosophy that is embedded in the poetry.

As in his essay on the function of criticism, Arnold identified poetic creation as an activity in which a person may find happiness. Arnold spoke first about the recognition or glory that follows the accomplished work; he took his text from Renan: to be recognized as "a seriously and eminently worthy workman, in one's own line of intellectual or spiritual activity, is indeed glory" (*PW*, 9:38). Except for *glory*, the terms are those of Aristotle's *Ethics:* the emphasis falls on *work* and on *activity*, whether intellectual or spiritual, the highest achievement being that which is "seriously and eminently worthy"— or poetry at the level of excellence.

Now Arnold set out to define more precisely what kind of activity poetry is and how it is to be ranked in comparison to philosophy. In separating poetry from philosophy, Arnold also was suggesting that poetry is a higher activity than philosophy.

Arnold proceeded by focusing on what he called *ideas*, in a sentence that he recalled from the essays on Homer: "The noble and profound application of ideas to life is the most essential part of poetic greatness" (*PW*, 9:44). What Arnold meant by *ideas* here was not philosophy; Arnold denied that formal philosophy, or "a scientific system of thought," had anything to do with poetic truth, thereby answering Leslie Stephen's article "Wordsworth's Ethics."[10] Arnold argued that the nearer Wordsworth came to putting forth a formal philosophy— whether in ideas of duty or in religious or philosophic thought— the further he moved from either poetry or truth. Thus, Wordsworth's speculations in *The Excursion* on " 'an abstract Intelligence,' " Arnold said, were "alien to the very nature of poetry" (*PW*, 9:49); passages of religious or philosophic doctrine had "none of the characters of *poetic* truth"; the ideas of the "Ode: Intimations of Immortality" had "no real solidity" (*PW*, 9:49). Philosophic poetry, according to Arnold, was neither poetry nor philosophy. This is not to say, however, that poetry does not possess its own kind of truth.

We might ordinarily ask whether the difference between poetic and philosophic truth lies in modes of reasoning or in language or in art. One might look for the difference between the general and the particular. S. H. Butcher, in his commentary on Aristotle's statement that poetry is more philosophical than history, said that poetry "expresses the universal not as it is in itself, but as seen through the medium of sensuous imagery" and hence approaches, but does not reach, philosophy.[11] Arnold had in fact copied out of Sir Leslie Stephen's essays just such a formulation, by which Stephen had tried to show that Wordsworth was a philosopher: " 'The *philosophic mind* is that which habitually sees the general in the particular, and finds food for the deepest thought in the simplest objects.' "[12] But Arnold copied out passages that he intended to attack as often as he copied those of which he approved. Although Arnold had earlier pointed out the difference in style between the poetry of Sophocles and the philosophical language of Aristotle, it is not evident, from the passage that he then quoted from *Oedipus at Colonus,* that he saw the difference as lying in generals and particulars (*PW,* 6:21). Since Arnold quoted from Aristotle the passage that asserts that poetry has a higher truth than history because poetry deals with universals, but without any obvious intention of turning Aristotle upside down, as Romantic critics had done, it seems unlikely that Arnold thought (as Butcher and Stephen did) that poetic truth meant that poetry translates philosophic generals into particulars. Poetry, rather, may deal with universal truth.

When Arnold tried to define the unique achievement of Wordsworth, he suggested what he meant by poetic truth. Wordsworth not only felt the joy in nature, the joy that inspires "simple primary affections and duties"; he also showed this joy and makes us feel it (*PW,* 9:51). The poetic truth of Wordsworth's poetry can be confirmed by experience: "The source of joy from which he thus draws is the truest and most unfailing source of joy accessible to man. It is also accessible universally" (*PW,* 9:51). Poetic truth thus seems to lie in observations that can be tested by reflection or experience, as Arnold said he had tested on his own pulses the "philosophy" of childhood in the "Ode: Intimations of Immortality" and had found it to be untrue. Arnold found more truth in the poetry than in the philosophy:

His poetry is the reality, his philosophy,—so far, at least, as it may be put on the form and habit of "a scientific system of thought," and the more that it puts them on,—is the illusion. Perhaps we shall one day learn to make this proposition general, and to say: Poetry is the reality, philosophy the illusion. But in Wordsworth's case, at any rate, we cannot do him justice until we dismiss his formal philosophy. (*PW*, 9:48)

Finally, as this passage clearly shows, Arnold saw a difference between the forms of poetry and philosophy: the "performance" of poetry is art; formal philosophy is a system of thought. Poetic truth differs from philosophic truth in form, in the tests, and in language. But Arnold did not claim for Wordsworth a poetic truth that is prophetic, apocalyptic, or visionary; Arnold's poetic truth was connected rather to what he calls the "criticism of life."

When Arnold called poetry "a criticism of life," he was thinking first of Homer; he used the phrase first in the essays on translating Homer. Indeed, Arnold's "criticism" or examination of life is close to the neoclassical precept that Homer followed Nature—that is, observed Nature or human nature—faithfully. When Arnold said that the "noble and profound application of ideas to life is the most essential part of poetic greatness," he was referring to "moral ideas" in the widest possible sense, ideas on *"how to live"* (*PW*, 9:44–45). Where Arnold earlier had allowed to the critic a share in poetic activity, here he allowed the poet a share in critical activity: "poetry is at bottom a criticism of life," for "the greatness of a poet lies in his powerful and beautiful application of ideas to life,—to the question: How to live" (*PW*, 9:46). As with style, the ideas of poetry are connected to the discipline of moral choice governed by judgment. What Arnold meant here by *ideas* were the meditations, intuitions, or observations of a powerful and disciplined mind.

I think it is unlikely that Arnold was claiming for poetry a higher truth seen by the imaginative reason, as contrasted to analytic or logical reason. Arnold nowhere mentioned the imaginative reason in these last essays. Earlier he had used the phrase specifically in reference to the great age of Greece from Simonides to Plato. It seems also to have been connected to the "imaginative intellect" that Arnold had assigned to Plato in *God and the Bible* and in *Literature and Dogma*.[13] Arnold appears to have been including Plato among those who lived by the imaginative reason or imaginative intellect. But Plato was a philosopher, not a poet, and there is no evidence that Arnold claimed that Plato was a poet. Arnold's examples of the great poets are Homer, Sophocles, and Shakespeare. If Arnold had thought of "imaginative reason" as something like Aristotle's *sophia*, or wisdom, he now determinedly rejected what is systematic and philosophical in Wordsworth's *Excursion*.

After having detached poetry from philosophy, Arnold's task now was to avoid moving to the opposite pole and making poetry a confession, an allegory of the state of one's mind. When, however, Arnold connected high seriousness and sincerity, he seems to have been suggesting some such test of truth and feeling. The connection was made late in the essay, when Arnold took up the poetry of Burns; he spoke about the "high seriousness which comes from absolute sincerity" and "the accent of high seriousness, born of absolute sincerity" (*PW*, 9:184). This single reference to sincerity has been used as the hook on which to hang Arnold's later criticism. But there are clearly problems in connecting high seriousness and sincerity. High seriousness, as Arnold's derivation of the term shows, is a classical concept. Arnold did not, as we might expect, think of sincerity as exclusively Romantic. True, the question of sincerity naturally arises in any discussion of the Romantic poets, as it did for Arnold in the essay on Wordsworth and later in the essays on Keats and Byron. But Arnold also discussed it in connection with the grand style of Milton. Although Arnold in his earliest criticism had been thought to have made a case against sincerity in favor of classical imitation, Arnold from the beginning had claimed sincerity for his own criticism and poetry, even that based on classical subjects and aesthetics. In "The Function of Criticism at the Present Time" Arnold had held that criticism approaches creative activity when it is serious and sincere. In "The Study of Poetry" Arnold claimed sincerity for poetry that is classic and gave to sincerity a classical meaning by attaching it to high seriousness.

The larger context of Arnold's reference to sincerity is the discussion that was begun during the 1840s and 1850s with his friends Clough, Shairp, Sellar, and Froude. The essay on Wordsworth looks back to earlier essays by Shairp and by Clough; the criticism of Burns also looks back to the early discussions between Clough and Arnold on lyric form, but also to recent criticism of Burns by Shairp. Before turning to that debate, I will look at the immediate context of the discussion in the several essays and reviews collected in *Mixed Essays*, primarily those dealing with French literature and criticism, but here important because Arnold takes up the question of sincerity in his discussion of Milton. Arnold found Milton's greatness in his style, the grand style, which was marked by *"elevation"* arising from the moral character of Milton (*PW*, 8:184). As evidence of Milton's moral character, Arnold quoted from Milton's prose a profession of knightly virtue; he commented: "What gives to Milton's professions such a stamp of their own is their accent of absolute sincerity. In this elevated strain of moral pureness his life was really pitched; its strong, immortal beauty passed into the diction and rhythm of his poetry" (*PW*, 8:185–86). Arnold attributed sincerity to Milton's autobiographical prose; what he found in Milton's poetry was beauty of diction and rhythm. The distinction is important: the test of good poetry is not sincerity; it is beauty of diction and rhythm. Arnold implied an indirect connection between character and poetry; the habits of discipline that result in character (as Arnold argued in this essay) also make for an artistic discipline that is necessary for the grand style (as Arnold implied). Even if Milton's poetry is marked by sincerity, we have the sincerity of the grand style, something very far from Romantic sincerity.

Arnold was quite clear that poetry did not aim at sincerity in the sense of a revelation of one's true feelings or real self. In reviewing Stopford Brooke's *A Primer of English Literature* in December, 1877, Arnold approved Brooke's declaration that the artist is "to please the public, not to reveal himself." Arnold, however, added that there was more to the art of poetry: "We mean by art . . . a law of pure and flawless workmanship" (*PW,* 8:245). In taking up style in the poetry of Wordsworth, however, Arnold seems to derive the power of style from sincerity; the power of Wordsworth's plain style, Arnold said, "arises from two causes: from the profound sincereness with which Wordsworth feels his subject, and also from the profoundly sincere and natural character of his subject itself" (*PW,* 9:53).[14] Arnold's expression of his idea is puzzling because it runs counter to ordinary expectations of what sincerity should be (an expression of deeply held feelings or beliefs); the notion of a sincere subject is especially baffling.[15]

Perhaps it would not be possible to talk about Wordsworth without speaking of sincerity; but evidently Arnold was not at ease with the usual notions of sincerity. To understand this, one must look at the long debate between Arnold and his friends on Wordsworth. Shairp's 1864 essay on Wordsworth was followed by the publication of the papers of Clough, which included a lecture on Wordsworth.[16] Here Clough took up the question that had troubled both himself and Arnold as young poets: how to know and to say what you mean; how to find the genuine poetic self. Clough found that Wordsworth "really derives from his style and his diction his chief and special charm" (*PR,* p. 311). Clough, indeed, found the source of style in character: "His poems do more perfectly and exquisitely and unintermittedly express his real meaning and significance and character than do the poems of either Scott or Byron" (*PR,* p. 312). Furthermore, Clough said, neither Scott nor Byron attained "permanent beauty of expression" or "harmony between thought and word."

To explain this kind of harmony, Clough turned to geometry: "For poetry, like science, has its final precision; and there are expressions of poetic knowledge which can no more be rewritten than could the elements of geometry" (*PR*, p. 313). Style, in some sense, fixes knowledge:

> It is as though you should suppose that to each poetic thought some particular geometric figure, or curve, it might be, specially appertained: just as to a particular definition the circle appertains, and no figure but the circle. . . . To draw the figure which may truly stand as the model and the pattern, the unmisleading, safe representative—this is the gift and the excellence of style. (*PR*, p. 314)

What Clough had in mind was not so much a neoclassical theory of poetry—what often was thought but never so well expressed—as a theory that poetry expresses the "real meaning and significance and character" of the poet himself. Thus, "Wordsworth succeeded beyond the other poets of the time in giving a perfect expression to his meaning, in making his verse permanently true to his genius and moral frame" (*PR*, p. 316). Although Clough did not use the term *sincerity*, what he said here falls within the general meaning of that word.

Having linked character and style, Clough could judge the poetry by judging the poet. Thus, if Wordsworth's poetry expressed "his genius and moral frame," Clough must inquire into the "worth of that genius and moral frame, the sum of the real significance of his character and view of life" (*PR*, p. 316). Clough found "a certain elevation and fixity" in Wordsworth's character: "To have attained a law, to exercise a lordship by right divine over passions and desires—this is Wordsworth's pre-eminence" (*PR*, p. 316). Thus Clough appealed to the standard of the *phronimos*, the one who achieves self-control and discipline in life and art. Clough, however, thought that Wordsworth's discipline was made easier by removing himself from the great world: "A certain withdrawal and separation, a moral and almost religious selectiveness, a rigid refusal and a nice picking and choosing, are essential to Wordsworth's being" (PR, p. 316). Thus Wordsworth's moral effort was a lesser one: "Retiring early from all conflict and even contact with the busy world, he shut himself from the elements which it was his business to encounter and to master" (PR, p. 319). As a result, there was in Wordsworth's poetry "an appearance of sterility and unreality" (PR, p. 319); "he is a poet rather of a country-house or a picturesque tour, not of life and business, action, and fact" (PR, p. 319). Thus Clough judged Wordsworth's "high moral tone" to be not such a great achievement, since it is easy, Clough implied, to be good in a village. Furthermore, Clough held, Wordsworth too often chose trivial subjects, such as the daisy and the celandine, and therefore his poetry is often mawkish (PR, p. 320–21). Thus far, Clough has followed Arnold in judging Wordsworth by the classical norms of the serious subject, the style derived from character; and Clough's criticism of Wordsworth was similar to what Arnold had said about Lucretius—namely, that he had withdrawn from the world and failed to arrive at an adequate interpretation of life.

In the concluding paragraphs of the lecture, which were not reprinted until Trawick's edition, Clough launched out on another subject, the comparison of poetry and science. Speculating on natural science and the poetry of the future, Clough suggested: "Poetry also is a sort of Science—a register at any rate of phenomena—and phenomena of the most subtle, evanescent, intangible nature; whose chemistry far transcends in strangeness and in dignity all the experiments of all existing retorts and crucibles" (SPW, p. 122). Clough was not referring to the phenomena that Wordsworth had recorded, because he had earlier criticized Wordsworth for his failure to look at reality:

[Wordsworth] instead of looking directly at an object, and considering it as a thing in itself, and allowing it to operate upon him as a fact in itself, . . . takes the sentiment produced by it in his own mind as the thing, as the important and really real fact. The real things cease to be real; the world no longer exists; all that exists is the feeling, somehow generated in the poet's sensibility. (*PR*, p. 315)

Here Clough, anticipating more recent critics who advocate the poets of reality, dismissed romantic introspection. He did not see in Wordsworth's recording of his own sensibility the value of sincerity, but he remarked that Wordsworth was "sentimentalising over sentiment."

The questions that Clough raised about Wordsworth's style and character provoked the discussion of these ideas in the later essays by Shairp and Arnold. Clough said that Wordsworth's charm lies in his style; Arnold said that Wordsworth had no style. Clough said that Wordsworth too often chose trivial subjects such as the daisy and that he often fell into sentimentality. Shairp argued for the importance of the ideas, even the philosophy, of Wordsworth. Arnold denied the significance of Wordsworth's philosophy but made a case for the power of his interpretation of nature.

Shairp's second essay on Wordsworth answered Clough's charge about the triviality of Wordsworth's poetic subjects.[17] Shairp had clearly read Clough, for he quoted from Clough's essay on the influence that the external nature of his boyhood home in the North country had had on the formation of Wordsworth's character (*PIN*, p. 241; *PR*, p. 305) and picked up occasional phrases. Shairp, however, gave a fuller and fairer account of the poetry of *The Prelude* and the view of Nature revealed in that poem. Shairp, moreover, referred to Leslie Stephen's article on the philosophy of Wordsworth, a philosophy "based on the 'identity between the instincts of our childhood and our enlightened reason' " (*PIN*, p. 264). Shairp ended by considering the question of Nature as interpreted by poetry and by science; poetry sees nature by the light of the "moral imagination" (*PIN*, p. 279). On these points, then, Shairp turned to Stephen for an argument to use against Clough's criticism of Wordsworth.

Principally, Shairp's argument depended on reading *The Prelude* as a key to the lyrical ballads. Clough had read *The Prelude*, but in his essay he referred chiefly to the passages on Hawkshead and the Simplon Pass (*PR*, pp. 305–6). Shairp answered Clough's criticism that Wordsworth had withdrawn from the world to write about nature and trivial subjects such as daisies. Shairp argued that Wordsworth's subject was really human nature and that Wordsworth's view of Nature was never trivial, even in "the smaller poems," which must be referred to the whole view of Nature expounded in *The Prelude* (*PIN*, p. 275). Like Stephen, Shairp emphasized the value of Wordsworth's philosophy: "Wordsworth alone, adding the philosopher to the poet, has speculated widely and deeply on the relation in which Nature stands to the soul of man, and on the truths suggested by this relation" (*PIN*, p. 279). Shairp thus defended Wordsworth by taking Stephen's line and arguing for the poet as a philosopher.

Arnold, in taking up the poetry of Wordsworth, had to avoid both Clough's skepticism, which dismissed much of Wordsworth's poetry as trivial and sentimental, and also Shairp's enthusiasm, which made the poetry depend upon the philosophy. Clough offered the myth of the simple Wordsworth; Shairp, the myth of the inspired visionary. Clough had created the simple Wordsworth, the homely man who retired from the world to sing about the daisy, the celandine, and the simple rustics; Wordsworth's style, when it was not sentimental or mawkish, expressed the character of the poet. Arnold understood the moral and intellectual energy of Wordsworth too well to adopt Clough's view of the simple poet; earlier, in fact, Arnold had ranked Wordsworth with Lucretius as the kind of poet who had too little of "natural magic" and too much of intellect (*PW*, 3:33–34).

Now Arnold's problem was to keep the complex character of Wordsworth while explaining the plain style of his poetry. To do this, Arnold invented his own myth, or poetic fable: Wordsworth, he said, had no style at all; rather, Nature seized the pen and wrote for him (*PW*, 9:52–53). What Arnold did in this fable was to separate the character of the poet from his art, so that character was not, as it was for Clough, the direct source of style. Nature herself had intervened to cancel Wordsworth's character and to inspire him to the "natural" style of his lyrical ballads. That is, Wordsworth mastered the craft of his poetry, the natural and simple style that is appropriate to his subject. To return to Arnold's larger theory of character and poetry, it could be said that Wordsworth possessed a flexibility that allowed him to master an art that was almost contrary to his nature. And this was why Arnold attributed sincerity, not to Wordsworth, but to the subject itself, meaning that Wordsworth responded to the requirements of the subject—an effect of sincerity and naturalness—rather than expressing (as Clough supposed) his own simple soul. Thus it was not because Wordsworth was a simple or a plain man that he wrote in a simple, plain style; it was because he was a poet, and the effect of sincerity in the lyric poems is explained, not by character, but by art.

Arnold pursued the distinction between character and art in "A French Play in London" (1879), which came between the brief essay "On Poetry," in which Arnold first explored the notion of seriousness in poetry, and "The Study of Poetry," in which he made high seriousness the criterion of great poetry. In the essay on French drama, Arnold again detached seriousness in art from seriousness of character. Arnold offered the seeming paradox that Molière, because of his seriousness of character and (Arnold insisted that Molière had "profound seriousness") recognizing that he lacked the highest poetic power, chose to write, not tragedy, but comedy, which by its nature lacks seriousness (PW, 9:72–73). In this context, "high seriousness" included an idea of excellence in performance: Molière, a serious artist who was aiming at the highest art of which he was capable, chose to write comedy, in which he could achieve excellence. Yet at the same time Arnold assumed that greatness inheres in some kinds of poetry rather than in others. In this essay the distinction between tragedy and comedy suggests that he connected high seriousness with genre:

Tragedy breasts the pressure of life. Comedy eludes it, half liberates itself from it by irony. . . .

Comedy, too, escapes as has been already said, the test of entire seriousness; it remains, by the law of its being, in a region of comparative lightness and irony. (PW, 9:72–73)

Thus far, Arnold has remained consistent in implying that greatness inheres in the subject, the genre, and the style but not in the character of the artist. In "The Study of Poetry," however, Arnold detached seriousness from the kinds of poetry, and while one can see that there remained a vestige of the feeling that comedy and irony are not entirely serious art and that this is why the poetry of Burns did not reach high seriousness, Arnold was primarily concerned to allow greatness to any excellence in performance.

Turning now to the central problem in Arnold's "The Study of Poetry"—the linking of high seriousness and sincerity—we see that again there are certain problems with our ordinary sense of things. We do not ordinarily inquire whether tragedy or epic poetry is sincere; nor, in fact, does Arnold explicitly make such a claim. He connected "high seriousness" to "sincerity" only once, and that was in the criticism of the poetry of Burns. Because Burns was primarily a lyric poet—Arnold and Clough had discussed Burns and his "lyric fury" in their early letters—it is natural enough to speak about sincerity in Burns. But Arnold was now trying to say something not only about lyric poetry but about all poetry. Nor was Arnold trying to reconcile Romantic and Classical poetry or criticism; he was claiming for Classical poetry the sincerity that the Romantic poets and critics felt to be so important, and he was giving to sincerity a Classical meaning. In this sense, sincerity is not an expression of the poet's inmost feelings or a revelation of his private self or even character; rather, sincerity is an earnest dedication to his art, an intense concentration requiring force of thought and character, an energy that

informs the poetic style—in some sense a devotion to the life
of the poet as activity.

Again, the immediate context is instructive. Arnold was
answering the late Romantic criticism of Shairp, specifically
Shairp's work on Burns. In denying to Burns high seriousness, Arnold was responding to Shairp's criticism of Burns and
also to Shairp's attack on Arnold's own positions. Shairp's essays became increasingly conservative defenses of traditional
thought and morality, and in *Culture and Religion* (1872),
Shairp set out to defend what he took for established truths
against what he saw as Arnold's skepticism in *Culture and
Anarchy*. Shairp's attack on "The Function of Criticism at the
Present Time," however, came fourteen years after Arnold had
published his essay. In "Criticism and Creation" (1878) Shairp
took up the issue that Arnold had raised in his essay.[18] Shairp
challenged Arnold's claim that criticism prepares the way for
poetry; of Burns he said: "Wider knowledge . . . would have
paralysed his singing-power" (*AP*, pp. 44–47). Deriving from
Plato's *Ion* a theory of poetic inspiration, Shairp attacked Aristotelian criticism as a mechanical reliance on method (*AP*,
pp. 49–50). Inspiration, he claimed, is the source of truth: "By
the flashes of uncritical genius the world has gained its finest
truths" (*AP*, p. 51). Furthermore, in the year 1879, while
Arnold had postponed writing "The Study of Poetry," Shairp
had published, in July, "Shelley as a Lyric Poet," in October,
"Burns and Scotch Song," and a book on Robert Burns in the
English Men of Letters Series.[19] Shairp's work on Burns was
what provided the immediate impetus for "The Study of
Poetry," giving to Arnold both his examples of the personal
bias in criticism and also his example of the poet who is not
a classic because he lacks high seriousness. In response to
Shairp's reliance on Plato, Arnold turned once more to Aristotle to support his earlier judgment that Gray was a classic
and that Burns was not and found the measure of worth in
high seriousness. Also, by connecting sincerity to high seriousness, Arnold detached sincerity from the implications of pastoral or rustic simplicity and absorbed it into his idea of the

classic by attributing it to the great poets of civilization such as Dante and Milton. Arnold thus removed from sincerity any notion of simple goodness or innocence.

First it will be useful to look at the way in which Arnold, with an eye on Shairp's criticism of Burns, detached his criticism of life and high seriousness from a simple moral didacticism. Arnold here was careful to avoid Shairp's obvious moral stance. Shairp has served, perhaps unfairly, as the example of the rigid Victorian moralist in his criticism of Burns, a reputation that was acquired as soon as his *Robert Burns* appeared. Shairp was attacked for his genteel censorship of the facts of Burns's life. He defended this censorship in a letter to a friend: "I have suppressed, as far as I could, all the grosser details"; and to another, "I do not want to be sympathetic with the coarseness and immorality that stained his whole life, and in some degree his works." For these omissions, Shairp said, he had been attacked by the "Scotch prints" as "Prig, Prude, Pharisee."[20] The reviewers, among whom was Robert Louis Stevenson, attacked Shairp not only for having failed to give the whole story of Burns's life but also for having given a one-sided appreciation of Burns's poetry by expressing little but moral disapproval of "Holy Willie's Prayer," "The Holy Fair," and "The Jolly Beggars."[21]

Although Arnold is in some quarters regarded as a moralizing critic, it is clear that in fact he was far more ready to praise a poem such as "The Jolly Beggars" as a "superb poetic success" (*PW*, 9:186) and, indeed, to separate moralizing from moral criticism. Shairp argued for the "moral wisdom" of poems such as "To a Mouse" and "Address to the Unco' Guid," and said of Burns, "He would not have been a Scotchman, if he had not been a moralizer; but then his moralizings are not platitudes, but truths winged with wit and wisdom" (*Burns*, p. 196). Quoting from "To a Mouse" and similar poems, Shairp ended by asking, "Who on the text, 'He that is without sin among you, let him first cast a stone,' ever preached such a sermon as Burns in his *Address to the unco Guid?*" (*Burns*, p. 197). Arnold's criticism of the poem gave the obvious answer to that rhetorical question: namely, that the poem, does, after all, merely preach a sermon (*PW*, 9:185). Poetry at the level of excellence is not merely preaching.

Arnold's theoretical attack on Shairp's criticism of Burns was aimed primarily at what Arnold called the personal estimate and the national bias. The effectiveness, though not the validity, of Arnold's criticism is here marred, it is true, by Arnold's apparent blindness to his own bias, which appeared in his description of Burns's world: "Burns's world of Scotch drink, Scotch religion, and Scotch manners, is often harsh, a sordid, a repulsive world" (*PW*, 9:182). In his letters, he was even more intolerant and intemperate in his expression: "Burns is a beast, with splendid gleams, and the medium in which he lived, Scotch peasants, Scotch Presbyterianism, and Scotch drink, is repulsive" (*PW*, 9:379). Although Shairp, like Arnold, deplored the coarser aspects of the life that Burns had depicted in his comic poems, Shairp as a critic had also expressed enthusiasm for the more attractive features of peasant life, and Shairp's enthusiasm was certainly more attractive than Arnold's rather finicky displeasure.

Yet as a theoretical critic, Arnold was arguing once more against the Balliol group's elevation of folk literature. Shairp had made folk literature the source of the art and the traditions of Burns's poetry. In "Burns and Scotch Song before Him," Shairp had traced the growth of folk poetry in Scotland and had seen Burns's importance as part of the Scottish folk tradition. In the concluding chapter of his book on Burns, he praised Burns as "the interpreter of Scotland's peasantry"; Burns "interpreted the lives, thoughts, feelings, manners of the Scottish peasantry to whom he belonged, as they had never been interpreted before, and never can be again" (*Burns*, pp. 194, 191). Arnold, however, insisted that poetry must be judged as art; and he proceeded to show how the feelings of "a partial countryman" had in fact misled Shairp in his judgment of Burns. If Shairp had failed to learn one of the lessons of "The Function of Criticism"—namely, the danger of provinciality—Arnold would again demonstrate it in the danger of a per-

sonal or a national bias. Shairp had praised Burns as a great
national poet, the "restorer of [Scotland's] nationality" (Burns,
p. 194). Arnold, however, would not allow even Shairp's praise
of the great national song or of "For A' That and A' That" but
spoke generally about the critics who were "admirers of
Burns": "With still more confidence will his admirers tell us
that we have the genuine Burns, the great poet, when his strain
asserts the independence, equality, dignity, of men" (PW,
9:183). Arnold was using phrases from Shairp's essay—"independence," "equality," and "dignity"—and from the biography—
"personal independence, and sturdy, if self-asserting man-
hood" (Burns, p. 204). In the earlier version of the essay, Shairp
had praised "the sense of the native dignity of man and the
essential equality of all men" ("Burns and Scotch Song," p.
510). Arnold here set aside his own bias, his faith in the "ideas
of 1789"; however fine the theme, the test of great poetry
is not patriotism or even democratic feeling. When Shairp revised the essays for Aspects of Poetry, he himself silently
acknowledged that his comparing Burns to Shakespeare was
an extravagant judgment by dropping the comparison as well
as the praise of the themes of independence and equality (AP,
p. 218). Responding to Arnold's criticism or not being willing
to be linked with the intemperate critics whom Arnold labeled
the "admirers of Burns," Shairp revised his claims for the Scottish poet.

The estimate of Burns as a poet and the ideas of the equality and the dignity of man were not as important in this last
debate as the larger issue of the poetry of the folk. When
Arnold had turned to the classical past for his subjects, themes,
and models, Shairp had discouraged him from taking that "old
greek form" and with Clough and Froude had preferred subjects from contemporary life. The debate over the choice of
the ancient or modern subjects led to the general question
of the rural people or the working classes as the source and
the audience of poetry. Were the folk the source of wisdom,
poetic forms, and traditions that nourished literature; or were
the common people illiterate rustics, with no real language or

poetry? Shairp, with some reservations, made a case for Burns as the poet of the Scottish people, deriving his poetry from folk songs and ballads, preserving ancient speech, and recording the ancient rural customs. Arnold felt that the actual life of the poor was often harsh and ugly. Burns could only by the strength of his poetic genius create great poetry from this material.

Moreover, the ballad form (whatever its origins), Arnold had said in the lectures on Homer, although of limited use in lyric poetry, was not adequate to the demands of great narrative poetry. The aesthetic or poetic question was mixed, however, with the social and practical question of what ought to be done for the poor. In *Culture and Religion*, Shairp had emphasized the virtues of the rural poor and had thought that they might be left to their own life and customs, needing only the solace of religion. Arnold, on the other hand, in *Culture and Anarchy*, had envisioned a state in which the life of the poor, either urban or rural, would be changed, largely through education, as the poor entered into the life of the nation. In the earlier debates in the circle, the question had taken an aesthetic form: What was the responsibility of the poet to the ordinary people, as subject or as audience? Should the poet take a subject from contemporary or ordinary life?

Clough attempted in *The Bothie* (risking the unknown language) to make heroes of the Scottish farmers and to let the Oxford scholar find that untutored wisdom was greater than the philosophy of Aristotle and that a pioneering life in New Zealand was better than a professional life in England. Arnold's brother, Thomas Arnold, actually went off to live a pioneering life in New Zealand, but in fact, he found the untutored English rustics, who had also emigrated, rather an alien species, with whom he tried to communicate by reading Wordsworth to them.[22] Matthew Arnold, who labored among the schools of the middle classes, had no sentimental feeling for the life of the poor. He dismissed the kind of primitivism that Clough and Shairp were inclined to adopt in theory. He did not find any special virtue in the country life or any sincerity in the peasant. It is in this context that the question of sincerity is to be considered. Arnold's problem was to detach sincerity as a critical idea from its romantic associations with the country, the simple poor, the uneducated, and to give it a classical sense, as at the same time he detached *classic* from an exclusive connection with Greek and Latin literature and thus made *classic* available to all the people and not only to the educated few.

The question of sincerity and high seriousness became a central one in Arnold's essays on the Romantic poets—on Gray, Byron, Keats, and Shelley. Arnold had taken up the question of sincerity in Wordsworth and Burns; now he turned to the various kinds of sincerity—that of the melancholy poet, Gray; of the immoral man, Byron; of the sensuous man, Keats; and of the undisciplined man, Shelley.

Arnold's first reference to sincerity in Byron's poetry appeared in the article on Wordsworth, where he cited Scherer (in a passage that he later canceled).[23] Arnold's strategy in rescuing Byron from Scherer's charge of insincerity was to admit that the man was theatrical but to claim that the poet, when he was inspired, was another person altogether. This argument recalls Shelley's defense of the poet as a good man: when he is in the process of composing a poem, he is a good man, and hence as a poet is always good; when he is not composing poetry, he lives the ordinary life of a man and is to be judged like other men. The argument is not a piece of sophistry; it is derived from the Aristotelian notion of the highest activity, the activity in which human beings find their greatest good. Because for Arnold this activity was poetry, it must then follow that to be a poet is to live the good life. But as Arnold and Shelley both seem to have thought, such activity is not continuous but is intermittent, and indeed, even Aristotle could be interpreted as having thought that one did not always philosophize. Commentators such as Grant had arrived at the idea that the highest activity was possible only at rare moments, moments of pure consciousness, perhaps even visionary moments (*Ethics*, 1857 ed., pp. 193–94). While it does not appear that Arnold was thinking of visionary moments, his defense of Byron indicates that he had a notion that poetic activity is intermittent.

The question of Shelley's character had been raised by Shairp in "Shelley as a Lyric Poet." In this essay, Shairp pushed to an extreme the view that lyric poetry is the outpouring of personal feeling: "Lyric poetry . . . is the vivid expression of personal experience."[24] Shairp argued that the critic must therefore know the "reality" behind the lyrics—namely, Shelley's life and thought (*AP*, pp. 228-29). The key to Shelley's character, Shairp found, was that Shelley was a child of impulse: "He was preeminently, one who followed his passions unquestioningly; and Aristotle, we know, tells us that such an one is no fit judge of moral truth" (*AP*, p. 230). Shairp clearly had in mind the discussion in the *Nicomachean Ethics* which (as I have shown) lay behind Arnold's analysis of the character of Maurice de Guérin and of Keats and of the poet who lacks judgment, although Arnold had focused on the temperament of the nature poet, on the susceptibility to impressions and a failure to order them. Instead Shairp was working towards the idea of the morally healthy imagination. Thus Shairp defined "the highest order of lyric poem" as that which "will interest all healthy and truthful minds in all stages of culture, and in all ages" (*AP*, p. 248). Shairp, however, fell into the inconsistency of saying that Shelley's impulsive nature had made him a lyric poet but also had made him a bad man and hence a bad lyric poet (*AP*, p. 231). Shairp's essay exemplifies the difficulties that arise from attempting to derive poetry directly from personal experience and from moral character and from attempting to judge the poet rather than the poem.

What Arnold did was to distinguish between the high seriousness of the individual and of the artist. The artist achieves high seriousness in performance at the level of excellence. The individual, on the other hand, may achieve high seriousness in other ways, perhaps even in moral earnestness. It is possible, on Arnold's theory, to be serious as an individual and yet not achieve seriousness as an artist.

Arnold began, in his essay on Shelley, the last essay on the Romantic poets in the second *Essays in Criticism*, by defending Shelley's character and establishing the goodness of the poet who achieved, along with other virtues, "high and tender seriousness," "a reverent enthusiasm for the great and wise," and "heroic generosity" (*PW*, 11:324). Arnold did note a defect of character, unexpectedly perhaps to those who think of Arnold's high seriousness as solemnity, but one that is quite in line with Arnold's discussion of *eutrapelia*—namely, Shelley's lack of humor and a resulting self-delusion. Although Arnold allowed to Shelley high seriousness of character, he did not make a case for the high seriousness of the poetry. Instead, Arnold argued that the defects of Shelley's character had led to defects in his poetry:

> But let no one suppose that a want of humor and a self-delusion such as Shelley's have no effect upon a man's poetry. The man, Shelley, in very truth, is not entirely sane, and Shelley's poetry is not entirely sane either. The Shelley of actual life is a vision of beauty and radiance, indeed, but availing nothing, effecting nothing. And in poetry, no less than in life, he is "a beautiful *and ineffectual* angel, beating in the void his luminous wings in vain." (*PW*, 11:327)

By pointing out the beauty and radiance of Shelley's poetry, Arnold seems to have been laying out the theme of the essay that he intended to write later (*PW*, 11:471).

Certainly, Arnold left a number of unresolved difficulties in the essay, and he answered only part of Shairp's criticism of Shelley: "I am inclined to believe that, for all his noble impulses and aims, he was in some way deficient in rational and moral sanity" (*AP*, p. 232). Arnold defended Shelley against the charge of moral insanity but convicted him of unreason. Furthermore, by saying that Shelley's poetry was ineffectual, Arnold seems to be contradicting the basic premise of his criticism—namely, that the highest activity is an end in itself.

It is here, perhaps, that we see most clearly that Arnold never quite separated poetry from politics; Arnold valued Shelley for his revolutionary fervor but blamed him for his failure to help to bring in the new age. Byron and Shelley, Arnold had said in "The Function of Criticism at the Present Time," did understand the new age and did attempt to usher in the new ideas. Yet here again there is an inconsistency, for Shelley can hardly have been right in understanding the new age, the new ideas, and yet have been not quite sane. Whatever distinction Arnold might have drawn—a distinction that might have resolved this apparent contradiction—remains in the unknown and unfinished business of Arnold's critical thought. Yet Arnold did once more establish the point that high seriousness in poetry is a matter of performance, not of the poet's character; and unsatisfactory as this last essay is on some points, it does make a case against Shairp's moralistic condemnation of Shelley by pointing to the moral deficiency of a lack of humor.

In three essays succeeding "The Study of Poetry," Arnold took up the idea of sincerity, high seriousness, and the question, proposed by Shairp in his essay on Shelley, of whether the character of the poet must determine the worth of the poetry. Insofar as sincerity is the honest expression of the poet's feeling or of his character, the test of poetry is sincerity: this, as I have indicated, was Shairp's position. Arnold, instead, separated the character of the poet from the performance of poetry. In the case of Thomas Gray, Arnold showed that there was no doubt about the poet's character as revealed in his biography; "and of Gray's high qualities of soul, of his [*spoudaiotēs*], his excellent seriousness, we may gather abundant proof from his letters" (*PW,* 9:195)

Citing passages from the letters that attest to Gray's admirable conduct during certain crises in his life, Arnold concluded, "Seriousness, character, was the foundation of things with him" (*PW,* 9:196). Yet, as Arnold had said about Molière, seriousness of character is not sufficient for the creation of great art. What is required is high seriousness in the activity of poetry. True, poets may fall short of excellence for various reasons; one cause may be the aridity of the times: "Gray, a born poet, fell upon an age of prose. He fell upon an age whose task was such as to call forth in general men's powers of understanding, wit and cleverness, rather than their deepest powers of mind and soul" (PW, 9:200). The view that the age of the eighteenth century produced a poetry that was deficient in imagination is a common one in Romantic criticism of the earlier poets.

Clough had outlined the history of that literary age, which, he said, relied on the senses and the understanding.[25] Arnold did not carry the criticism of the Age of Reason much further. The poetry of the eighteenth century, he said, was "intellectual, argumentative, ingenious; not seeing things in their truth and beauty, not interpretative" (PW, 9:200). What was required for *interpretation*, a term that Arnold tended to fall back on in his uninspired moments, may have been imaginative reason, but here Arnold was speaking about the "deepest powers of the mind and soul." Practically, the age prevented the high seriousness of Gray from achieving high seriousness in art; but poetry must finally be judged by its performance, not by the sincerity or the good character of the poet.

In the essay on Keats, again, Arnold struggled with the question of Keats's character and the importance of his ideas before he finally pronounced judgment on Keats's poetry. Once again, it is instructive to see how Arnold, without denying the importance of character to great poetry, still escaped a narrow moralism. To the man Keats, as to the man Burns, Arnold had always had some aversion. Reading the letters of Keats, probably in 1848 or 1849, Arnold had confessed to feeling a deep moral shock, a shock connected with his sense that Keats had no control over his life or his poetry.[26] At a time when Arnold was himself struggling for control, he could only flee, like his scholar-gipsy, the contagion of the merry Grecian coaster, the exotic luxuriance of Keats's imagery. Some years later, when analyzing Keats's temperament in the essay on Maurice de Guérin, Arnold thought that Keats's melancholy had derived from his lack of self-control, from his cultivation

of sensibility, of impulse, of emotions, and from a corresponding refusal to listen to reason, thus having been carried away
by emotion or passion. In short, Arnold had judged that Keats
had lacked the discipline of the *phronimos*.

Now Arnold began his new essay with a similar analysis:
"Character and self-control, the *virtus verusque labor* so
necessary for every kind of greatness, and for the great artist,
too, indispensable, appear to be wanting, certainly, to this
Keats of Haydon's portraiture" (*PW*, 9:205). Arnold again deplored the publication of the letters to Fanny Brawne, which re-
inforced the impression of Benjamin Robert Haydon's *Journals*:

> We who believe Keats to have been by his promise, at any
> rate, if not fully by his performance, one of the very great-
> est of English poets, and who believe also that a merely
> sensuous man cannot either by promise or by performance
> be a very great poet, because poetry interprets life, and
> so large and noble a part of life is outside of such a man's
> ken,—we cannot but look for signs in him of something
> more than sensuousness, for signs of character and virtue.
> And indeed the elements of high character Keats undoubt-
> edly has. (*PW*, 9:207)

Arnold showed that Keats was in fact capable of self-discipline:
Keats "had flint and iron in him, . . . he had character" (*PW*,
9:221).

Arnold went on to show how character and intellect may
work together in the pursuit of a high activity that is in itself
good: "Even in his pursuit of 'the pleasures of song,' however,
there is that stamp of high work which is akin to character,
which is character passing into intellectual production" (*PW*,
9:212). Arnold, although he separated character and poetry,
came close to saying that the poet who is working at the level
of excellence is by definition a good man because he is engaged
in an activity in which character, intellect, and art combine
to produce great poetry. Arnold went on to try to define this
activity as it manifested itself in Keats's poetry:

The truth is that the "yearning passion for the Beautiful," which was with Keats, as he himself truly says, the master-passion, is not a passion of the sensuous or sentimental man, is not a passion of the sensuous or sentimental poet. It is an intellectual and spiritual passion. It is "connected and made one," as Keats declares that in his case it was, "with the ambition of the intellect." It is, as he again says, "the mighty *abstract idea* of Beauty in all things." And in his last days Keats wrote, . . . *I have loved the principle of beauty in all things."* (PW, 9:213)

Thus the great insight in Keats's poetry, Arnold thought, was the idea that the perception of beauty is also the perception of truth: " 'What the Imagination seizes as Beauty must be Truth.' " Arnold quoted Keats as having said: "And with beauty goes not only truth, joy goes with her also. It is no small thing to have so loved the principle of beauty as to perceive the necessary relation of beauty with truth, and both with joy" (PW, 9:213–14).

Arnold illustrated these ideas by quoting passages from Keats's prose and verse, including the enigmatic ending of the "Ode on a Grecian Urn" and the first line of *Endymion*, evidence that confirmed Arnold's judgment: "By virtue of his feeling for beauty and of his perception of the vital connection of beauty with truth, Keats accomplished so much in poetry, that in one of the two great modes by which poetry interprets, in the faculty of naturalistic interpretation, in what we call natural magic, he ranks with Shakespeare" (PW, 9:214). Now Arnold said that Keats had failed to achieve a high "moral interpretation" only because his poetry had not matured; Keats had not yet been capable of the "high architectonics which go with complete poetic development" and which are evident in works such as *Agamemnon* and *King Lear* (PW, 9:215). Keats thus failed to achieve poetic greatness because he had not enough mortal time to learn and to perfect the art of poetry. Character he had; ideas and insights he had; "high architectonics" he had not. For Arnold, then, high seriousness was finally a matter of performance; it was the most demanding of the poetic forms.

In the essay on Byron, Arnold drew together his major criticism of the Romantic poets, taking up Wordsworth and, briefly, Keats and Shelley. The essay also drew together "The Function of Criticism at the Present Time" and the later essays, and it looked back to the 1853 Preface. Arnold touched once more on the importance of a great subject, on the character of the poet, on criticism of life according to the laws of poetic truth and beauty, on the superiority of poetry over philosophy, and on sincerity as connected to high seriousness. In this, one of his last essays, Arnold connected his major ideas in a way that points to the coherence of his theory and illuminates and clarifies its parts.

Arnold's defense of Byron is, more than any of the other essays on the Romantic poets, written *con amore*, for like other Victorian poets, Arnold responded to Byron's passionate intellect and his revolutionary fervor. Byron, more than any of the other Romantic poets, had taken as his subject the Revolution and had remained faithful to the end to the ideals of 1789. As Arnold had said in "The Function of Criticism at the Present Time," Byron had attempted to bring about the new age of criticism, the new modern age, in England. Therefore, once more, Arnold took as his first premise Byron's grasp of a great subject: "Byron found our nation, after its long and victorious struggle with revolutionary France, fixed in a system of established facts and dominant ideas which revolted him" (*PW*, 9:232). Byron, although he himself was an aristocrat, did not join the other aristocrats in accepting the cant of the middle class. He had been made indignant by the retreat from the great democratic principles, and he had continued to look forward to the establishment of a genuine republic governed by the people.

Byron had taken as his subject, Arnold said, not the fantasy of Shelley but the "upholders of the old order, George the Third and Lord Castlereagh and the Duke of Wellington and Southey, and they were the canters and tramplers of the great world, and they were his enemies and himself" (*PW*, 9:233). Byron's greatness, Arnold thought, lay in his having seized the great subject and in having pursued it with great poetic energy. Insofar as the character of the man is significant, this was his character: "Such was Byron's personality, by which 'he is different from all the rest of the English poets, and in the main greater' " (PW, 9:233). To those, such as Scherer, who saw Byron as a theatrical personality, Arnold addressed the argument that he had used in the case of Shelley and of Wordsworth. Arnold once more invented a myth of poetic creation, corresponding to the one by which he had separated Wordsworth's character from his creation. When Byron had begun to write poetry, Arnold said, he had set aside his ordinary self, and "he became another man . . . ; then a higher power took possession of him and filled him; then at last came forth into light that true and puissant personality, with its direct strokes, its ever-welling force, its satire, its energy, and its agony. This is the real Byron" (PW, 9:233). But the real Byron was the Byron of the poetry.

As in the essay on Shelley, Arnold did not separate the practical effect of poetry from social and political effect. Byron could not lead the way to the future: "The way out of the false state of things which enraged him he did not see,—the slow and laborious way upward; he had not the patience, knowledge, self-discipline, virtue, requisite for seeing it" (PW, 9:234). What Arnold was looking for was not the visionary or the prophetic poet; it was the patient, disciplined thinker; Byron had lacked judgment. What he could accomplish in poetry through feeling he had done:

Along with his astounding power and passion he had a strong and deep sense for what is beautiful in nature, and for what is beautiful in human action and suffering. When he warms to his work, when he is inspired, Nature herself seems to take the pen from him as she took it from Wordsworth, and to write for him as she wrote for Wordsworth, though in a different fashion, with her own penetrating simplicity. (PW, 9:234)

In the same way, then, Arnold attributed to Byron's poetry an effect of sincerity, which has been achieved in the myth by Nature and in fact by the art of the poet.

If we look at the famous passage in which Arnold attributed sincerity to Byron, we see that what Arnold was praising was Byron's sincerity in political feeling, his devotion to a cause. This is shown by the context in which Arnold, writing, as he may have sensed, one of his last essays, outlined the future for which he himself hoped:

> As the inevitable break-up of the old order comes, as the English middle-class slowly awakens from its intellectual sleep of two centuries, as our actual present world, to which this sleep has condemned us, shows itself more clearly,—our world of an aristocracy materialised and null, a middle class purblind and hideous, a lower class crude and brutal,—we shall turn our eyes again, and to more purpose, upon this passionate and dauntless soldier of a forlorn hope, who, ignorant of the future and unconsoled by its promises, nevertheless waged against the conservation of the old impossible world so fiery a battle; waged it till he fell,—waged it with splendid and imperishable excellence of sincerity and strength. (PW, 9:236)

Again, in the use of the word *sincerity* there is something unexpected, which defeats both our usual sense of the word and the sense in which Algernon Charles Swinburne (from whom Arnold borrowed the phrase "sincerity and strength") used it. Arnold spoke about an excellence of sincerity, and we see that what Arnold meant was the excellence of the performance, the intense energy that Byron had given to his cause and to the poetry that he had written in that cause. Sincerity thus becomes indistinguishable from the poetic activity.

In comparing Byron to Wordsworth, Arnold threw some light on what he meant by poetic truth: "Wordsworth has an insight into permanent sources of joy and consolation for mankind which Byron has not; his poetry gives us more which we may rest upon than Byron's,—more which we can rest upon now, and which men may rest upon always" (*PW*, 9:236). Poetic truth—a criticism of life—is derived from insight (a function also of the *phronimos*, the rational man who has an insight into the rational order of the universe and into man's place within that order). It is this insight, not any system of philosophic truth, that is the truth of poetry.

Like the essay on Byron, the essay "Amiel" stated once more Arnold's critical positions; it clarified and illuminated what he had worked out in the better-known essays.[27] Arnold first took up the question of sincerity. Critics, Arnold said, had praised Amiel's journal for its sincerity, and Arnold agreed: "The sincerity is unquestionable" (*PW*, 11:267). Arnold denied, however, that Henri Frédéric Amiel possessed great gifts of eloquence and expression, and Arnold tried to define the "magic of style" by an appeal to creative activity: "Magic of style is creative: its possessor himself creates, and he inspires and enables his reader in some sort to create after him. And creation gives the sense of life and joy; hence its extraordinary value" (*PW*, 11:268). Thus, Arnold once more stated his essential position: poetry is a creative activity, and in such activity is to be found happiness. Here, Arnold made clear the link between creation and style, a link that he had implied, as we have seen, in "The Function of Criticism at the Present Time," when Arnold had held that criticism, so far as it was art, was also a creative activity. Moreover, great artists find a unique style and in this sense discover or create their selves. Finally, Arnold suggested that the reader shares in this creative activity and, hence, in the sense of life and joy of creation. Arnold did not develop the idea of the reader's sharing in the creation of poetry through the magic of style, but some such idea is implicit in Arnold's idea of a poetry for a democracy, in which the poetry for the people is not only the folk ballad, which is thought to be their own creation, but also the poetry of Homer, Dante, and Shakespeare or of Byron and Wordsworth.

Arnold once more dismissed the pretensions to philosophic thought which are claimed by poets and their critics. Scherer found that Amiel's philosophy was profound; Arnold, who had labored in the study of far greater philosophies, picked up Scherer's empty phrase "on a far other scale of vastness" and took it as the key to this "profound" philosophy, quoting passages that are nonsensical, which Arnold labels "perfectly futile" (PW, 11:269–70). Arnold admitted the attraction of the yearning for the infinite, but he insisted that

> the thoughts which have positive truth and value, the thoughts to be lived with and dwelt upon, the thoughts which are a real acquisition for our minds, are precisely thoughts which counteract the "vague aspiration and indeterminate desire" possessing Amiel and filling his Journal: they are thoughts insisting on the need of limit, the feasibility of performance. (PW, 11:272)

Arnold, like Locke, insisted on the need for limits: "The ideas to live with," according to Arnold, were "ideas staunchly counteracting and reducing the power of the infinite and indeterminate, not paralysing us with it" (PW, 11:272). Arnold approved of Amiel's resolve that men have a calling to be happy: " 'To live is to conquer incessantly; one must have the courage to be happy. I turn in a vicious circle; I have never had clear sight of my true vocation' " (PW, 11:273). What Arnold could not approve was the vague "philosophising," the claim to visionary insight: "I cannot join in celebrating his prodigies of speculative intuition, the glow and splendour of his beautific vision of absolute knowledge, the marvellous pages in which his deep and vast philosophic thought is laid bare, the secret of his malady is expressed" (PW, 11:273). Arnold thus set limits to the function of literature; he set it off from philosophic thought, from speculative intuition, from visionary dreaming.

The essay on Amiel asserted once more the Arnoldian principles. Sincerity is not a test of literary worth. Arnold agreed that Amiel had sincerity, but he showed that sincerity was not enough for greatness in art. Amiel, critics said, had a profound philosophy; Arnold reduced this pretentious claim to absurdity. Most important of all is Arnold's criticism of what has come to be seen as one of the defining characteristics of Romanticism—the aspiration for the infinite. Arnold's distrust of the yearning for the infinite, his feeling that only paralysis follows from dreaming or dwelling upon the infinite and the indeterminate, was a corollary of his insistence on performance, on "the feasibility of performance." This is the essential basis for Arnold's criticism: poetry is an activity, as criticism in an activity; and in the performance of the activity, as poet or as reader, lies happiness. Arnold's judgment of the poets confirm this view. Byron, judged by his performance, ranked with Wordsworth as one of the two great poets of the century. Although there were explanations for the inferior performance of Shelley, Keats, and Gray in the obstructions of the external world or in the deficiencies of the self, finally what mattered was not what the poet dreamed but what he did—not his promise, but his performance.

Chapter Eight

The Classic and Classical Poetry

The connection between Arnold's idea of the classic, which in "The Study of Poetry" referred to the best poetry, and his idea of classical poetry is both obvious and subtle. In part, the idea of the classic arises out of Arnold's early conviction that the Greek poets of the Periclean Age should be models for the young English poets, advice that he gave in the 1853 Preface; and in part it extends the notion of the modern spirit which, he thought, could be found in the ancients. But in a more subtle way, the idea expressed Arnold's early vision of the perfect freedom of poetry. Poetry should be bound neither by place nor by time, by nation nor by party, by culture nor by people. It should not be required to be anything at all but the best possible poetry. The best poetry should be known, not by any set of rules or conventions, but by a free-ranging criticism of a reader who is well versed in the poetry of the world. Even the high seriousness that Arnold, almost reluctantly, identified as the mark of a classic was the art achieved by a poet who is totally dedicated to the craft and is performing at the highest level.

That Arnold's classic was also a poetry for the people must seem inconsistent, if not paradoxical, to those who assume that the people, if they have a literature of their own, must have folk songs or music-hall songs, Border ballads or the Beatles. Such criticism continues the arguments of Shairp, an interesting example of how the ideas of a nineteenth-century conservative come to seem very like those of some twen-

173

tieth-century critics. Shairp's ideas, however, were corrected by the Classical scholar Sellar, who wrote with a strong sense of reality learned form his study of Roman literature. In this chapter, I will review the later criticism of Shairp and Sellar, both as representative of a body of criticism and as a background for Arnold's idea of the classic.

Shairp attacked Arnold's positions that were set out in the criticism of the 1860s—the assertion that Homer did "refine the raw natural man" (*PW*, 1:139) and the belief that classical poetry is accessible to the ordinary person, given an intelligent and educated people. Arnold's ideas came under attack in Shairp's *Culture and Religion* (1872), in which Shairp argued, in "The Literary Theory of Culture," that culture that is literary and aesthetic is accessible, not to the ordinary people, to the multitude, but only to the few.[1] Shairp's argument was essentially conservative; it was opposed, as he himself said, to the Enlightenment, to humanism, and to ideas of progress and perfectibility; it is not dissimilar to some of the conservative thought of the twentieth century. The evil in the heart of man, he argued, cannot be touched by humanism (*CR*, p. 99).

In respect to the lower classes, it is clear that Shairp thought of the common people as static and as incapable of intellectual thought or appreciation of complex aesthetic works though able to make songs and ballads; Arnold's criticism, Shairp feared, would not only destroy their creativity but also their faith (*CR*, pp. 109–20). In his Oxford lectures, collected in *Aspects of Poetry* (1881), Shairp reiterated points in the old debate, which had begun in his review of Arnold's poems in 1854, and argued for a poetry of the people. Not from books or from the classical past come the materials for such poetry; nor are the classical writers either models or standards of criticism. Rather, the sources of poetry are in the folk: "From the poetry of the people has been drawn most of what is truest, most human-hearted, in the greatest poems."[2] Modern poets must follow the popular balladists in observing life: "If the poetry of any, even the most advanced, age, is to retain that eternal freshness, which is its finest grace, it must draw both its materials and its impulses more from sympathy with the people than from past poets, more from the heart of man than from books" (*AP*, p. 21). Poems are made, in Shairp's view, not from other poems, but from incidents of actual life and from the actual language of genuine emotion, especially of the common people (*AP*, p. 22), even though actual life, in Shairp's view, was not so broad as to include the "morbid self-analysis" of some modern poets (*AP*, p. 23). Shairp, it should be remarked, had not liked Clough's *Amours de Voyage*; nor did Shairp think that life was to be recorded "objectively."

Summarizing what he called the aesthetic critics, he quoted Arnold's phrase, " 'to see life steadily and to see it whole' "; this, as Shairp understood the "aesthetic poets," was their aim—to represent life faithfully as it is and without moral judgment (*AP*, pp. 29–30). This seems to be an odd reading of Arnold's phrase, and perhaps Shairp meant other poets than Arnold. But Shairp was using the phrase from his early review of Arnold—that the poets fail to lay "a strong hearthold of any side of human interest" (*AP*, p. 29).

In a lecture on the early poetry of Scotland, Shairp returned to the distinction that he had made in his review of Arnold's poems—the difference between literary and popular poetry. The first borrows from other cultures forms such as meter, language, and even sentiments; the second is written in native forms and in the vernacular.[3] In his early review, Shairp had made it evident that poetry is bound to its culture, in the sense of regional or national life. For this reason, the poetry of the Greeks could no longer be of any interest to modern Europeans or to the English, let alone to the Scottish.

Here Shairp took up another question—the effect that civilization and a learned literature have on popular poetry. In the earlier history of the ballad, the "rude but genuine poetry of the people" had been crushed, or so he thought, by a literary poetry; but the recovery of the ballad had "revivified the whole body of England's poetry" ("EP," pp. 224–26), as Scott, Burns, and Wordsworth were inspired by the old forms. Now, for the young poet, Shairp prescribed, along with the *Iliad* and the *Odyssey*, the ballads as "the finest, freshest, most inspiring poetic education that is possible in our age. So furnished [a young poet] might well neglect more than half of modern poetry" ("EP," p. 238). It will be recalled that Shairp had seen Homer as being like the ballad poets or even the modern novelists in his direct transcription of life; it is for this reason, perhaps, that Shairp allowed the young poets to study the *Iliad* and the *Odyssey.* Shairp thus was attempting to overturn the principle that Arnold had set forth in the 1853 Preface— namely, that the Greek tragic writers were the best models for young poets—and to overturn Arnold's assertion in "The Function of Criticism at the Present Time" that criticism prepares the way for poetry. Rather, the sources of the great Romantic poetry lay in the creative imagination and in the spontaneity of the native and popular poetry.

In the next lecture, "Criticism and Creation," Shairp continued to argue against Arnold that criticism, by setting in motion a current of new ideas, would not produce an age of poetry, but would, in fact, crush poetry. Of Burns, Shairp said "Wider knowledge would have paralysed his singing power" (*AP,* p. 46). Genuine poetry, Shairp said, "originates in a high enthusiasm, a noble passion overmastering the soul" (*AP,* p. 48). Indeed, Shairp went so far as to say: "By the flashes of uncritical genius the world has gained its finest truths"(*AP,* p. 51). Furthermore, Shairp thought, poets must speak to the young and to the majority of their audience, who are neither learned nor moved by learning. Like the great English poets, they would find their materials in "the actual life of men, the face of nature, their own hearts" (*AP,* p. 53). Shairp did not subscribe to the Aristotelian principle that all men desire to learn.

Although at first glance Shairp's view seems to be democratic, because he advocated a poetry of and for the people, Shairp's ideas were essentially feudal, as appears in his discussion of Scott and Wordsworth. Shairp praised Scott because he had turned "the tide against the Illumination"—that is,

the Enlightenment—had begun the medieval revival, had revived Scottish nationalism, and above all, had discovered the
peasant: "And not the past only, with its heroic figures, but
the lowly peasant life of his own time, he first revealed to the
world in its worth and beauty" (*AP,* pp. 105-7).[4] Scott was
linked, in Shairp's view, to a feudal hierarchy, in which the
peasants kept their place in the social order, where they exhibited noble virtues. Shairp, indeed, opposed the radicalism that
would change the life or character of the peasant.

Much of Shairp's view of the rustics as the source of
poetry was derived from his reading of Wordsworth, and here,
too, his discussion revealed a preference for a feudal order.
Shairp saw Wordsworth, not as democratic, but as aiming at
"a moral and spiritual aristocracy," though not one that is exclusive, but one that is open to those who have the strength
to rise to "moral heights" (*AP,* p. 116). Wordsworth, Shairp
thought, did not care for either education or "culture, literary,
aesthetic, scientific." None of these, Shairp implied, would
improve the condition of the lowliest, who already possessed
moral worth and character. (*AP,* pp. 115-16).

As for the rustics being the source of poetry and poetic
language, in "Poetic Style in Modern English Poetry," Shairp
noticed an argument that told against his theory. Coleridge
had pointed out the deficiencies in Wordsworth's theory that
the language of peasants was a "real," and therefore a poetic,
language (*AP,* p. 135); and Shairp, in a brief summary of Coleridge's argument, showed that he was aware of Coleridge's
questions about a "real" language: "The language of the most
educated writers, Hooker, Bacon, Burke, is as real as that of
any peasant, while it covers a far wider range of ideas, feelings,
and experiences" (*AP,* p. 137). Yet Shairp did not, in this essay
or in any other, show that he thought Coleridge's criticism
of Wordsworth's theory of poetic language had had any effect
on his own argument that the people are creators, uttering
in their own language a natural, spontaneous song.

One reason, no doubt, was that Shairp's attention was on
another question; he had called Coleridge in as a witness

against Arnold, who had observed that Wordsworth had no style. In fact, Coleridge's main argument would have supported Arnold in regard to the importance of culture and education to literary style. It is true that in this essay, which is mainly about style, Shairp came closest to Arnold in recognizing that the "natural" was an effect of art, that it was not really effortless or unconscious: "To be able to be natural, yet artistic, it is this which distinguishes true literary genius" (AP, p. 125). Although this essay contains signs that Shairp was aware of arguments against his belief in the people as artists, he continued to use the arguments that he had announced in his first review of Arnold's poems.

Although Shairp did not recommend the classical poets as models for English poets, he was looking, as Froude had done, for evidence of the love of the country people in classical poets, thus attempting to rescue some of Vergil for the modern age. In "Virgil as a Religious Poet," in which Shairp began by quoting Froude's *Caesar* on the death of the old religions in Rome, Shairp noted that Vergil, who still retained faith in the old gods, was isolated in the Augustan world (AP, p. 165).[5] Vergil had shaped a "composite . . . theology," which had begun with his "love for the old rustic gods," for "his first impressions were of the country and the country people" (AP, p. 167). Shairp said of the *Georgics:* "That greatest of didactic poems is Virgil's tribute to his love of Italian scenery, and to his interest in Italian rustics, among whom he had spent his childhood and youth" (AP, p. 175). Even in the *Aeneid*, Vergil had turned to the country people: "The country housewife going about her work pleases him more than the grandest of patrician matrons" (AP, p. 188). Vergil's great and famous phrase "These are the things of tears" was interpreted to indicate his "remembrance of the poor, and his feeling for the miserable" (AP, p. 188). In this way, Shairp turned the Augustan poet into one who had loved the rustic life. The classic, by inference, is the poem that reaches the common people.

Shairp's idealization of country life was different from the world that was being drawn in the Victorian novels, and it was

certainly different from the life of the farmers and miners that
Hardy and Lawrence were to write about, when the morbid
self-analysis that Shairp deplored in the modern poets was
claimed as a right of the people. Shairp's people have more
in common with the Scottish farmers of Clough's *Bothie*,
which the Balliol group admired, and are in part derived from
his own travels in the Scottish highlands. Shairp tended to
see the people as being blessed in their simple life; they are
moral and worthy, a source and subject of poetry. Nonetheless,
Shairp's respect for them contained a determinism as fixed
as that of the naturalists, since Shairp held that any change
would destroy their life and character. Arnold, in contrast,
allowed to the people as much range of character as he allowed
the middle or upper classes, and Arnold's plan for education
would have allowed the people as much range of literature.

Arnold had argued in 1853 that the Greek poets were the
best models for the young poets; but Shairp and others had
condemned this as sterile imitation. In writing the history
of Roman literature, Sellar had to deal with the fact that the
Romans had, for the most part, translated and imitated the
epics and plays of Greece; he had to consider whether they
had thus failed to create a new and original literature. Sellar
began by dismissing the notion that imitation was necessarily
failure; he asserted that "Roman poetry was the living heir,
not the lifeless reproduction of the genius of Greece."[6] He
ended his opening survey of Roman literature by saying that
the Romans indeed had used the forms of "a foreign art" but
that these had been "executed with native energy, and expres-
sive of native character" (*RPR*, p. 26). Sellar thought, as Shairp
did, that there were dangers in using the forms of Greek art—
the danger that poetry would be imitative, not original, and
that it would not be entirely a "native" art. Concerned about
a national and even an ethnic art, as Shairp was, Sellar considered Greek literature to be foreign, as alien to the Romans as
to modern Europeans. Shairp had gone even further in asserting that a "Teutonic" mind could take no interest in Greek

gods and heroes. Arnold, on the other hand, saw art as universal; his idea of the classic held that poetry could transcend local and national boundaries.

Connected to the notion of a local or national poetry was the idea of a poetry of a people. Shairp had argued that a great national poetry was a natural outgrowth from the early songs and ballads of the people and thus that a great poetry was necessarily a creation of the folk. The question that Sellar had to consider for Roman poetry was the one raised by Barthold Georg Niebuhr and by Thomas Macaulay—namely, whether the early Romans had had a "native minstrelsy," one "of plebeian origin, strongly animated by plebeian sentiment, and familiarly known among the mass of the people (*RPR*, pp. 28–29). Niebuhr and Macaulay had thought that they saw traces of such ballads and epic poems surviving in the early legends of Roman history (*RPR*, pp. 28–29). Sellar, after reviewing the evidence for an early native poetry, finally decided against Niebuhr's theory. Sellar thought that no such poetry had ever existed, nor, given the life of the Roman farmers, that it could have arisen. In the Saturnian and Fescennine poetry, Sellar saw evidence of a hearty but rude, primitive, and uncouth peasantry (*RPR*, pp. 30–38). Although Sellar was willing to allow that a "native minstrelsy" could arise and had arisen on the Scottish Border, he did not find in primitive life any inspiration for spontaneous poetry. Further, in arguing against Niebuhr, Sellar pointed out that if there had been a great national poetry or a rich popular poetry in early Rome, it would not have disappeared so quickly and completely as Niebuhr supposed (*RPR*, p. 39). In developing this point, Sellar acknowledged the importance of a long literary tradition for the creation of a great poetry. Homer was not, Sellar thought, a rude or primitive bard; rather, Homer had drawn on a tradition that had been perfected by a long line of poets. In contrast, the Roman poet Ennius, had written in the rough and unpolished verse of a poet who had no such tradition behind him (*RPR*, p. 39).

The other question that Sellar illuminated was the division between a small educated class and the people. Roman comedy had drawn on a tradition of popular entertainment; "Naevius and Plautus might thus be poets of the people more truly than and later Roman poet could be" (*RPR*, pp. 156–57). Although Plautus could thus appeal to both classes, with Ennius begins the division between the classes; in the later Roman Empire, the lower classes turned to games and sports, while the aristocrats preferred imitations of Greek literature, such as the plays of Terence (*RPR*, pp. 206–11). Sellar thus saw in Rome some of the problems that Shairp and Arnold thought were important in the Victorian age, especially the separation between the classes and the rise of a literature that was polished and urbane but imitative.

The idea of the classic is illuminated by Sellar's criticism of Lucretius. Sellar points out that Lucretius was not in any sense a popular poet, either among the educated class in Rome or among the people, nor did Lucretius himself have any illusions about the people or about primitive life: "The privations and rude misery of savage life are painted in as sombre colours as the satiety and discontent of his own age" (*RPR*, p. 376). For Sellar, as for Arnold, Lucretius was the most interesting of the Roman poets of the Republic. But where Arnold had in 1857 seen Lucretius as a melancholic who had turned away from the great spectacle of Roman life, Sellar found in the Roman poet the exemplar of the Victorian idea of the creative genius, a poet who had found his own nature, found his own subject, and pursued it with "impassioned earnestness" (*RPR*, p. 295).

Sellar, indeed, escaped from a false opposition of intellect and emotion; he borrowed from Plato the idea of a philosophical passion or an intellectual emotion. Although as a literary artist, Lucretius had failed to combine the disparate elements of his poem—art, science, scientific discourse, poetic intuition, detailed observation, and poetic fancy—still his intellectual passion carries the reader along; the effect is that of being

borne along by a strong enthusiasm,—the philosophical *erōs* of Plato,—different from, but akin to, the impulses of poetry. That marvellous intensity of feeling in conjunction with the operations of the intellect, which the Greeks regarded as a kind of divine possession and which Lucretius, by the use of such phrases as "divinitus invenientes," ascribes to the earliest enquirers, animates all his interpretation of the facts and laws of Nature. (RPR, p. 388)

Although Sellar had little sympathy with the Epicurean moral philosophy of the poem and had still less with the scientific theory, he admired the poet who had found his great theme, to which he had devoted all his powers, with "impassioned earnestness."

As I have suggested earlier, Sellar's discussion of "imaginative reason" clarified Arnold's use of that term. "Impassioned earnestness" seems to recall the "high seriousness" of Arnold. Although there is a similarity in the dedication of the poet, who commits his entire intellectual and emotional energy to his work, Arnold meant by "high seriousness," not the enthusiastic exposition of an idea, but the skillful performance of a great art. Both Shairp and Sellar made literary art secondary to philosophical thought or to inspiration or to feeling. It was Lucretius's passion, Sellar argued, that gave to the whole poem its effect, carrying the reader, as it were, in great flights over the deserts and dry places of scientific exposition. Nonetheless, Sellar did grasp the fact that there is joy in intellectual inquiry (an idea that is important to Arnold's idea of criticism), that there is a philosophical erōs. Thus Sellar escaped from the trap of the romantic cliché of the cold intellect or reason—Tennyson's "the freezing reason's colder part." Escaping from the false dilemma of choosing between intellect and emotion, Sellar thus could assign to Lucretius the rank of classic poet.

When Sellar turned to the poetry of the Augustan age, he came to see Vergil as a classic in Arnold's sense of the word. Sellar's book on Vergil showed that he had much in mind both Arnold's criticism and his poetry. Although Sellar did not refer to Arnold's 1853 Preface, he confirmed Arnold's point that the Greek tragic writers wisely had chosen subjects from the past rather than from contemporary life.[7] Sellar referred to Arnold's phrase the "disinterested objectivity" of Greek art (*RPA*, p. 158), and Sellar's ideas about the epic and contemporary life paralleled those of Arnold in the 1857 lecture. More than once, Sellar called on Arnold to illustrate a point about Vergil. Sellar quoted from "The Scholar-Gipsy" on Dido's flying from Aeneas in Hades (*RPA*, p. 408); he cited "Thyrsis" as one of the modern pastoral elegies descended from the "Lament of Bion" (*RPA*, pp. 155–56); and on "the stream of epic poetry" he quoted from the concluding lines of Arnold's epic fragment "Sohrab and Rustum" (*RPA*, p. 310). Clearly, Sellar had thought about Arnold's classical poetry and his criticism.

After his long study of Vergil, which was preceded by his study of Lucretius, Sellar had by 1876 moved nearer to Arnold's positions; he asserted the value of the great classics of the civilized eras; and he included Homer, once more, not among the primitive or ballad poets, but among the great artists. Sellar saw Homer and Sophocles as "poets of a whole people" (*RPA*, p. 30), as he had in the early essays of the 1850s; in contrast, he saw Vergil as a poet who had written for a small aristocratic class (*RPA*, p. 307). In looking at the distinction between "primitive" and "literary epic," "one of the commonplaces of criticism," Sellar corrected some of the ideas that had been generated by these categories. True, he agreed that the primitive had developed "out of some germ of popular ballad or national legend" and that it had arisen from an "immediate sympathy between poet and people" (*RPA*, p. 280).

So far, Sellar agreed with Shairp in the characteristics of a poetry of the people. But although Homer belonged, Sellar thought, to the early stages of Greek poetry, yet Homer's poems were "masterpieces of art and great monuments of the national mind":

It was the peculiar glory of Greece, that in the earlier stage of her literary development she manifested not only a perfection of expression and of art, but a maturity of intelligence, a true insight into the meaning of life, a nobility of imagination in union with a clearness and sanity of judgment which the most advanced eras of other literatures scarcely equal. (*RPA*, pp. 280–81)

This passage might have been intended as a summary of Arnold's Homeric criticism were it not that the phrases are demonstrably Sellar's in his own early essay on Thucydides. Like Arnold, Sellar would not include Homer among the ballad poets or among the primitive bards. In Sellar's view, Homer did not belong to the earliest times, but Homer had succeeded in "living the imaginative life of an earlier time" (*RPA*, p. 361) by the force of his art and by his imagination's negating the limits of time and place. Sellar has come close to Arnold's idea of the classic, the great work of art that is not bound by time, place, or literary tradition. But Sellar offers a criticism of life that is valid universally and a perfection of art that cannot be explained by literary history.

Sellar, like Arnold, did not set aside the artist in favor of the unsophisticated poet. Sellar observed that the reputation of Vergil had declined as interest had grown in the primitive epics of various nations and in the history of the language (*RPA*, pp. 71–74). But while he approved these useful studies, he did not give to science the rights of literary criticism. Rather, he deplored "the disparagement of the great works of cultivated areas" and the neglect of "the superior grace, richness, and power which are imparted to ordinary speech by the labours of intellect and imagination employed in creating a national literature" (*RPA*, p. 75). Sellar, in this book, which he wrote as part of a long study of the national literature of Rome, gave to Arnold's positions the support of a scholarly critic. Sellar affirmed the value of the great Roman classics, and at the same time he affirmed the even greater value of the Greek classics, the poets of a great democracy.

At the conclusion of "The Study of Poetry," Arnold turned from the idea of the classic—to be known simply by "using

the poetry" of the great classics as a sort of touchstone"—to
the opposite idea, that of a popular literature intended for the
masses:

> We are often told that an era is opening in which we are
> to see multitudes of a common sort of readers, and masses
> of a common sort of literature; that such readers do not
> want and could not relish anything better than such litera-
> ture, and that to provide it is becoming a vast and profit-
> able industry. Even if good literature entirely lost currency
> with the world, it would still be abundantly worth while
> to continue to enjoy it by oneself. But it never will lose
> currency with the world, in spite of momentary appear-
> ances; it never will lose supremacy. Currency and suprem-
> acy are insured to it, not indeed by the world's deliberate
> and conscious choice, but by something far deeper,—by
> the instinct of self-preservation in humanity. (PW, 9:188)

Arnold's criticism had been addressed as much to the common reader as to the educated few. He invited the reader to
share in his inquiry, as in the Preface to *Merope* he described
the Greek theater in a way that neither condescends to the
common reader nor offends the scholar. In the *Essays in Criticism*, by means of frequent illustration, copious quotation,
and lively passages of translation, as of Theocritus, Arnold
brings his reader into the critical activity, into the business
of reading, understanding, and even judging. In "The Study
of Poetry" the touchstones allow the reader to share in the
activity of reading poetry, of trying on the individual palate
the taste of the classic. Arnold did not offer complex definitions, numbered sets of characteristics of epic or tragedy, and
an arcane or scientific-looking set of terms. Criticism, Arnold
insisted, is open-minded and flexible. He relied instead on that
he called *tact*, a word akin to *flexibility*—keeping a light
touch, not being carried away into elaborate systems. His critical essays, including those that he gave as lectures at Oxford,
were addressed to those who read only English; he spoke on

the translation of Homer, not on Homer's Greek; and he delivered his lectures in English, not in Latin, as had been the tradition. His last critical essays were almost entirely on the English poets. Even his occasional quotations in Greek or Latin or Italian were usually brief, like the touchstones, and were intended, not as a display of erudite or esoteric learning, but as illustrations of his point that a classic is independent of time or place.

One of the unfinished projects that Arnold planned between 1867 and 1872 was a guide to Greek poetry.[8] William Buckler has suggested a reason why Arnold postponed the book in the decade from 1865 to 1875: "Like Ruskin at almost the same time, he [Arnold] felt that he must turn from the pleasures of the few to the welfare of the many" (p. 267). Yet the project seems to have been directed at least to the common reader; Buckler has pointed out that Arnold's revisions in *Culture and Anarchy* in 1875 were directed toward "the popular reader" (p. 264). If one looks about in Arnold's published works for essays that might have gone into the anthology, the translation and commentary on Theocritus's "Fifteenth Idyll" comes to mind; on drama, there is the Preface to *Merope*; and on epic, there are the essays on translating Homer. Arnold at one time proposed "The Modern Element on Literature" as an introduction, although he had some doubts about its "antiquity" in 1869, when *Macmillan's* published the article, and about its "high-horse academic style" (p. 265). The guide, Buckler has noted, was encouraged by the publisher because he sensed a "popular interest in the classics" (p. 267). To this project may be added Arnold's editions of the English poets. Arnold, in choosing to discuss the poetry of Robert Burns in "The Study of Poetry" must have been aware that Burns was one of the poets whose works had continued to sell during the nineteenth century.[9] Arnold, then, was trying, in these editions, to make the classics available to the common reader. In the activities, Arnold does not seem to have been defending the classics against democratic masses; rather, he was trying to make them available.[10]

Arnold's criticism was not exclusive; he admitted some of Burns's poetry to the rank of the classic and compared poems such as "The Jolly Beggars" to the best poems in the language. Although the test of a good poem is not, finally, its national or regional tradition, Arnold did not exclude poems in any tradition. Indeed, the range of literatures considered throughout Arnold's criticism is wide, embracing the Persian as well as the Russian, welcoming the new as well as the old. Again, an open mind and flexibility were characteristics of Arnold's criticism. Arnold's defense of Greek poetry was against critics such as Shairp, who insisted that the Greeks had nothing to say to modern England or to Scotland or to any of the "Teutonic" race. Such criticism rested on a dangerously narrow ethnocentrism, not in making a claim for the value of Scottish poetry but in asserting that there was no value in the poetry of the ancient Greeks and that the Greeks were too remote from modern life to arouse any emotional or intellectual response.

The matter of the availability of a classic to people in other places or times continues to be a subject for critical discussion. In Arnold's time there was the question not only of whether the English people in the Victorian period could read the Greek classical writers but also of whether the people of the United States could read British literature. When Arnold looked at the literature of the United States, he found little that was adequate for the new political and social life that had been brought forth in the new world. In the last of Arnold's essays, "Civilisation in the United States," Arnold pointed out how far short the civilization falls of any distinction. In reading Arnold's criticism of the nineteenth-century American civilization, one must be aware that he tended to see the United States of the age of Jackson. Arnold still relied on the study by Alexis de Tocqueville and continued to quote a phrase from Michelet which had appeared in one of his early letters in 1848. There is something rather grand in Arnold's sweeping condemnation of a continent as having no interesting landscapes, or entire cities as having no interesting archi-

tecture, and of American statesmen as being without distinction, especially when his list does not include either Thomas
Jefferson or James Madison.

Yet, although Arnold's idea of the landscapes of America
was limited, it is clear that in this essay he was concerned,
as he had been all his life, with the literature of a democracy.
The feature of the literary landscape that he hit upon was "a
native author called Roe": "the Western States are at this
moment being nourished and formed, we hear, on the novels
of a native author called Roe, instead of those of Scott and
Dickens" (PW, 11:364).[11] Edward Payson Roe, a popular writer,
duly noted and resented Arnold's allusion in a brief piece in
which he took the title from Arnold's phrase.[12] Roe saw himself as the champion of democratic literature: "Certainly, if
I had my choice, I would rather write a book interesting to
the young and to the common people, whom Lincoln said,
'God must love, since He made so many of them' " (p. 23).
Roe thus took his stand with the popular hero who Arnold
had said lacked distinction, though he was a representative
American. Roe's defense of culture in the western states, however, rested on the fact that people were buying the books of
Scott and Dickens.

Although there is no evidence that Arnold had ever read
any novel by Roe, if he had read only the opening chapter of
Roe's most famous novel, *Barriers Burned Away*, he would have
recognized the story that in *Culture and Anarchy* Arnold himself had made the emblem of the present state of culture in
England, the story of the young man who feared that " 'he
would come to poverty, and that he was eternally lost' " (PW,
5:186– 87). The twin fears of Arnold's young man were reflected
in the story of the father of the young hero, a failure and a skep-
tic. All of the father's schemes for new inventions and hoped-
for wealth have failed; although there is still time for his religious conversion, nothing can be done to change his permanent
consignment to the ranks of the poor.[13] Arnold, although he
was too optimistic in assuring the Americans that they had
solved their social and political problems, had an insight into

the general life that Roe unintentionally confirmed in the opening scene of his novel.

Although Arnold was not inclined to see any distinction in American civilization, in an earlier essay, "Numbers," he had advanced the idea that the "remnant" might eventually leaven the culture (PW, 10:145–46). Although it appears that Arnold's appeal to the "remnant" was to a select few, actually Arnold thought that, given the size of populations in modern society, the remnant would be a great power: "A remnant of how great numbers, how mighty strength, how irresistible efficacy!" (PW, 10:163). The notion of the remnant ceases to have the meaning of a select group, and such a remnant might change American society.

The question of whether anyone can read a classic of another time and place became important as emphasis shifted in criticism from the idea of a general human nature and universal truths to a emphasis on national, regional, or class culture; a sense of barriers raised between past and present increased the difficulty, so that an extreme view is that it becomes impossible to read any work as the author and the audience understood it.[14] Arnold addressed some of these questions, especially in the lectures "On the Modern Element in Literature" and on Homer. Although Arnold in the earlier lectures had said that literature appeals to the "great primary human affections" (PW, 1:4), in his criticism of epic poetry he acknowledged that epic relied for effect on descriptions of customs and manners that were "local and transient"; it was for this reason that he thought that the Aeneid failed in trying to report the historical details of a past time. Homer, Arnold thought, described a time near to Homer's own (PW, 1:34–35).

In arguing the question of how Homer's language was to be translated into English, Arnold acknowledged that there was a barrier of language between the translator and the ancient poet, "alien modes of thinking, speaking, and feeling," but he thought the barrier could be surmounted by a poet and the judgment might be referred to a scholar with poetic sensibility, such as Jowett (PW, 1:103, 99). Certainly, Arnold found differences in national character such as influenced the kind of natural description found in Greek and Celtic poetry. Yet in general he held that it was not only possible but also salutary to try to comprehend the literature of another time and place.

Indeed, this was the function of criticism, to make known the best that has been thought and said. As in his drama *Merope*, to make either the new or the old available depended on the effort of the critic and the reader; Arnold hoped to show through *Merope* the Greek imagination—that is, the imagination that shapes a work of art. Although in part what is universal is a certain kind of truth, some poets whose work possesses truth are not classics, such as Dryden, Pope, and Chaucer, though in Chaucer there is to be found "a criticism of life" that "has largeness, freedom, shrewdness, benignity" (*PW*, 9:176–77). Arnold, though he did not say this, may in fact have been thinking that comedy and irony are least likely to be understood in another time or place, but there is another explanation in "high seriousness."

The "high seriousness" of the classic is connected to the highest performance in poetry, the greatest art, as in drama, a structure of plot or action deriving from character. Such structures may have a universal appeal. What Arnold had arrived at through the idea of poetry as an activity was a recognition that poetry was not directed towards a passive audience but that the reader of poetry or the audience of a drama in some degree shared in creative activity. As Arnold had described the *catharsis* of drama, the response is complex: the audience, through a high state of thought and emotion, is brought to a sense of understanding the complexity of life. In the same way, in "The Function of Criticism at the Present Time," Arnold had said that the reader has a sense of sharing in creative activity, whether of the poet or the critic—the joy of discovering new ideas. In "Amiel," Arnold said: "Magic of style is creative: its possessor himself creates, and he inspires and enables his reader in some sort to create after him. And creation gives the sense of life and joy; hence its extraordinary value" (*PW*, 11:268). This kind of creation Arnold had tried to make available to the public in his poetry and his criticism; in his selections of poems from Wordsworth and Byron he wrote introductions aimed at the "common intelligence" (*PW*, 9:337–38).

Arnold's last great critical essays grew out of his faith that the best poetry could be made available to all the people. Even earlier he was not defending the classics against the democratic masses; he was aiming to make the classics available to the people. As he had said in "Democracy," "They arrive, these masses, eager to enter into possession of the world, to gain a more vivid sense of their own life and activity" (*PW*, 2:26). From great poetry comes this sense of life and joy. For this reason and for the sake of all the people, the poetry for a democratic age is the classic.

Notes

Acronyms and short forms used in the notes:

Arnoldian	*The Arnoldian: A Review of Mid-Victorian Culture*
ELH	*ELH*
MLR	*Modern Language Review*
MP	*Modern Philology*
PMLA	*Publications of the Modern Language Association of America*
VN	*Victorian Newsletter*
VP	*Victorian Poetry*
VS	*Victorian Studies: A Journal of the Humanities, Arts, and Sciences*

Chapter 1. Literary Critics and Democratic Ideas

    1. Benjamin Evans Lippincott, *Victorian Critics of Democracy* (1938; reprint, New York: Octagon Books, 1964), pp. 93-133.
    2. Matthew Arnold, "Democracy," in *The Complete Prose Works of Matthew Arnold*, ed. R. H. Super, 11 vols. (Ann Arbor: University of Michigan Press, 1960-77), 2:3-29, 330-31, hereafter cited as *Prose Works* in the notes and as *PW* in the text.
    3. Lionel Trilling, *Matthew Arnold* (New York: Meridian, 1955), pp. 147-148.
    4. David J. DeLaura, *Hebrew and Hellene in Victorian England: Newman, Arnold, and Pater* (Austin: University of Texas Press, 1969), p. 70; idem, "Arnold and Literary Criticism: (1) Critical Ideas," in *Matthew Arnold*, ed. Kenneth Allott (Athens: Ohio University Press, 1976), pp. 135-41.
    5. R. H. Super, *The Time-Spirit of Matthew Arnold* (Ann Arbor: University of Michigan Press, 1970), p. 36.

6. R. H. Super, "Arnold and Literary Criticism: (2) Critical Practice," in Allott, *Matthew Arnold*, pp. 162-63.

7. Sidney Coulling, *Matthew Arnold and His Critics: A Study of Arnold's Controversies* (Athens: Ohio University Press, 1974), pp. 55-59.

8. Dorothy Deering, "The Antithetical Poetics of Arnold and Clough," *VP* 16 (1978): 16-31.

9. Essays that consider the conflicts between objective and subjective thought include Manfred Dietrich, "Arnold's *Empedocles on Etna* and the 1853 Preface," *VP* 14 (1976): 311-24; Kenneth Allott, "A Background for *Empedocles on Etna*," in *Matthew Arnold: A Collection of Critical Essays*, ed. David J. DeLaura (Englewood Cliffs, N.J.: Prentice-Hall, 1973), pp. 55-70; J. Hillis Miller, "Matthew Arnold," ibid., pp. 24-45, reprinted from *The Disappearance of God: Five Nineteenth Century Writers* (Cambridge, Mass.: Harvard University Press, 1963).

10. William A. Madden, *Matthew Arnold: A Study of the Aesthetic Temperament* (Bloomington: Indiana University Press, 1967), pp. 170, 185, 187.

11. Raymond Williams, *Culture and Society, 1790-1950* (New York: Columbia University Press, 1958), pp. xiii-xviii.

12. T. S. Eliot, *Notes towards the Definition of Culture* (New York: Harcourt Brace, 1949), pp. 110-11.

13. Ian Watson, *Song and Democratic Culture in Britain: An Approach to Popular Culture in Social Movements* (New York: St. Martin's Press, 1983), pp. 135-54, 215. A general survey of cultural theory and a criticism of its assumptions are found in Gerald Graff, *Literature against Itself: Literary Ideas in Modern Society* (Chicago: University of Chicago Press, 1979); he notes the faulty assumption that "since popular culture, as its name indicates, is the culture enjoyed by the masses, it seems to follow that popular culture is *democratic*" (p. 84).

14. Frank Kermode, *The Classic: Literary Images of Permanence and Change* (New York: Viking, 1975), pp. 18-19.

15. Arnold, *Prose Works*, 1:103, 105; a general discussion of Arnold's awareness of some problems in regard to knowing universal human nature is found in my Ph.D. dissertation, "The Classical Poetry of Matthew Arnold" (University of Minnesota, 1964), pp. 6-24.

16. Walt Whitman, "Democratic Vistas," in *Walt Whitman: Complete Poetry and Collected Prose*, ed. Justin Kaplan (New York: Library of America, 1982), p. 930; idem, "A Backward Glance o'er Travel'd Roads," in *The Norton Anthology of American Literature*,

ed. Ronald Gottesman et al., 2 vols. (New York: Norton, 1979), 1:994–95; idem, *Goodbye, My Fancy,* in *Library of America,* p. 1261.

17. John Henry Raleigh, *Matthew Arnold and American Culture* (Berkeley and Los Angeles: University of California Press, 1961), pp. 58–61.

18. Gerald F. Else, *Plato and Aristotle on Poetry,* ed. Peter Burian (Chapel Hill: University of North Carolina Press, 1986), pp. 90, 155.

Chapter 2. The Balliol Group

1. Thomas Arnold the Younger, *Passages in a Wandering Life* (London: Edward Arnold, 1900), p. 58.

2. [John Campbell Shairp], "English Poets and Oxford Critics," *Quarterly Review* 153 (1882): 463.

3. Henry Sidgwick, *Miscellaneous Essays and Addresses* (London: Macmillan, 1904), p. 61.

4. John Campbell Shairp, *Portraits of Friends, with a Sketch of Principal Shairp by William Young Sellar* (Boston and New York: Houghton Mifflin, 1889), pp. 199–212; also in [Blanche Smith] Clough, "Memoirs of Clough," in *Prose Remains of Arthur Hugh Clough* (London: Macmillan, 1888), pp. 20–21, 23–31. An account of the Oxford life is found in Park Honan, *Matthew Arnold: A Life* (New York: McGraw-Hill, 1981), pp. 48–80. This is the indispensable background for Arnold's life; but Professor Honan, although he has drawn on the letters of Shairp, Palgrave, and others, does not examine the life of this circle of friends in any detail; he focuses on Arnold's friendship with Clough.

5. Lewis Campbell and Evelyn Abbott, *The Life and Letters of Benjamin Jowett,* 2 vols. (New York: E. P. Dutton, 1897), 1:81, 100–104; on the friendship of Stanley and Jowett see 1:167–68 and 2:6, 184, 205–6, cited in text as *LL.* See also Geoffrey Faber, *Jowett: A Portrait with a Background* (Cambridge, Mass.: Harvard University Press, 1957), pp. 116–22.

6. Yale ms., Osborn file, 73.7.65, Oct. 31, 1871.

7. Kenneth Allott, "Matthew Arnold's Reading-Lists in Three Early Diaries," *VS* 2 (1959): 258.

8. Gwenllian F. Palgrave, *Francis Turner Palgrave: His Journals and Memories of His Life* (London: Longmans, Green, & Co., 1899), p. 255, cited in the text as *FTP.*

9. Andrew Lang, "Memoirs of William Young Sellar," in *The*

Roman Poets of the Augustan Age . . . Horace and the Elegiac Poets,
ed. W. P. Ker (Oxford: Clarendon Press, 1892), p. xxxv.

10. Shairp, *Portraits of Friends,* pp. 206-12; see also T.
Arnold, *Passages in a Wandering Life,* pp. 59-63.

11. The letters are included in *The Correspondence of Arthur
Hugh Clough,* ed. Frederick L. Mulhauser, 2 vols. (Oxford: Clarendon Press, 1957), cited in the text as *Correspondence.*

12. Ibid., 1:246-47.

13. Palgrave, *Francis Turner Palgrave,* pp. 25-26, 33, 36.

14. *Letters of Matthew Arnold, 1848-1888,* ed. George W. E.
Russell, 2 vols. (New York: Macmillan, 1900), 1:375, Mar. 17, 1866.

15. Christopher Clausen, "The Palgrave Version," in *The Place
of Poetry: Two Centuries of an Art in Crisis* (Lexington: University
Press of Kentucky, 1981), pp. 64-82.

16. Arthur Penrhyn Stanley, *The Life and Correspondence of
Thomas Arnold,* 4th ed., 2 vols. (London: B. Fellowes, 1845), 1:77 and
2:300; see also *Quarterly Review,* 32 (1827): 70.

17. Frank M. Turner, *The Greek Heritage in Victorian Britain* (New Haven, Conn.: Yale University Press, 1981), pp. 340-58.
This valuable work came out while I was writing an early version of this study; especially helpful to me was the section on
Alexander Grant's edition of Aristotle. Although Turner does discuss Matthew Arnold in his opening chapter, largely summarizing earlier work, he does not mention Arnold in the chapter on
Aristotle.

18. Arnold's recollection of his study of Aristotle is confirmed
by college examination registers; see Warren D. Anderson, "Arnold's
Undergraduate Syllabus," *Arnoldian* 6 (Winter 1979): 3.

19. Arthur Hugh Clough, *The Bothie,* ed. Patrick Scott (St.
Lucia, Queensland, Australia: University of Queensland Press, 1976),
p. 18 (1848 text, 2:305, 312-13).

20. Ibid., p. 14 (2:181-83); see Scott's notes on 2:182, 184-89,
190-91, and "Explanatory Notes," pp. 34-35.

21. *The Letters of Matthew Arnold to Arthur Hugh Clough,* ed.
Howard Foster Lowry (London and New York: Oxford University
Press, 1932), pp. 109-12; Lowry cites Aristotle's definition of virtue.
On Arnold's reading of Aristotle in general, see Warren D. Anderson, *Matthew Arnold and the Classical Tradition* (Ann Arbor: University of Michigan Press, 1965), pp. 125-29. Anderson concludes that
Arnold's reading of Aristotle mainly prepared Arnold for the Stoic
and Epicurean thinkers who were more congenial to Arnold's
thought; hence, Anderson does little with the Aristotelian concepts
in Arnold's criticism.

Chapter 3. "Poetry as Such": Arnold's Early Criticism

1. *The Letters of Matthew Arnold to Arthur Hugh Clough*, ed. Howard Foster Lowry (London and New York: Oxford University Press, 1932), p. 146, hereafter cited as *LC* in the notes and the text; see also *Letters of Matthew Arnold, 1848–1888*, ed. George W. E. Russell, 2 vols. (New York: Macmillan, 1900), 1:34–35, hereafter cited as *Letters*.

2. James Anthony Froude, "Arnold's Poems," *Westminster Review* o.s. 61, n.s. 5 (Jan., 1854): 158–59; idem, "The Science of History," in *Short Studies on Great Subjects*, 4 vols. (London: Longmans, Green, & Co., 1915), 1:29, cited in the text as *SSGS*.

3. Arthur Penrhyn Stanley, *The Life and Correspondence of Thomas Arnold*, 4th ed., 2 vols. (London: B. Fellowes, 1845), 2:53, to A. P. Stanley, Oct. 21, 1836.

4. Matthew Arnold, *Empedocles on Etna*, 2:394–96, in *The Poems of Matthew Arnold*, ed. Kenneth Allott; 2d ed., ed. Miriam Allott (London and New York: Longman, 1979), p. 203.

5. *Letters*, 1:62, to "K," Dec. 6, 1856. See Warren D. Anderson, *Matthew Arnold and the Classical Tradition* (Ann Arbor: University of Michigan Press, 1965), p. 140.

6. *The Correspondence of Arthur Hugh Clough*, ed. Frederick L. Mulhauser, 2 vols. (Oxford: Clarendon Press, 1957), 1:250–51, cited in the text as *Correspondence*.

7. *Correspondence* 2:467; also *Letters to Clough*, pp. 126–27; Arnold said of his new volume, "Froude will review it in the April Westminster, calling me by name" (p. 126). Froude's review, however, appeared in January 1854 (see note 1).

8. *The Ethics of Aristotle*, ed. Alexander Grant, 2 vols. (London: John W. Parker, 1857), 1:170: "The forms of thought which Aristotle worked out for himself are the most remarkable feature of his system; he applied them to all subjects, and to a great extent has left them stamped on language ever since."

9. James Anthony Froude, *Shadows of the Clouds* (London: John Ollivier, 1847; reprint, Westmead, Farnborough, Hants., Eng.: Gregg International Publishers, 1971), pp. 168–78.

10. Waldo Hilary Dunn, *James Anthony Froude: A Biography*, 2 vols. (Oxford: Clarendon Press, 1961, 1963), 1:104–5. Dunn says earlier: "It is well to remember that the 'Arthur' of Clough's *Bothie* was understood in their little circle to be Froude himself" (1:52).

11. James Anthony Froude, *The Nemesis of Faith*, 2d ed. (London: John Chapman, 1849; reprint, Westmead, Farnborough, Hants., Eng.: Gregg International Publishers, 1969).

12. John Campbell Shairp, "Balliol Scholars, 1840–1843," in *Glen Dessaray and Other Poems Lyrical and Elegiac*, ed. Francis Turner Palgrave (London and New York: Macmillan, 1888), pp. 209–20.

13. "Review of Some Poems by Alexander Smith and Matthew Arnold," in *Prose Remains of Arthur Hugh Clough*, ed. by His Wife [Blanche Smith Clough] (London: Macmillan, 1888), pp. 355–78; originally published as "Recent English Poetry: A Review of Several Volumes of Poems by Alexander Smith, Matthew Arnold, and Others" in *North American Review* 77 (July 1853): 1–30; reprinted in its entirety in *Selected Prose Works of Arthur Hugh Clough*, ed. Buckner B. Trawick (University: University of Alabama Press, 1964), pp. 143–71.

14. Froude, "Arnold's Poems," pp. 158–59.

15. Gerald Else, *Plato and Aristotle on Poetry*, ed. Peter Burian (Chapel Hill: University of North Carolina Press, 1986), pp. 75, 90, cited as *Plato* in the text.

16. John Campbell Shairp, "Poems by Matthew Arnold," *North British Review* 21 (Aug., 1854): 494.

17. Trilling misses the point in seeing the play only as an antiquarian exercise (*Matthew Arnold*, pp. 141–44). A. Dwight Culler sees that the interest of the play lies in its political theme: see *Imaginative Reason: The Poetry of Matthew Arnold* (New Haven, Conn.: Yale University Press, 1966), pp. 223–28. Arnold's source for the account of Greek drama was Karl Otfried Müller, *A History of the Literature of Ancient Greece*, trans. George Cornewall Lewis and John William Donaldson, 3 vols. (London: John W. Parker & Son, 1858), 1:377 (the maturity of the audience), 1:395 (the size of the audience), and 1:411 (the chorus as ideal spectator; see also Super's notes, in *Prose-Works*, 1:229, 232–33. Müller emphasizes the influence of Pericles (leader of the democratic party) in the growth of a national literature (pp. 364, 371). Arnold used the 1840 edition (see Super's note, in *Prose-Works*, 1:232). Frank M. Turner, in *The Greek Heritage in Victorian Britain* (New Haven, Conn.: Yale University Press, 1981), gives an account of Arnold's humanistic Hellenism that emphasizes his indebtedness to German Hellenists and to his father's Viconian theory on the parallels between ancient Greece and modern England; but Turner does not discuss the importance of Greek democracy (pp. 23, 25, 27). However, in his chapter on the Athenian constitution, Turner attributes to George Grote the glorification of Greek democracy (pp. 216–19). Arnold read in Grote's history in 1857 when he was writing *Merope* and preparing the lecture: see *The Note-Books of Matthew Arnold*, ed. Howard Foster Lowry, Karl Young, and Waldo

Hilary Dunn (London: Oxford University Press, 1952), pp. 561-62.
Grote, in his account of Greek drama, emphasizes the popular audience: "All this abundance found its way to the minds of the great
body of the citizens, not excepting even the poorest"; Grote also
describes Pericles' efforts to make cheap tickets available to the poor.
Grote comments also on the moral effect of Greek tragedy on the
multitude: "The tastes, the sentiments, and the intellectual standard, of the Athenian multitude, must have been sensibly improved
and exalted by such lessons." And of Aristophanes, Grote notes: "His
comedies are popular in the largest sense of the word, addressed to
the entire body of male citizens on a day consecrated to festivity";
see *A History of Greece from the Earliest Period to the Close of the
Generation Contemporary with Alexander the Great*, 4 vols. (New
York: American Book Exchange, 1881), 3:386, 387, 391.
    18. See my note, "Arnold's Two Regions of Form," *VN* 49 (Spring,
1976): 22-24.

Chapter 4. Subjects from the Past

    1. On Thomas Arnold and Niebuhr see G. P. Gooch, *History
and Historians in the Nineteenth Century* (London: Longmans,
Green, 1913), pp. 319-21; Patrick McCarthy, *Matthew Arnold and
the Three Classes* (New York: Columbia University Press, 1964), pp.
31-32.
    2. *The Letters of Matthew Arnold to Arthur Hugh Clough*, ed.
Howard Foster Lowry (London and New York: Oxford University
Press, 1932), p. 121, hereafter cited as *Letters to Clough*.
    3. Arthur Penrhyn Stanley, *The Life and Correspondence of
Thomas Arnold*, 4th ed., 2 vols. (London: B. Fellowes, 1845), 1:209;
Thomas Arnold, *History of the Later Roman Commonwealth*, 2 vols.
(London: B. Fellowes, 1845), 1:487-89 cited as *LRC* in the text.
Clough, in a letter of 1845, noted the reprint of the articles from the
Encyclopedia Metropolitana (*Correspondence*, 1:153). The three-
volume *History of Rome* (1838-42) was also republished in 1845.
    4. This theory was most fully and recently developed by Peter
Allan Dale, *The Victorian Critic and the Idea of History: Carlyle,
Arnold, Pater* (Cambridge, Mass.: Harvard University Press, 1977),
pp. 91-104. On Thomas Arnold see also Duncan Forbes, *The Liberal
Anglican Idea of History* (Cambridge, Eng.: Cambridge University
Press, 1952), pp. 12-20, 43-44. Earlier articles on Thomas Arnold
and Matthew Arnold include Charles R. Moyer, "The Idea of History
in Thomas and Matthew Arnold," *MP* 67 (1969): 160-67; R. A. For-

syth, " 'The Buried Life': The Contrasting Views of Arnold and Clough in the Context of Dr. Arnold's Historiography," *ELH* 35 (1968): 218–53. The importance of Arnold's reading of history has not been fully examined. From his father, Arnold had acquired some knowledge of and acquaintance with several important earlier historians of the nineteenth century—e.g., B. G. Niebuhr; Arnold knew Jules Michelet and François-Pierre-Guillaume Guizot. Of the historians of Greece, Arnold knew the work of Connop Thirlwall, who was admired by his father, as well as that of George Grote, both of which he probably used in preparing *Merope*; Arnold mentioned these histories in his reviews of Curtius' *History of Greece* (*PW*,5:258–9). On Rome, besides his father's histories, he had also read Drumann and evidently knew Mommsen's works. In addition, he knew Sellar's literary history of Rome and Müller's literary history of Greece. Arnold also read the histories of Macaulay and Froude as the various volumes were published. A. Dwight Culler reviews historical ideas of the important poets and prose writers in his recent *The Victorian Mirror of History* (New Haven, Conn.: Yale University Press, 1985); in his chapter on Matthew Arnold, he notes that in the 1840s, Arnold read in the Romantic German philosophers and historians, but Culler does not refer specifically to the German historians; Culler also discusses Thomas Arnold and Niebuhr (pp. 83–85).

5. Waldo Hilary Dunn, *James Anthony Froude*, 2 vols. (Oxford: Clarendon Press, 1961, 1963), 1:18, 27.

6. Richard C. Jebb, "Froude's Caesar," in *Essays and Addresses* (Cambridge, Eng.: Cambridge University Press, 1907), p. 299: "The peculiar fascination of Caesar's career for our days depends partly on the rather delusive facility with which modern society, especially perhaps English society, thinks to recognize its own features in the Roman society of Caesar's time."

7. *The Complete Prose Works of Matthew Arnold*, ed. R. H. Super, 11 vols. (Ann Arbor: University of Michigan Press, 1960–77), 1:4–5, 9.

8. C. B. Tinker and H. F. Lowry, *The Poetry of Matthew Arnold: A Commentary* (London: Oxford University Press, 1940), pp. 287–88, hereafter cited as *Commentary.*

9. *The Note-Books of Matthew Arnold*, ed. Howard Foster Lowry, Karl Young, and Waldo Hilary Dunn (London: Oxford University Press, 1952), pp. 5–8, 459 (translation), cited as *Note-Books* in the text; "katharsis" is defined as "treatment of the obstructed person," driving out the obstruction.

10. Robert Liddell Lowe, "Two Arnold Letters," *MP* 52 (May,

1955): 262–64, letter written on Dec. 18, 1847; on the Elizabethan Age, compare the Preface to the 1853 *Poems* (1:24–28) and "The Function of Criticism at the Present Time" (3:262–63); by 1864 Arnold thought that the England of Shakespeare was equal to the Greece of Pindar and Sophocles.

11. Karl Otfried Müller, *A History of the Literature of Ancient Greece*, trans. George Cornewall Lewis and John William Donaldson, 3 vols. (London: John W. Parker & Son, 1858), 1:471; this part of the history had appeared in 1840; see Super, *PW*, 1:232; on the use of Müller elsewhere. The identification of the "modern" with the "critical spirit" is implicit in Thomas Arnold's writings on history.

12. *Oxford Essays, 1857*, contributed by members of the university (London: John W. Parker, 1857), pp. 218–313, cited as *1857 Essays* in the text.

13. Arnold, *Note-Books*, p. 558; *Letters of Matthew Arnold, 1848–1888*, ed. George W. E. Russell, 2 vols. (New York: Macmillan, 1900), 1:56–57, hereafter cited as *Letters*; Tinker and Lowry, *Commentary*, pp. 340–47; A. Dwight Culler, *Imaginative Reason: The Poetry of Matthew Arnold* (New Haven, Conn.: Yale University Press, 1966), pp. 219–20.

14. William Young Sellar, "Lucretius and the Poetic Characteristics of His Age," *Oxford Essays, 1855*, contributed by members of the university (London: John W. Parker, 1855), p. 6, cited in the text as *1855 Essays*.

15. James Anthony Froude, *Caesar, a Sketch* (New York: Charles Scribner's, 1908); see reviews by William Young Sellar, "Mr. Froude's Caesar," *Fraser's Magazine* n.s. 20 (Sept., 1879): 315–37; Jebb, "Froude's Caesar," pp. 279–322.

16. Arnold, *Letters*, 1:12, May 7, 1848.

17. Thomas Arnold, *Introductory Lectures on Modern History*, 5th ed. (London: T. Fellowes, 1860), p. 140, cited in the text as *ILMH*.

18. Connop Thirlwall, *A History of Greece*, 2 vols. (New York: Harper, 1845), 1:140; Thomas Arnold, ed., *The History of the Peloponnesian War*, 3d ed., 2 vols. (Oxford: J. H. Parker, 1847), 1:530–31.

19. Warren D. Anderson, *Matthew Arnold and the Classical Tradition* (Ann Arbor: University of Michigan Press, 1965), pp. 103–4. The analysis of "To a Friend" and the 1857 lecture and of Arnold's view of Sophocles are found in the chapter on tragedy, especially pp. 93–103. Anderson writes: "Moralist rather than aesthetician in art, he took his stand not with Aristotle but with Plato. For him the good writer is the good man" (p. 95); but I see Arnold as an aesthetician, especially where he follows Aristotle.

20. *Plutarch's Lives, The Translation called Dryden's*, rev. A. H.

Clough (London: J. M. Dent, 1957), p. xvi; *Greek History from Themistocles to Alexander, in a Series of Lives from Plutarch,* rev. A. H. Clough, new ed. (London: Longmans, Green, 1870), pp. vii–ix.

21. *The Correspondence of Arthur Hugh Clough,* ed. Frederick L. Mulhouser, 2 vols. (Oxford: Clarendon Press, 1957), 2:482, 569.

22. *Letters to Clough,* pp. 151–52, Sept. 29, 1859.

23. James Anthony Froude, "The Science of History," in *Short Studies on Great Subjects,* 4 vols. (London: Longmans, Green, 1915), 1:16–21, cited in the text as *SSGS.*

Chapter 5. "That Natural Heart of Humanity":
Homer and the Ballad Poets

1. "On Translating Homer," in *The Complete Prose Works of Matthew Arnold,* ed. R. H. Super, 11 vols. (Ann Arbor: University of Michigan Press, 1960–77), 1:98. On the background of this essay, especially Arnold's answer to Francis Newman, see Sidney Coulling, *Matthew Arnold and His Critics: A Study of Arnold's Controversies* (Athens: Ohio University Press, 1974), pp. 62–99, esp. pp. 65–75.

2. Coulling, *Matthew Arnold,* pp. 74–75; Henry Hill Lancaster, "Recent Homeric Critics and Translators," *North British Review* 36 (May, 1862): 183–201. Lancaster, however, agreed with Arnold on the latter's main critical principle: "The future translator of Homer must regard him not condescendingly as a barbarian, nor familiarly as a balladist" (p. 201).

3. By "ballad-poets," Arnold meant composers of the traditional English ballad, the "Percy" ballads, as well as songs and ballads collected by Scott. Clough, who had known F. J. Child in the United States, flatly told Child, when Clough began the project of collecting ballads, that he himself did not like ballads. Shairp, on the other hand, wrote about the tradition of the Scottish folk song. All were of course aware of the "lyrical ballads" of Wordsworth and Coleridge. There is no indication, however, that Arnold was aware of the "street ballads" of Victorian cities that are now taken as the literature of the working class or of the broadside ballads that are seen as models for some of Wordsworth's lyrical ballads. On the ballad as popular literature see Victor E. Neuburg, *Popular Literature: A History and a Guide* (Harmondsworth, Eng.: Penguin, 1977), pp. 141–42, and J. S. Bratton, *The Victorian Popular Ballad* (London: Macmillan, 1975), pp. 13–17; see also Albert B. Friedman, *The Ballad Revival: Studies in the Influence of Popular on Sophisticated Poetry* (Chicago: University of Chicago Press, 1961), and David C. Fowler, *A Literary History*

of the Popular Ballad (Durham, N.C.: Duke University Press, 1968)—both are useful for general background.

4. James Anthony Froude, *Short Studies on Great Subjects*, 4 vols. (London: Longmans, Green, 1915), 1:505–6, cited in the text as *SSGS*; this essay first appeared in *Fraser's Magazine* in 1851.

5. Elizabeth Barrett Browning, *Aurora Leigh*, with an introduction by Gardner B. Taplin (1864; reprint, Chicago: Academy Chicago, 1979), bk. 5, pp. 160–61.

6. Arthur Hugh Clough, "Macaulay's 'Battle of Ivry,' " *Rugby Magazine* 1 (Oct., 1855): 123–37, reprinted in *Selected Prose Works of Arthur Hugh Clough*, ed. Buckner B. Trawick (University: University of Alabama Press, 1964), pp. 29–38.

7. *Prose Remains of Arthur Hugh Clough*, ed. by His Wife [Blanche Smith Clough] (London: Macmillan, 1888), pp. 389–96, first published in *Putnam's Monthly Magazine* 2 (Aug., 1853): 138–40, cited in the text as *PR*.

8. William Young Sellar, "Poems by Arthur Hugh Clough," *North British Review* 37 (Nov., 1862): 328, cited in the text as "Poems."

9. John Campbell Shairp, "Poems by Matthew Arnold," *North British Review* 21 (Aug., 1854): 493–94.

10. John Campbell Shairp, "The Songs of Scotland before Burns," *Macmillan's* 3 (Mar., 1861): 399–410. Sellar, however, tended to agree with Arnold on the use of the old ballad style in modern poetry. In review of Shairp's *Kilmahoe: A Highland Pastoral*, Sellar made a number of points that suggested Shairp's own discussion of Homer and of Scott (*North British Review* 40 [Feb., 1864]: 169–83). Indeed, Sellar compared the poetry of Shairp to that of Scott, both of whom were trying to preserve the memory of a life that was coming to an end (p. 170); but Sellar thought that Shairp was too much attached to "ancient traditions" and "to all the terms of expression in our ancient ballads" (p. 171). Sellar was particularly disturbed by the "incongruous Scotch words" which did not harmonize with Shairp's own language.

11. John Campbell Shairp, *Aspects of Poetry, Being Lectures Delivered at Oxford* (Oxford: Clarendon Press, 1881), pp. 377–406, cited in the text as *AP*.

12. Thomas Arnold, *A Manual of English Literature, Historical and Critical*, 6th ed. (London: Longmans, Green, 1888), pp. 483–84. Shairp quotes from Matthew Arnold's "On Translating Homer," *Prose Works*, 1:127; Arnold refers to J. S. Blackie, "Homer and His Translators," *Macmillan's* 4 (Aug., 1861): 269–76; see *Prose Works*, 1:207–11, 252, also Coulling, *Matthew Arnold*, pp. 83–85.

13. See Kenneth Allott's *The Poems of Matthew Arnold*, 2d ed., ed. Miriam Allott (London and New York: Longman, 1979), p. 454 n. I noted the parallels between Scott's *Lady of the Lake* and *Merope* in "The Classical Poetry of Matthew Arnold" (Ph.D. diss., University of Minnesota, 1964), p. 144. Arnold also had a taste for Ossian and Gray and for Celtic literature. The lectures on Celtic literature, which follow the *Essays in Criticism*, deal largely with the branch of literary criticism that is concerned with natural description and thus are not, on the whole, relevant to the question of literature for a democratic age. Arnold did, however, see something Greek in the people of Wales. Reporting on the view of the Eisteddfod as "a kind of Olympic meeting," he suggested this conclusion: "That the common people of Wales should care for such a thing, shows something Greek in them, something spiritual, something humane, something (I am afraid I must add) which in the English common people is not to be found." The actual performance, however, did not suggest to Arnold "a multitude touched by the divine flame, and hanging on the lips of Pindar" (*Prose Works*, 3:296). Although Arnold went on to argue for the value of Celtic literature, in part as a way of understanding the Celtic people and their past, he did not see the literature as composed by the folk, but rather by the "great traditional poets" (*Prose Works*, 3:315-16; 366). Indeed, Arnold, considering the "ideal genius" of the Celts, wrote: "The same sensibility made the Celts full of reverence and enthusiasm for genius, learning, and the things of the mind; *to be a bard, freed a man,*—that is a characteristic stroke of this generous and ennobling ardour of theirs, which no race has ever shown more strongly" (*Prose Works*, 3:347). The lectures on Celtic literature, which follow the *Essays in Criticism*, thus continued Arnold's inquiry into the possibility of a great literature for a democratic age, one addressed by great poets to an intelligent audience.

Chapter 6. The Great Work of Criticism

1. *Ethica Nicomachea* (cited in the text and notes as *NE*), ed. Ingram Bywater (Oxford: Clarendon Press, 1949), pp. 212-13; William David Ross, *Aristotle*, 5th ed. (1949; reprint, New York: Barnes & Nobel, 1964), pp. 232-34; W. F. R. Hardie, *Aristotle's Ethical Theory*, 2nd ed. (Oxford: Clarendon Press, 1980), pp. 336-57.

2. Ross, *Aristotle*, p. 234; Hardie, *Aristotle's Ethical Theory*, pp. 338-40, quoting J. Burnet, *The Ethics of Aristotle* (London: Methuen, 1900), p. 438. Hardie says: "It may be suggested, however, that some

of Aristotle's reasons for commending theoretical activity, in contrast with practical and political pursuits, are applicable to artistic and aesthetic as well as to scientific interests" (p. 340).

3. *Ethics of Aristotle*, ed. Alexander Grant, 2 vols. (London: John W. Parker, 1857), 2:153; see also the 4th ed., 2 vols. (London: Longmans, Green & Co., 1885), 2:335, hereafter cited as *Ethics*. See Frank M. Turner, *The Greek Heritage in Victorian Britain* (New Haven, Conn.: Yale University Press, 1981), pp. 326–27, 340–52. Turner sees Grant's work as a dividing point in studies of Aristotle during the nineteenth century. It seems evident to me that Arnold's reading of Aristotle in "The Function of Criticism at the Present Time" belongs to the earlier interpretations, especially of "activity"; but the presence of Grant in the circle of the friends of Benjamin Jowett, who was so important to Arnold and his friends as a guide to Greek studies, cannot be ignored. I have found Grant's commentary on certain words to be a useful illustration of points that Arnold made in his criticism.

4. Peter Allan Dale, *The Victorian Critic and the Idea of History: Carlyle, Arnold, Pater* (Cambridge, Mass.: Harvard University Press, 1977), pp. 10, 107–9.

5. See *Ethics*, 1857 ed., 2:83, 256–57.

6. *NE* 1150b25–28, p. 144; *The Works of Aristotle*, vol. 9, ed. W. D. Ross (Oxford: Clarendon Press, 1925).

7. *Ethics*, 4th ed., 2:223–24; *The Poems of Tennyson*, ed. Christopher Ricks (London: Longman, 1969; reprint, New York: Norton, 1972), p. 1050.

8. John Campbell Shairp, "Wordsworth: The Man and the Poet," in *Studies in Poetry and Philosophy* (Boston and New York: Houghton Mifflin, 1872), pp. 1–4; this first appeared in *North British Review* 41 (Aug., 1864): 1–54.

9. John Campbell Shairp, "Criticism and Creation," *Aspects of Poetry, Being Lectures Delivered at Oxford* (Oxford: Clarendon Press, 1881), pp. 49–53; this essay was first published in *Macmillan's Magazine* 38 (July, 1878): 246–56. On the *Ion* as satire see Gerald F. Else, *Plato and Aristotle on Poetry*, ed. Peter Burian (Chapel Hill: University of North Carolina Press, 1986), pp. 5–9.

10. Geoffrey Hartman, *Criticism in the Wilderness* (New Haven, Conn.: Yale University Press, 1980), p. 6.

11. *NE* 1170; see Ross's note; Turner, *Greek Heritage*, pp. 350–51; *Ethics*, 1857 ed., 1:193–94, 200–201.

12. David J. DeLaura, "Arnold's Imaginative Reason: The Oxford Sources and the Tradition," *Prose Studies* 1 (1977): 7–18, "Imaginative Reason: A Further Note," ibid., 2 (1979): 103–6, and "Imaginative Reason: Yet Again," ibid., 188–89.

13. Ross, *Aristotle*, pp. 216–18; Hardie, *Aristotle's Ethical Theory*, pp. 345–57; on difficulties of *nous* in Aristotle's theory see *Ethics*, 1857 ed., 1:261–63 ("a union of reason and science").

14. Karl Otfried Müller, *A History of the Literature of Ancient Greece*, trans. George Cornewall Lewis and John William Donaldson, 3 vols. (London: John W. Parker, 1858), 2:258.

15. William Young Sellar, *The Roman Poets of the Republic* (Edinburgh: Edmonston & Douglas, 1863), p. 279.

16. *The Note-Books of Matthew Arnold*, ed. Howard Foster Lowry, Karl Young, and Waldo Hilary Dunn (London: Oxford University Press, 1952), p. 571, July, 1863; William Bell Guthrie, "Matthew Arnold's Diaries: The Unpublished Items: A Transcription and Commentary" 4 vols. (Ph.D. diss., University of Virginia, 1957; Ann Arbor, Mich.: University Microfilms, 1981), 2:402–4: Arnold entered "Sellar's Roman Poets" on July 23, 25, 27, 28, 29, and 30 and Aug. 4 and 5, 1863; on August 7 he wrote "finish Sellar's Roman Poets." The letter that Arnold wrote to Shairp is included in E. M. (Eleanour Denniston) Sellar's *Recollections and Impressions* (Edinburgh and London: William Blackwood & Sons, 1907), pp. 164–65. Arnold wrote, "I have now read every word of it, some of it more than once, and with extreme satisfaction" (p. 164); on Lucretius, he wrote: "The delicacy and interestingness of the criticism in certain places I say little about, because these are chiefly shown in the chapters on Lucretius, most of which I had read and liked, as such criticism deserved to be liked, before"; Arnold thus indicated that he had read the essay on Lucretius in the *Oxford Essays* of 1855.

17. William Young Sellar, *The Roman Poets of the Augustan Age: Virgil*, 3d ed. (London: Oxford University Press, 1908; reprint, New York: Biblo & Tannen, 1965), p. 240.

18. The lecture "The Influence of Academies on National Spirit and Literature" was given on June 4, 1864, and was revised for *Cornhill*. In chronological order, it thus immediately precedes "The Function of Criticism at the Present Time," but in the order of the essays in the collection, Arnold placed it immediately after the introductory essay, in part to show a function of the "critic" (*PW*, 3:463).

19. See Super's notes on *PW*, 2:331; the essay was composed as an introduction to *The Popular Education of France* (1861) and was considered in 1864 as part of the collection of *Essays in Criticism*.

20. The lecture "A Modern French Poet" was given on Nov. 15, 1862; it appeared in *Fraser's Magazine* in Jan., 1863 (See Super's notes on pp. 407–8).

21. The essay was first published in June, 1863, in *Cornhill* (see Super's notes *PW*, 3:428). "The French Academy voted a prize to her

[Eugénie de Guérin's] posthumously published *Journal"* (ibid.). Eugénie de Guérin died in 1848.

22. Super notes that the lecture "The Modern Element in Romanticism" was not published; it was delivered on Mar. 26, 1863. The lecture "Heinrich Heine" was given on June 13 and was subsequently published in *Cornhill* (*PW*, 3:433).

23. *PW*, 3:215. The Oxford lecture "Pagan and Christian Religious Sentiment," which was given on Mar. 5, 1864, was published in *Cornhill* in April (see Super's notes in *PW*, 3:458). Between this essay and the earlier one on Heine, Arnold had published "Marcus Aurelius," "Spinoza and the Bible," and "Joubert"; that is, he had given considerable thought to popular religion, as well as to Stoic morality, and to the emotional appeal of morality and religion.

24. The lecture "A French Coleridge" was delivered on Nov. 28, 1863, and was published in the *National Review* in Jan., 1864 (*PW*, 3:452).

25. The essay first appeared in *Victoria Magazine* in Nov., 1863; see Super's notes in *PW*, 3:440.

Chapter 7. The Activity of Poetry

1. *The Complete Prose Works of Matthew Arnold*, ed. R. H. Super, 11 vols. (Ann Arbor: University of Michigan Press, 1960–77), 1:188.

2. See notes on p. 347. The essay was written sometime between Oct., 1878, and Aug., 1879; it clearly preceded the composition of "The Study of Poetry." For the *Poetics*, I use Bywater second edition (Oxford: Clarendon Press, 1911; reprint, 1953) and commentaries by S. H. Butcher, *Aristotle's Theory of Poetry and Fine Art*, 4th ed. (1902: reprint, New York: Dover, 1951), and Gerald F. Else, *Aristotle's Poetics: The Argument* (Cambridge, Mass.: Harvard University Press, 1963). For the *Nicomachean Ethics*, I use Bywater's edition (Oxford: Clarendon Press, 1894; reprint, 1949), and these commentaries: Harold Henry Joachim, *Aristotle: The "Nicomachean Ethics*," ed. D. A. Rees (Oxford: Clarendon Press, 1955); W. F. R. Hardie, *Aristotle's Ethical Theory*, 2d ed. (Oxford: Clarendon Press, 1980); William David Ross, *Aristotle*, 5th ed. (1949; reprint, New York: Barnes & Noble, 1964), and Ross's translation in *The Works of Aristotle*, ed. W. D. Ross (Oxford: Clarendon Press, 1925), vol. 9. The importance of Alexander Grant's edition of the *Ethics* in the late nineteenth century has been shown by Frank M. Turner in *The Greek Heritage in Victorian Britain* (New Haven, Conn.: Yale University

Press, 1981), pp. 340-58. I have consulted Grant's 1857 edition of *The Ethics of Aristotle*, 2 vols. (London: John W. Parker, 1857; hereafter cited as *Ethics*, 1857 ed.) and *The Ethics of Aristotle*, ed. Alexander Grant, 4th ed., 2 vols. (London: Longmans, Green, & Co., 1885); hereafter cited as *Ethics*, 4th ed.

   3. *PW,* 6:115, 219, 299-301, 326-27, 442, and 8:28. See *Ethics*, 4th ed., 2:138-39; also *Ethics*, 1857 ed., 2:233-34.

   4. *PW,* 6:456: "I have been reading this year in connexion with the New Testament a good deal of Aristotle and Plato, and this has brought papa very much to my mind again" (*Letters of Matthew Arnold, 1848-1888*, ed. George W. E. Russell, 2 vols. [New York: Macmillan, 1900], 1:442).

   5. See Grant on *Ethics* 113a23-33: "The good man is made here again, as above (II.vi.15), that standard of right and wrong, that exponent of universal reason, by which Aristotle escapes being forced into an utterly relative system of morals" (4th ed., 2:24; 1857 ed., 2:118). See also Joachim, *Aristotle*, p. 104.

   6. "A Speech at Eton," *PW,* 9:20-35; the speech was given on Apr. 5, 1879, and was published in *Cornhill* in May, 1879; see *PW,* 9:334. See Grant on *eutrapelia* or *tact:* " 'This then will be the attitude of the refined and liberal man, he being as it were a law to himself.' Aristotle usually escapes from pure indefiniteness and relativity by asserting that the standard in each case is to be found in the good, the wise, the refined man. It is not to be supposed that wit, beauty, or goodness are mere matters of taste, as Aristotle would seem for a moment to imply. . . . When he adds afterwards that the educated man must be the standard of appeal, he means that the laws of reason must decide" (4th ed., 2:91, commentary on IV.viii.9-10).

   7. Super notes that the list earlier appeared in "Equality" and again in the Preface to *Mixed Essays* (*PW,* 8:287, 382; note in *PW,* 9:335.

   8. Butcher says that *spoudaios* "can denote any one that is good or excellent in his kind or in his special line" but referring to man in general means " 'morally good' " (*Aristotle's Theory*, pp. 228-29). See also Else, *Aristotle's Poetics*, pp. 68-79, especially on "those who take themselves and life seriously" (p. 77).

   9. Arthur Hugh Clough, *Amours de Voyage*, ed. Patrick Scott (St. Lucia, Queensland, Australia: University of Queensland Press, 1974), app. 3, pp. 81-82.

   10. Leslie Stephen, "Wordsworth's Ethics," *Cornhill Magazine* 34 (Aug., 1876): 219; for Arnold's notes on Stephen see *The Note-Books of Matthew Arnold*, ed. Howard Foster Lowry, Karl Young, and Waldo Hilary Dunn (London: Oxford University Press, 1952), pp. 318-19, 329, and from Wordsworth, p. 514.

   11. Butcher, *Aristotle's Theory*, p. 191.

12. Arnold, *Note-Books*, p. 319; from Stephen, "Wordsworth's Ethics," p. 219.

13. *PW*, 7:310, 323; here, in *God and the Bible*, the "imaginative intellect" is contrasted to "soul."

14. On dates of composition and publication see *PW*, 9:336–39. The essay was first published in *Macmillan's Magazine* in July, 1879. Shairp's "Wordsworth: The Man and the Poet" appeared in *North British Review* 41 (Aug., 1864): 1–54; Arnold referred to it in "The Function of Criticism at the Present Time," *PW*, 3:258. On Arnold and Shairp see John P. Farrell, "Homeward Bound: Arnold's Late Criticism," *Victorian Studies* 17 (1973): 187–206.

15. Leon Gottfried, *Matthew Arnold and the Romantics* (Lincoln: University of Nebraska Press, 1963), p. 431. Other discussions of Arnold and sincerity are: Patricia M. Ball, "Sincerity: The Rise and Fall of a Critical Term," *MLR* 59 (1964): 1–11, and also *The Central Self: A Study in Victorian and Romantic Imagination* (London: University of London, Athlone Press, 1968), pp. 158–59; Cleanth Brooks, "Wit and High Seriousness," in *Modern Poetry and the Tradition* (Chapel Hill: University of North Carolina Press, 1939), pp. 18–38; David Perkins, *Wordsworth and the Poetry of Sincerity* (Cambridge, Mass.: Harvard University Press, 1964), p. 11.

16. *Prose Remains of Arthur Hugh Clough*, edited by His Wife [Blanche Smith Clough] (London: Macmillan, 1888), pp. 305–21, cited in the text as *PR*; see also *Selected Prose Works of Arthur Hugh Clough*, ed. Buckner B. Trawick (University: University of Alabama Press, 1964), pp. 107–22, cited in the text as *SPW*.

17. John Campbell Shairp, "Wordsworth as an Interpreter of Nature," in *On Poetic Interpretation of Nature* (New York: Hurd & Houghton, 1878), pp. 235–79, cited in the text as *PIN*.

18. John Campbell Shairp, "Criticism and Creation," in *Aspects of Poetry, Being Lectures Delivered at Oxford* (Oxford: Clarendon Press, 1881), pp. 37–65; the essay first appeared in *Macmillan's Magazine* 38 (July, 1878): 246–56.

19. John Campbell Shairp, "Shelley as a Lyric Poet," in *Aspects of Poetry*, pp. 227–55; it first appeared in *Fraser's Magazine*, o.s. 100, n.s. 20 (July, 1879): 38–53. The lecture on Burns appeared as "Burns and Scotch Song before Him" in the *Atlantic Monthly* 46 (Oct., 1879): 502–13, and as "Scottish Song and Burns" in *Aspects of Poetry* (pp. 192–226). References in the text are to the 1881 edition of *Aspects of Poetry* unless otherwise noted. The monograph on Burns appeared as *Robert Burns* in the English Men of Letters series (New York: Harper, 1879); it is cited in the text as *Burns*.

210 Notes to Pages 156-177

210 Notes to Pages 156-177

20. William Angus Knight, *Principal Shairp and His Friends* (London: John Murray, 1888), pp. 364, 361.

21. R. L. Stevenson, "Some Aspects of Robert Burns," *Cornhill Magazine* 40 (Oct., 1879): 408-9; see also William Wallace's review in *Academy* 15 (May 24, 1879): 448-49. On Shairp's reputation at the present time see Donald A. Low, ed., *Robert Burns: The Critical Heritage* (London and Boston: Routledge & Kegan Paul, 1974), p. 74.

22. Thomas Arnold, *New Zealand Letters of Thomas Arnold the Younger*, ed. James Bertram (London and Wellington, New Zealand: Oxford University Press, 1966), pp. 63-64.

23. *PW*, 9:432. The essay on Byron was first published in *Macmillan's Magazine* in Mar., 1881 (*PW*, 9:396). On Arnold, Byron, and Swinburne see Sidney Coulling, *Matthew Arnold and His Critics: A Study of Arnold's Controversies* (Athens: Ohio University Press, 1974), pp. 276-81; see also John P. Farrell, "Arnold, Byron and Taine," *English Studies* 55 (Oct., 1974): 435-39.

24. Shairp, *Aspects of Poetry*, p. 228.

25. Arthur Hugh Clough, "Lecture on the Development of English Literature from Chaucer to Wordsworth," in *Prose Remains*, pp. 346-50; "Dryden and His Times," in *Selected Prose Works*, pp. 85-106; from Lecture I, VI: "It is a period, I confess, rather of the senses and the understanding than of the spirit and the imagination" (p. 105).

26. *The Letters of Matthew Arnold to Arthur Hugh Clough*, ed. Howard Foster Lowry (London and New York: Oxford University Press, 1932), pp. 96-97.

27. Arnold, "Amiel," in *PW*, 11:265-81, see notes on pp. 459-60; the essay was written in July, 1887, and was published in *Macmillan's Magazine* in September. On Aristotle and the finite see *Ethics*, 1857 ed., 1:180, and *Ethics*, 4th ed., 1:231 (on *orismenon*).

Chapter 8. The Classic and Classical Poetry

1. John Campbell Shairp, *Culture and Religion in Some of Their Relations* (New York: Hurd & Houghton, 1872), p. 94, cited in the text as *CR*.

2. John Campbell Shairp, *Aspects of Poetry, Being Lectures Delivered at Oxford* (Oxford: Clarendon Press, 1881), p. 20, cited in the text as *AP*.

3. John Campbell Shairp, "The Early Poetry of Scotland," in *Sketches in History and Poetry*, ed. John Veitch (Edinburgh: David Douglas, 1887), p. 203, cited in the text as "EP."

4. John Campbell Shairp, "The Poet a Revealer," in *Aspects of Poetry*.

5. John Campbell Shairp, "Virgil as a Religious Poet," in *Aspects of Poetry*.

6. William Young Sellar, *The Roman Poets of the Republic*, 3d ed. (London: Oxford University Press, 1905; reprint London: Humphrey Milford, 1932), p. 5, cited in the text as *RPR*.

7. William Young Sellar, *The Roman Poets of the Augustan Age: Virgil*, 3d ed. (London: Oxford University Press, 1908; reprint, New York: Biblo & Tannen, 1965), p. 286, cited in the text as *RPA*.

8. William E. Buckler, "Studies in Three Arnold Problems," *PLMA* 73 (1958): 264–68.

9. Victor E. Neuburg, *Popular Literature: A History and a Guide* (Harmondsworth, Eng.: Penguin Books, 1977), p. 183.

10. Patrick Brantlinger, *Bread and Circuses: Theories of Mass Culture as Social Decay* (Ithaca, N.Y.: Cornell University Press, 1983), p. 63. In tracing the "classical roots of the mass culture debate," Brantlinger calls Arnold "the key figure in the defense of the classics against the threats of democracy and of 'ignorant armies clashing by night' " (p. 61). Misquoting from "Dover Beach," Brantlinger seems to equate the "ignorant armies" with the lower classes; but the allusions in the poem to Sophocles and to Thucydides, indirectly in the image of the night battle, suggest instead the greatness of the Athenian democracy. Brantlinger also sees Arnold's ideas of education as a "pacification" for the masses (p. 42). Yet Brantlinger sees a connection between the democratic society of Athens and its high culture (p. 81).

11. Matthew Arnold, "Civilization in the United States," *PW*, 11:350–69; see also Super's notes, p. 493.

12. Edward Payson Roe, " 'A Native Author Called Roe': An Autobiography," in *The Works of E. P. Roe*, 11 vols. (New York: P. F. Collier, 1902), 11:24–25. A brief account of Arnold's criticism is found in Glenn O. Carey, *Edward Payson Roe* (Boston: Twayne Publishers, 1985), pp. 3–4. The essay was first published in *Lippincott's* 42 (Oct., 1888): 479–97.

13. Edward Payson Roe, *Barriers Burned Away*, in *Works*, 5:13–15, 23–27.

14. Frank Kermode, *The Classic: Literary Images of Permanence and Change* (New York: Viking, 1975), pp. 17–19.

Bibliography

MATTHEW ARNOLD

Editions

The Complete Prose Works of Matthew Arnold. Edited by R. H. Super.
11 vols. Ann Arbor: Michigan University Press, 1960–77.
The Poems of Matthew Arnold. Edited by Kenneth Allott. London:
Longmans, 1965. 2d ed., edited by Miriam Allott. London and New
York: Longman, 1979.
The Poetical Works of Matthew Arnold. Edited by C. B. Tinker and
H. F. Lowry. London: Oxford University Press, 1950.

Letter, Diaries, Notebooks, and Manuscripts

Allott, Kenneth. "Matthew Arnold's Reading-Lists in Three Early
Diaries: *Victorian Studies* 2 (1959): 254–66.
Guthrie, William B. "Matthew Arnold's Diaries: The Unpublished
Items: A Transcription and Commentary." Ph.D. diss., University
of Virginia, 1957. 4 vols. Ann Arbor, Mich.: University Microfilms,
1981. (Diaries, 1852–88.)
Letters of Matthew Arnold, 1848–1888. Edited by George W. E.
Russell. 2 vols. New York: Macmillan, 1900.
The Letters of Matthew Arnold to Arthur Hugh Clough. Edited by
Howard Foster Lowry. London and New York: Oxford University
Press, 1932.
Unpublished Letters of Matthew Arnold. Edited by Arnold Whitridge.
New Haven, Conn.: Yale University Press, 1923.
Yale Papers: Tinker 21, a miscellany, not published.

DR. THOMAS ARNOLD

History of Rome. 3 vols. London. B. Fellowes, 1838–42; republished in 1845.

History of the Later Roman Commonwealth. 2 vols. London: B. Fellowes, 1845.

Introductory Lectures on Modern History. 5th ed. London: T. Fellowes, 1860.

Stanley, Arthur Penrhyn. *The Life and Correspondence of Thomas Arnold.* 4th ed. 2 vols. London: B. Fellowes, 1845.

THOMAS ARNOLD THE YOUNGER

Letters of Thomas Arnold the Younger, 1850–1900. Edited by James Bertram. Auckland, New Zealand, and London: Auckland University Press and Oxford University Press, 1980.

New Zealand Letters of Thomas Arnold the Younger. Edited by James Bertram. London and Wellington, New Zealand: Oxford University Press, 1966.

Passages in a Wandering Life. London: Edwin Arnold, 1900.

ARTHUR HUGH CLOUGH

Amours de Voyage. Edited by Patrick Scott. St. Lucia, Queensland, Australia: University of Queensland Press, 1974.

The Bothie. Edited by Patrick Scott. St. Lucia, Queensland, Australia: University of Queensland Press, 1976.

The Bothie of Toper-na-Fuosich, A Long-Vacation Pastoral. Oxford: Francis Macpherson, 1848.

The Correspondence of Arthur Hugh Clough. Edited by Frederick L. Mulhauser. 2 vols. Oxford: Clarendon Press, 1957.

Greek History from Themistocles to Alexander, in a Series of Lives from Plutarch. Revised by Arthur Hugh Clough. London: Longmans, Green, 1870.

Plutarch's Lives, The Translation Called Dryden's. Revised by Arthur Hugh Clough. 5 vols. Boston, Mass.: Little Brown, 1882; London: J. M. Dent, 1957.

The Poems of Arthur Hugh Clough. Edited by H. F. Lowry, A. L. P. Norrington, and F. L. Mulhauser. Oxford: Clarendon Press, 1951.

Prose Remains of Arthur Hugh Clough. Edited by His Wife [Blanche Smith Clough]. London: Macmillan, 1888.

Selected Prose Works of Arthur Hugh Clough. Edited by Buckner B. Trawick. University: University of Alabama Press, 1964.

JAMES ANTHONY FROUDE

"Arnold's Poems." *Westminster Review,* o.s. 61, n.s. 5 (Jan., 1854): 146–59.

Caesar, a Sketch. New York: Charles Scribner's, 1908.

Jebb, Richard C. "Froude's Caesar." In *Essays and Addresses.* Cambridge, Eng.: Cambridge University Press, 1907. Originally printed in *Edinburgh Review* 150 (Oct., 1879): 498–523.

The Nemesis of Faith. 2d ed. London: John Chapman, 1849; reprint, Westmead, Farnborough, Hants., Eng.: Gregg International Publishers, 1969.

Shadows of the Clouds. London: John Ollivier, 1847; reprint, Westmead, Farnborough, Hants., Eng.: Gregg International Publishers, 1971.

Short Studies on Great Subjects. 4 vols. London: Longmans, Green, 1915.

FRANCIS TURNER PALGRAVE

The Golden Treasury of the Best Songs and Lyrical Poems in the English Language. 5th ed. London: Oxford University Press, 1964.

Idyls and Songs, 1848–1854. London: John W. Parker & Son, 1854.

Landscape in Poetry: From Homer to Tennyson. London: Macmillan, 1897.

Palgrave, Gwenllian F. *Francis Turner Palgrave: His Journals and Memories of His Life.* London, New York, and Bombay: Longmans, Green, & Co., 1899.

Preface to John Campbell Shairp's *Glen Dessaray and Other Poems.* Edited by Francis T. Palgrave. London and New York: Macmillan, 1888.

The Visions of England. London: Macmillan, 1881.

WILLIAM YOUNG SELLAR

"Characteristics of Thucydides." In *Oxford Essays, 1857,* pp. 282–313. London: John W. Parker, 1857.

Horace and the Elegiac Poets. Edited by W. P. Ker, with a Memoir by Andrew Lang. Oxford: Clarendon Press, 1892.

"Lucretius and the Poetic Characteristics of His Age." In *Oxford Essays, 1855*, pp. 1–46. London: John W. Parker & Son, 1855.

"Mr. Froude's Caesar." *Fraser's Magazine*, n.s. 20 (Sept., 1878): 315–37.

"Poems by Arthur Hugh Clough." *North British Review* 37 (Nov., 1862): 323–43.

Review of *Kilmahoe: A Highland Pastoral. North British Review* 39 (Aug., 1863): 169–83.

The Roman Poets of the Augustan Age: Virgil. 3d ed. London: Oxford University Press, 1908; reprint, New York: Biblo & Tannen, 1965.

The Roman Poets of the Republic. Edinburgh: Edmonston & Douglas, 1863.

JOHN CAMPBELL SHAIRP

Aspects of Poetry. Oxford: Clarendon Press, 1881.

Culture and Religion in Some of Their Relations. New York: Hurd & Houghton, 1872.

"English Poets and Oxford Critics." *Quarterly Review* 153 (1882): 431–63.

Kilmahoe: A Highland Pastoral. London and Cambridge: Macmillan, 1864.

On Poetic Interpretation of Nature. New York: Hurd & Houghton, 1878.

Robert Burns. New York: Harper & Brothers, 1879.

Sketches in History and Poetry. Edited by John Veitch. Edinburgh: David Douglas, 1887.

Studies in Poetry and Philosophy. 2d ed. Boston and New York: Houghton Mifflin, 1872.

THE CIRCLE

Dunn, Waldo Hilary. *James Anthony Froude: A Biography.* 2 vols. Oxford: Clarendon Press, 1961, 1963.

Goetzman, Robert. *James Anthony Froude: A Bibliography of Studies.* New York and London: Garland, 1977.

Gollin, Richard M.; Walter E. Houghton; and Michael Timko. *Arthur Hugh Clough: A Descriptive Catalogue: Poetry, Prose, Bi-*

ography, and Criticism. New York: New York Public Library, 1967.

Honan, Park. *Matthew Arnold: A Life.* New York: McGraw-Hill, 1981.

Knight, William Angus. *Principal Shairp and His Friends.* London: John Murray, 1888.

Sellar, E. M. [Eleanour Denniston]. *Recollections and Impressions.* Edinburgh and London: William Blackwoord & Sons, 1907.

Shairp, John Campbell. *Portraits of Friends, with a Sketch of Principal Shairp by William Young Sellar.* Boston and New York: Houghton Mifflin, 1889.

SELECTED GENERAL BIBLIOGRAPHY

Alexander, Edward. *Arnold and John Stuart Mill.* New York: Columbia University Press, 1965.

_____. *Matthew Arnold, John Ruskin, and the Modern Temper.* Columbus: University of Ohio Press, 1973.

Anderson, Warren D. *Matthew Arnold and the Classical Tradition.* Ann Arbor: University of Michigan Press, 1965.

Ball, Patricia M. *The Central Self: A Study in Victorian and Romantic Imagination.* London: University of London, Athlone Press, 1968.

Bamford, T. W. *Thomas Arnold.* London: Cresset, 1960.

Blackburn, William. "Matthew Arnold and the Oriel Noetics." *Philological Quarterly* 35 (1946): 70–78.

Brantlinger, Patrick. *Bread and Circuses: Theories of Mass Culture as Social Decay.* Ithaca, N.Y.: Cornell University Press, 1983.

Bratton, J. S. *The Victorian Popular Ballad.* London: Macmillan, 1975.

Brooks, Cleanth. "Wit and High Seriousness." In *Modern Poetry and the Tradition.* Chapel Hill: University of North Carolina Press, 1939.

Buckley, Vincent. *Poetry and Morality: Studies on the Criticism of Matthew Arnold, T. S. Eliot, and F. R. Leavis.* London: Chatto & Windus, 1959.

Clausen, Christopher. *The Place of Poetry: Two Centuries of Art in Crisis.* Lexington: University Press of Kentucky, 1981.

Coulling, Sidney. *Matthew Arnold and His Critics: A Study of Arnold's Controversies.* Athens: Ohio University Press, 1974.

Culler, A. Dwight. *Imaginative Reason: The Poetry of Matthew Arnold.* New Haven, Conn.: Yale University Press, 1966.

_____. *The Victorian Mirror of History.* New Haven, Conn.: Yale University Press, 1985.

Dale, Peter Allan. *The Victorian Critic and the Idea of History: Carlyle, Arnold, Pater.* Cambridge, Mass.: Harvard University Press, 1977.

Deering, Dorothy. "The Antithetical Poetics of Arnold and Clough." *Victorian Poetry* 16 (1978): 16-31.

DeLaura, David J. "Arnold and Carlyle." *PMLA* 79 (1964): 104-29.

———. "Arnold and Literary Criticism: (1) Critical Ideas." In *Matthew Arnold*, edited by Kenneth Allott, pp. 118-48. Athens: Ohio University Press, 1976.

———. "Arnold's Imaginative Reason: The Oxford Sources and the Tradition." *Prose Studies* 1 (1977): 7-18, and 2 (1979): 103-6, 188-89.

———. *Hebrew and Hellene in Victorian England: Newman, Arnold, Pater.* Austin: University of Texas Press, 1969.

———. "Matthew Arnold and the Nightmare of History." *Victorian Poetry.* Edited by M. Bradbury and D. Palmer. Stratford-upon-Avon Studies no. 15. London: Edward Arnold, 1972.

———. "The Wordsworth of Pater and Arnold: 'The Supreme Artistic View of Life.' " *Studies in English Literature* 6 (1966): 651-57.

Dietrich, Manfred. "Arnold's *Empedocles on Etna* and the 1853 Preface." *Victorian Poetry* 14 (1976): 311-24.

Douglas, Dennis. "Matthew Arnold and the 'Critical Spirit.' " *English Studies* 59 (1978): 344-52.

Eliot, T. S. *Notes towards the Definition of Culture.* New York: Harcourt Brace, 1949.

Else, Gerald. *Aristotle's Poetics: The Argument.* Cambridge, Mass.: Harvard University Press, 1963.

———. *Plato and Aristotle on Poetry.* Edited by Peter Burian. Chapel Hill: University of North Carolina Press, 1986.

Faber, Geoffrey. *Jowett: A Portrait with a Background.* Cambridge, Mass.: Harvard University Press, 1957.

Farrell, John P. "Arnold, Byron and Taine." *English Studies* 55 (1974): 435-39.

———. "Homeward Bound: Arnold's Late Criticism." *Victorian Studies* 17 (1973): 187-206.

———. "Matthew Arnold's Tragic Vision." *PMLA* 85 (1970): 107-17.

———. *Revolution as Tragedy: The Dilemma of the Moderate from Scott to Arnold.* Ithaca, N.Y.: Cornell University Press, 1980.

Forsyth, R. A. " 'The Buried Life': The Contrasting Views of Arnold and Clough in the Context of Dr. Arnold's Historiography." *ELH* 35 (1968): 218-53.

Friedman, Albert B. *The Ballad Revival: Studies of the Influence of Popular on Sophisticated Poetry.* Chicago: University of Chicago Press, 1961.

Frierson, J. W. "Matthew Arnold, Philosophe." *Studies on Voltaire and the Eighteenth Century* 25 (1963): 645–56.

Garrod, H. W. "Matthew Arnold's 1853 Preface." *Review of English Studies* 17 (1941): 310–21.

Gooch, G. P. *History and Historians in the Nineteenth Century.* London: Longmans, Green, 1913.

Gottfried, Leon. *Matthew Arnold and the Romantics.* Lincoln: University of Nebraska Press, 1963.

Graff, Gerald. *Literature against Itself: Literary Ideas in Modern Society.* Chicago: University of Chicago Press, 1979.

Harris, Wendell V. *Arthur Hugh Clough.* New York: Twayne, 1970.

——. "Eighteenth-Century Straws in Arnoldian Amber and a Conjecture 'How the Devil They Got There,' " *Victorian Poetry* 13 (1975): 70–74.

Hartman, Geoffrey. *Criticism in the Wilderness.* New Haven, Conn.: Yale University Press, 1980.

James, D. G. *Matthew Arnold and the Decline of English Romanticism.* Oxford: Oxford University Press, 1961.

Kermode, Frank. *The Classic: Literary Images of Permanence and Change.* New York: Viking, 1975.

Leavis, F. R. "Revaluations, XI: Arnold as Critic." *Scrutiny* 7 (Dec., 1938): 319–32.

Lippincott, Benjamin Evans. *Victorian Critics of Democracy.* Minneapolis: University of Minnesota Press, 1938; reprint, New York: Octagon Books, 1964.

Low, Donald A., ed. *Robert Burns: The Critical Heritage.* London and Boston: Routledge & Kegan Paul, 1974.

Lowry, Howard F. *Matthew Arnold and the Modern Spirit.* Princeton, N.J.: Princeton University Press, 1941.

McCarthy, Patrick J. *Matthew Arnold and the Three Classes.* New York: Columbia University Press, 1964.

Madden, William A. *Matthew Arnold: A Study of the Aesthetic Temperament.* Bloomington: Indiana University Press, 1967.

Moyer, Charles R. "The Idea of History in Thomas and Matthew Arnold." *Modern Philology* 67 (1969): 160–67.

Müller, Karl Otfried. *A History of the Literature of Ancient Greece.* Translated by George Cornewall Lewis and John William Donaldson. 3 vols. London: John Parker & Son, 1858.

Neuburg, Victor E. *Popular Literature: A History and a Guide.* Harmondsworth, Eng.: Penguin, 1977.

Perkins, David. *Wordsworth and the Poetry of Sincerity.* Cambridge, Mass.: Harvard University Press, 1964.

Raleigh, John Henry. *Matthew Arnold and American Culture.* Berkeley and Los Angeles: University of California Press, 1961.

Robbins, William. *The Ethical Idealism of Matthew Arnold.* London: William Heinemann, 1959.

Sansom, E. Steve. "Forms of Humanistic Argument in Arnold and Johnson." *Enlightenment Essays* 5 (1974): 19–25.

_____. "Matthew Arnold: Literary Theories and Methods of Criticism." *Enlightenment Essays* 5 (1974): 34–47.

_____. "Matthew Arnold and the Power of Persuasion." *Enlightenment Essays* 4 (1973): 20–35.

Scott, Patrick Greig. "The Victorianism of Clough." *Victorian Poetry* 16 (1978): 32–42.

Super, R. H. "Arnold and Literary Criticism: (2) Critical Practice." In *Matthew Arnold,* edited by Kenneth Allott, pp. 149–77. Athens: Ohio University Press, 1976.

_____. *The Time Spirit of Matthew Arnold.* Ann Arbor: University of Michigan Press, 1970.

Tillotson, Geoffrey. *Criticism and the Nineteenth Century.* London: Athlone Press, 1951.

Tinker, C. B., and H. F. Lowry. *The Poetry of Matthew Arnold: A Commentary.* London: Oxford University Press, 1940.

Trilling, Lionel. *Matthew Arnold.* New York: Meridian, 1955.

Turner, Frank M. *The Greek Heritage in Victorian Britain.* New Haven, Conn.: Yale University Press, 1981.

Warren, Alba H. *English Poetic Theory, 1825–1865.* Princeton, N.J.: Princeton University Press, 1950.

Watson, Edward A. "Matthew Arnold's 'The Study of Poetry' in the Context of T. H. Ward's *The English Poets." Arnoldian* 7 (1979): 2–7.

Watson, Ian. *Song and Democratic Culture in Britain: An Approach to Popular Culture in Social Movements.* New York: St. Martin's Press, 1983.

Wellek, René. *A History of Modern Criticism, 1750–1950.* 5 vols. New Haven, Conn.: Yale University Press, 1965. Vol. 4: *The Later Nineteenth Century.*

Williams, Raymond. *Culture and Society, 1798–1950.* New York: Columbia University Press, 1958.

Index

Activity
 of criticism, 103-15
 of poetry, 135-37, 142-43, 161,
  170-72, 185, 190-91
Aeschylus, 30, 54, 74, 130
Amiel, Henri Frédéric, 170-71
Anderson, Warren DeWitt,
  196 nn18, 21; 201 n19
Aristotle
 Arnold on, 13, 27-31, 109
 on Homer and the tragic
  poets, 12-13
 Nicomachean Ethics, 12, 104,
  106-9, 135, 161, 196 nn18,
  21, 197 n8
 Poetics, 2, 12-13, 51-54, 135-
  36; catharsis in, 67-68; high
  seriousness in, 138-41; imitation in, 52-59; poetry and
  history in, 82, 138
 Politics, 21, 27
 Shairp on, 112
Arnold, Matthew
 and Aristotle, 27-31, 51-59,
  104-7, 135-41
 on Greek genius, 29, 30, 70,
  74
 on poetry: art of, 1-2, 40-47,
  52-53, 63, 75-77, 164-65,
  168, 182; and genius, 115-
  23, 131; and history, 59-85;
  and politics, 32; and subjects of, 66-67, 73-74;

and truth, 143-45
 on style, 128; ballad, 99-101;
  of Clough, 89-90; distinc-
  tion in, 124-26; grand style,
  89-91, 100-101; of Homer,
  89-91, 96-102
 works, poetry
 —"Dover Beach," 47, 76,
  211 n10
 —*Empedocles on Etna*, 35,
  39-40, 46, 49-51, 58, 66-67
 —"The Forsaken Merman,"
  46-47, 51, 86
 —*Lucretius*, 63, 71
 —*Merope*, 40, 57, 59, 74-75,
  102, 190
 —"Morality," 51
 —*Poems* (1853), 97-98
 —"Resignation," 76
 —*The Strayed Reveller and
  Other Poems*, 49-51
 —"Switzerland," 47
 —"Thyrsis," 18, 81
 —"To a Friend," 75-76
 —"Tristram and Iseult," 51,
  102
 works, prose
 —"Amiel," 170-72, 190
 —"Byron," 167-70
 —"Civilization in the United
  States," 187-89
 —*Culture and Anarchy*, 8-10,
  61, 65, 81, 136, 140, 155,

221

Arnold, Matthew, *continued*
  159, 186, 188–89; and
  Shairp, 23, 155, 159, 174
—"Democracy," 3, 14–16,
  121–24, 191
—"Emerson," 30
—"England and the Italian
  Question," 3
—*Essays in Criticism*, First
  Series, 61, 103–4, 121–24
—*Essays in Criticism*, Second
  Series, 135–37, 162, 185
—"Eugénie de Guérin," 125–
  26
—"Falkland," 5
—"A French Critic on Mil-
  ton," 147
—"A French Play in London,"
  153
—"The Function of Criticism
  at the Present Time," 7, 65,
  81, 103–4, 137–38, 141, 147,
  155, 163, 167–70, 190,
  205 n3
—"Heinrich Heine," 111,
  126–27
—"John Keats," 164–66
—"Joubert," 131–32
—*Letters to Clough*, 28–29,
  32–39, 75–76
—"The Literary Influence of
  Academies," 115, 121–23
—"Literature and Science," 4,
  14
—"Marcus Aurelius," 80–81,
  132–34
—"Maurice de Guérin," 124–
  25, 141, 164
—"On Poetry," 138
—"On the Modern Element in
  Literature," 3–4, 10, 57–77,
  111, 127, 186, 189
—*On the Study of Celtic Lit-
  erature*, 204 n13
—*On Translating Homer*, 7,
  10, 19, 95, 189
—"Pagan and Medieval

Religious Sentiment," 116–
  17, 129–31
—*The Popular Education of
  France*, 14
—Preface to *Merope*, 47, 55–
  57, 59, 74, 185–86
—Preface to *Poems* (1853),
  51–55, 60, 65, 74, 167, 176,
  183; and Aristotle, 13, 51–
  54; and democracy, 51–54
—*St. Paul and Protestantism*,
  29–30
—"Shelley," 160–63
—"A Speech at Eton," 140
—"The Study of Poetry," 5,
  10, 129, 135–40, 185–86;
  and Aristotle, 13; and Burns,
  24, 146–47, 154–59; and
  Shairp, 24, 155–59
—"Thomas Gray," 163–64
—"The Twice-Revised Code,"
  14–15
—"Wordsworth," 135–36, 142,
  148
Arnold, Thomas (father)
  and Aristotle's *Politics*, 27
  ideas of history of, 60–61, 80
  and Roman history, 62, 64,
  71–72, 80
Arnold, Thomas (younger), 18,
  97, 159
Athens, Athenians, 130
  as audience of drama, 11, 55–
  56
  democracy of, 2, 14–16, 61,
  70, 77, 122, 129, 198–
  99 n17, 211 n10
  Periclean age of, 57, 69–70,
  130

Ballad poetry, ballad poets, 2,
  86–87, 88–90, 96–98, 100–
  102, 202 n3
Bernays, Jakob, 68
Blackie, John Stuart, on Homer,
  97

Bossuet, Jacques Bénigne, 126
Brantlinger, Patrick, 211 n10
Brooke, Stopford Augustus, 148
Brown, Huntington, 88
Brownell, William, 12
Browning, Elizabeth Barrett, 93
Browning, Robert, 37, 57
Buckler, William, 186
Burbidge, Thomas, 35
Burns, Robert, 2, 46, 146–47,
    154–56, 186
  Shairp on, 24, 55, 96, 155–59,
    175–76
Butcher, Samuel Henry, 22, 143–
    44, 208 n8
Byron, George Gordon, 2, 105,
    160
  Arnold on modern ideas of,
    127
  Arnold on sincerity of, 146,
    160
  Clough on style of, 148

Caesar, Julius, 63, 71, 80
Carlyle, Thomas, 24, 29, 33, 105
Catharsis, 67–68, 190, 200 n9
Classic, classical, 173–74, 179–
    84, 185–86, 187–88, 190–91
Clausen, Christopher, 26
Clough, Arthur Hugh, 8, 75, 147
  on Aristotle, 27, 141–42
  and Arnold, 19, 35–36, 40–44,
    76
  and Balliol scholars, 18–20
  criticism: of Arnold, 49–51,
    58; of Browning, 57; of
    Alexander Smith, 49–58
  on style, 142, 148, 150–51
  on subjects for poetry, 61
  translation of Plutarch of, 61,
    63, 77–82
  on Whitman, 58
  on Wordsworth, 148–52
  works, poetry
  —Ambarvalia, 35
  —Amours de Voyage, 19, 47–

49, 58, 175
—The Bothie of Toper-na-
  Fuosich: A Long-Vacation
  Pastoral (1848), 19, 22, 30,
  39, 47, 80, 107, 159, 179,
  197 n10; and Aristotle, 27–
  28; and Homeric style, 39–
  40, 86, 89, 95
—Mari Magno, 95–96
Colenso, John William (Bishop
  of Natal), 6, 105
Coleridge, Samuel Taylor, 127,
  177
Coulling, Sidney, 7–8
Criticism, 9
  activity of, 103–15
  art of, 106, 115
  and creation, 2, 106–8
  definition of, 107
  and ethics, 106
  function of, 106–7
  and poetry, 111–15
  standard of, 106, 110
Criticism of life, 2, 5, 9, 144–45
Culler, A. Dwight, 198 n17,
  200 n4
Curtius, Ernst, 15, 200 n4

Dale, Peter Allen, on Vico,
  199 n4
Dante Alighieri, 156
Decade (society), 18, 20
Deering, Dorothy, 8
DeLaura, David, 6
Democracy
  in Arnold's Essays in Criti-
    cism, First Series, 121
  in Athens, 2, 14–16, 61, 70,
    77, 122, 129, 198–99 n17,
    211 n10
  in England, 3, 123–24
  and French Revolution, 3, 90,
    121–24
  and ideas, 3–4, 6–7
  and poetry, 1–13, 17, 24, 32–
    34, 48–62, 73–75, 130–31,

224   Index

Democracy, *continued*
183-91
in United States, 11, 187-89
Demosthenes, 16
Dickens, Charles, 188
Diogenes Laërtius, *Lives*, 62
Disinterestedness, 5, 107, 183
Drama, Greek
Aeschylus, 30, 54, 74, 130
Aristotle, 12-13, 51-54
audience of, 11, 55-56, 198-
99 n17
Sophocles, 61, 67, 74-77, 130,
146, 183

Education, 3, 6, 14
Eliot, Thomas Stearns, 10
Else, Gerald Frank
on Aristotle, 13, 30, 59
on Aristotle and Plato, 52-54, 59
Emerson, Ralph Waldo, 105
Empedocles, 132
Enlightenment, 176-77
Ennius, 180
Epictetus, 75, 120
Epicurus, 39

Flexibility, 105, 136, 185
Francis of Assisi, Saint, 129-30
French Revolution, 90
Froude, James Anthony, 61, 147
Caesar, 64, 178
History of England, 24
on Homer, 91-94
Nemesis of Faith, 24, 47
on poetry of Arnold and
Clough, 24, 40
on poetry and history, 82-84
"The Science of History," 81- 85
Shadows of the Clouds, 47

Gibbon, Edward, 64, 83
Goethe, Johann Wolfgang von,
on Homer, 88

Graff, Gerald, 194 n13
Grand style, 89, 100
Grant, Alexander
and his edition of Aristotle's
Ethics, 21, 22, 196 n17
commentary: on *energeia,*
160; on imagination, 117; on
judgment, 110; on melan-
choly, 109; on play of mind,
107; on tact, 205 n3, 208 n6
and Jowett, 21-22
on Plato and imagination, 117-18
and Sellar, 22
Gray, Thomas, 160-64
Grote, George, 198-99 n17,
200 n4
Guérin, Eugénie de, 125-26
Guérin, Maurice de, 124-26, 161
Guizot, François Pierre Guil-
laume, 200 n4

Hartman, Geoffrey H., "Arnoldian concordat," 112
Haydon, Benjamin Robert, 164-65
Heine, Heinrich, 4, 120, 127-30
High seriousness, 5, 135-39
and flexibility, 140
and grand style, 137
and sincerity, 137, 146-48,
154-64
History and poetry, 2, 59-62,
67-69, 71-72, 74-75, 77,
79-81, 82-85
Homer, 174, 180-89
and ballad style, 2, 86-89, 176
and criticism of life, 145
Iliad, 54, 96-99, 176
Odyssey, 92-94, 176

Imaginative reason, 5, 8, 22,
116-20, 130-31, 145
Infinity, the infinite, 128, 171
Inspiration, 112, 116, 119, 131-32
Intellectual
activity, 105, 112, 123, 143, 181

deliverance, 67–68, 103, 127
elitism, 13, 52, 154
independence, 28–29, 38–39
pleasure, 53, 164–66
sleep, 169
Intuition, 117, 119
Inventive power, 115, 119
and creative power, 115–16
and critical faculty, 116

Jackson, Andrew, 11, 187
Jebb, Richard C., 22, 64, 200 n6
Johnson, Samuel, 68
Joubert, Joseph, 120, 131–32
Jowett, Benjamin
and Aristotle, 21–22
and Matthew Arnold, 20–21
and Thomas Arnold, 20
and Balliol scholars, 18–22
and Homeric translation, 10,
87
Judgment, the judicious, 109–10,
135, 149
derivation from Aristotle, 30–
31, 109

Keats, John, 160–61
and idea of beauty, 163–64
and idea of the world, 37
and judgment, 109, 161, 165–
66
and melancholy, 109–10
"Ode on a Grecian Urn," 166
Kermode, Frank, The Classic, 10

Lancaster, Henry Hill, on
Homer, 202 n2
Lang, Andrew, 22
Lippincott, Benjamin, 3
Locke, John, 171
Long, George, 80–81
Longfellow, Henry Wadsworth
Evangeline, 86, 89
Hiawatha, 57

Lucretius (Titus Lucretius Car-
us), 47, 73, 120, 181–83,
206 n16
Arnold compares to Words-
worth, 152
and poetry and science, 41
Sellar on imagination of,
118–20

Macaulay, Thomas Babington,
180
Roman Ballads, 89, 101
Madden, William, 8
Marcus Aurelius, 80–81, 120,
133–34
Merivale, Charles, 72
Michelet, Jules, 20, 189
Mill, John Stuart, 33, 123
Milton, John, 120, 140, 146–47
and grand style, 101, 146–47
and high seriousness, 156
and sincerity, 147–48
style and character of, 141–42,
147–48
Molière, 153, 164
Mommsen, Theodor, 72
Müller, Karl Otfried, History of
the Literature of Ancient
Greece, 61, 69, 75–76,
198 n17
on Sophocles, 75–76
Mysteries, Eleusinian, 129

Napoleon Bonaparte, 72
Newman, Francis William, 86–
89
Niebuhr, Barthold Georg, 62, 68,
180
Norton, Charles E., 81

Palgrave, Francis Turner, 18, 26
and Matthew Arnold, 24–26,
122–23
and Clough, 24–25

Palgrave, *continued*
and Alexander Grant, 25
and Sellar, 25
and Shairp, 25
on Alexander Smith, 49
and Tennyson, 25
works
—*Landscape in Poetry,* 25
—*Visions of England,* 26
—*Golden Treasury of English Lyrics,* 26
Pascal, Blaise, and Eugénie de Guérin, 125-26
Paul, Sherman (Arnoldian critic), 12
Pindar, 126, 130
Plato
contrasted to Demosthenes, 16
on Homer and the tragic poets, 13
and imaginative intellect, 146
Ion, 53, 112, 155
and literary art, 30
and Socrates, 15-16
Plautus, Titus Maccius, 181
Play of mind, 105, 107
Plutarch, 61, 63, 77-81
Clough on, 78-80
George Long on, 80-81
and Shakespeare, 82
Poetry
art of, 2, 35-36, 42-43, 55-57, 114
definition of, 128, 145
and drama, 55-57
form and feeling of, 40-47
form and matter of, 40-46
form and style of, 35
and form of expression and of conception, 42-43
high seriousness of, 141-43
and history, 34-35, 60
and interpretation of age, 69
lyric, 46-47, 155-56
materials of, 35, 37-38
unity of, 42
Politics, 32-34

Puritan, Puritanism, 128

Racine, 42
Reason. *See* Imaginative reason; Judgment, the judicious
Roe, Edward Payson, 188-89
Roman history, 71-73, 78-79. *See also* Arnold, Thomas (father)
Roman poets, 73, 179-84. *See also* Sellar, William Young
Roman Republic, 62, 71
Rome, 62, 71
Ruskin, John, 22, 87-88, 186

Sand, George, 38-39
Scherer, Edmond, 141, 160, 171
Science, and poetry, 41, 115, 149
Scott, Walter, 176, 188
Arnold on, 127
and ballad style, 99
and Homer, 86, 97-101
The Lady of the Lake, 102
Marmion, 98
Shairp on, 55, 96, 96-99, 175
Sellar, William Young, 18, 77, 147, 174, 203 n10
and Arnold, 22, 39
"Characteristics of Thucydides," 69-70
on imitation, 179
on Julius Caesar and the Roman Republic, 72
on Lucretius, 22, 61, 118-20, 181-82
"Poems by Arthur Hugh Clough," 95-96
on poetry and history, 84-85
on Roman poets, 179-85
The Roman Poets of the Augustan Age: Virgil, 118-20, 182
The Roman Poets of the Republic, 22, 118-20, 179-82, 206 n16

on Thucydides, 61, 82
on Vergil, 22
Shairp, John Campbell, 18, 23,
52, 61, 147, 173
Criticism of: Arnold's poetry,
40, 49, 54–55; Burns, 96,
155–59; Clough, 19, 22–23,
49; Homer, 55, 97–99; Plato
and Aristotle, 155; Scott,
96–97; Shelley, 142; Vergil,
86, 178; Wordsworth, 111,
151–53
works, poetry
—"Balliol Scholars," 47
—*Glen Dessaray and Other
Poems*, 23
—*Kilmahoe: A Highland Pastoral*, 23
works, prose
—*Aspects of Poetry*, 23, 96–97,
174, 209 n19
—"Burns and Scotch Song before Him," 155, 157, 158,
209 n19
—"Criticism and Creation,"
112, 137, 155, 176–77
—*Culture and Religion*, 155,
159, 174
—"English Poets and Oxford
Critics," 24
—"The Homeric Spirit in
Walter Scott," 97–99
—"Poems by Matthew Arnold," 96
—*On Poetic Interpretation of
Nature*, 23, 151–52
—"Poetic Style in Modern English Poetry," 177–78
—*Robert Burns*, 24, 155–59
—"Scottish Song, and Burns,"
96, 157–58, 209 n19
—"Shelley as a Lyric Poet,"
155, 161
—"The Songs of Scotland
before Burns," 96
—*Sketches in History and
Poetry*, 23

—*Studies in Poetry and Philosophy*, 23
—"Virgil as a Religious Poet,"
178
—"Wordsworth as an Interpreter of Nature," 151–52
Shakespeare, William, 35–36,
82–84, 120, 146
Shelley, Percy Bysshe, 105, 140,
160
Arnold on modern ideas of, 127
Shairp on character of, 161
Sidgwick, Henry, 19
Sincerity, 42, 146–48
and high seriousness, 137,
146–48
and plain style, 148
Smith, Alexander, 58, 49–50
Smith, Sir William, *Dictionary
of Greek and Roman Biography*, 81
Sophocles, 61, 67, 74–77, 130,
146, 183
Müller on, 75–76
Oedipus at Colonus, 144
Spinoza, Baruch, 68
Stanley, Arthur Penrhyn, 18, 71
Stephen, Leslie, 143–44, 151
Super, R. H., 6–7
Sweet reasonableness, 105, 110,
136, 139–40

Tacitus, Publius, 126
Tatham, Emma, 126
Tennyson, Alfred, 35–36, 66
In Memoriam, 66
Maud, 57, 109
Theocritus, 120, 129, 186
Thirlwall, Connop, 75, 200 n4
Thucydides, *History of the Peloponnesian War*, 67–70, 73,
120, 184
Tocqueville, Alexis de, 124, 189
Trilling, Lionel, 3–6, 59
Turner, Frank M., 196 n17,
198 n17

United States, democracy in, 11
  Arnold on, 187–89

Vergil, 22, 73, 182
  and Shairp, 86, 91
Vico, Giovanni Battista (also
  Giambattista), 62, 63
Voltaire, François Marie Arouet
  de, 91, 120

Walrond, Theodore, 18, 23
Ward, Thomas Humphrey, 135
Whitman, Walt, 11, 57
Williams, Raymond, 9
Wolf, Friedrich August, 97

Wordsworth, William, 127, 177
  Clough on subjects of poetry
    of, 150
  The Excursion, 146
  "Ode: Intimations of Immor-
    tality," 143–44
  philosophy of, 142–45
  on poetry and criticism, 104,
    111–12
  and poetry and philosophy,
    142–45
  The Prelude, 151–52
  Shairp on, 55, 175–77
  sincerity of, 146–53
  style of, 86, 90, 99–100, 148,
    151–53